About the author:

William Cash was born in London in 1966. He went to Westminster and Magdalene College, Cambridge, where he read English. In 1989 he covered the revolutions of East Germany and Czechoslovakia for various national publications. Formerly *The Times*'s correspondent on the West Coast of the United States, he is now American correspondent-at-large for the *Daily Mail*. He is a contributor to *Harper's & Queen* and *The Spectator*, and has written for *The Observer* and *Evening Standard*. TV and radio guest appearances include *Entertainment Tonight*, ITN, BBC *Six O'Clock News* and BBC World Service.

He lives in Hollywood Hills and is writing a novel set in LA.

Educating William

Memoirs of a Hollywood Correspondent

WILLIAM CASH

A Touchstone Book
LONDON · SYDNEY · NEW YORK · TOKYO
SINGAPORE · TORONTO

First published in Great Britain by
Simon & Schuster Ltd, 1993
First published in Great Britain by Touchstone, 1994
An imprint of Simon & Schuster Ltd
A Paramount Communications Company

Simon & Schuster Ltd
West Garden Place
Kendal Street
London W2 2AQ

Simon & Schuster of Australia Pty Ltd
Sydney

A CIP catalogue record for this book is
available from the British Library

ISBN 0-671-71277-2

Printed and bound in Great Britain by
HarperCollins*Manufacturing*, Glasgow

Acknowledgements

This book owes a very great deal to the generosity and support of *The Times* over the last three years. I would like to especially thank (in alphabetical order): John Bryant, Brigid Callaghan, Alan Copps, Andrew Harvey, Simon Jenkins, Gill Morgan, Richard Owen and all on the foreign desk, Peter Roberts, Peter Stothard, Nicholas Wapshott and all on *The Times Magazine* and Nigel Williamson. I would also like to thank the staff of the News International Library. In addition, very special thanks are due to Martin Ivens, for sending me to LA, and for standing by me in an awkward moment (see Chapter 9: Bad Boys), and to Graham Paterson, whose endless enthusiasm and encouragement never ceases to amaze.

I would also like to thank the following London editors for employing me in various capacities: Susan Boyd, Jane Mays, Heather McGlone, Rebecca Nicolson, Richard Preston and Vicki Woods. I am very grateful to Simon Tiffin for some inspired last-minute thinking. Above all, I would like to thank Dominic Lawson, editor of *The Spectator*, for jump-starting my career. Without his continued support this book would never have been written.

I am most grateful to the many people who appear in these pages for the time they gave me outside the usual publicity rounds – in particular Martin Amis, William Boyd, Joe Eszterhas, Jackie Collins, Hugh Hefner, David Hockney, Peggy Lee, Armistead Maupin, Jay and Helen McInerney and Hunter S. Thompson. In LA, I would like also to thank the staff of the Academy of Motion Picture Arts and Sciences Center for Motion Picture Studies, all at Fox TV, Henry

Brocklehurst, Xan Rufus Isaacs, Martin Cohen, Simon Kelton – with apologies for my disgraceful lack of application to matters domestic – and my friends John and Fev Micklethwait for putting up with me when I began to sound like a record player. For helping with research, or other matters, I am grateful to Victoria Hull, Anita Ferry and Birgit Cunningham.

I would also like to thank my agent Judy Martin; Dr Richard Luckett in Cambridge for reading the manuscript and offering useful suggestions; Rob Long and Toby Young for their candid and constructive comments. Finally, I would like to thank the editor of these pages, Carol O'Brien, along with Sian Parkhouse and everyone else at Simon & Schuster. Once more, I have been exceptionally fortunate to work with such dedicated and sharp-minded editors.

To my mother and father

Contents

Prologue		*page* 1
Introduction: A Mirror to Caliban		9
1	Dancing with Madonna	13
2	West from Wapping	27
3	Invitation to a Wedding	34
4	Sofa so Good	49
5	LA Lust	67
6	To Live and Die in LA	85
7	The Mousetrap	100
8	The Power and the Glitz	117
9	Bad Boys	138
10	Deathwatch	163
11	Postcard from South-Central	180
12	The Unloved Ones	199
13	The Graduate	216
14	Walking on Sunset	242
Epilogue: The Death of Celebrity		256
Index		285

None . . . will hold a mirror up to Caliban; all feel their own security threatened by a whisper of criticism. Artists and public men elsewhere live under a fusillade of detraction and derision; they accept it as a condition of their calling. Not so in Hollywood, where all is a continuous psalm of self-praise.

Evelyn Waugh, 'Why Hollywood is a Term of Disparagement',
Morning Post, 1 May 1947

Prologue

'THERE ARE NO CABS,' SAID an apologetic-looking Playboy Enterprises executive, turning off his mobile-phone. 'Sunset Boulevard is being closed off. Rioting has started in West Hollywood. Mayor Bradley has ordered everyone to stay inside. No one is going *anywhere*.'

It was shortly before 3p.m. on Thursday, 30 April 1992, just after the last Playmate of the Year luncheon guest had sped off in a black Mercedes coupé. Twenty-four hours after a Simi Valley jury had acquitted the four white LAPD police officers charged with beating Rodney King, I was marooned at Hugh Hefner's Playboy mansion – in the middle of the worst civil violence in modern American history.

When I woke up that morning, the view from my kitchen window was of thick clouds of sepia-brown smoke rising above the Hollywood Hills like a fog caused by badly burnt toast. Palm trees along the 110 Harbor Freeway were ablaze. Drive-by gang shootings were reported close to Beverly Hills. Thousands of armed troops were on their way to patrol the streets. Police had advised against *all* travel.

Lunch – I assumed – would be off.

I dialled the Playboy Studio West offices on Sunset Boulevard and asked for extension 370.

'Is Mr Hefner's party today still on?' I inquired.

'Oh, yes, yes, yes,' a bubbly voice assured me. 'It's on. Limousine-shuttle service from the Beverly Hilton to the Playboy Mansion starts in an hour.'

The invitation resembled the sort of candy-pink birthday card you might send your next-door neighbour's ten-year-old daughter.

PLEASE JOIN US IN HONORING PLAYBOY
MAGAZINE'S 1992 PLAYMATE OF THE YEAR.
COCKTAILS AND LUNCHEON.

By 12.30p.m. I was sitting on a wobbly plastic gold chair inside a giant fairy-white tent pitched on a patch of astroturf behind Hugh Hefner's mansion. Beside me was a buffet plate of salmon fillet in dill sauce, a fizzing champagne cocktail and the fleshy and sun-grilled thighs of a sherbert-lemon blonde 1982 Playmate of the Month (fifty-three former *Playboy* centrefolds were at lunch).

Two hours later I asked a Playboy executive to order me a taxi. On any other day, I might have been delighted to roam about inside the famous $50 million 'Tudor' manor in the Holmby Hills. But with Los Angeles's looting and mob violence growing by the minute my employers at *The Times* wanted me to file fresh accounts of the disturbance for each new edition. I needed a taxi from the Playboy Mansion because my car was being fitted with a new windscreen and doors after being pelted with rocks (with me inside) by rioters in South-Central LA the night before.

The LA riots had, in fact, nearly cancelled the Playmate of the Year pageant for the first time in its history. A decision had been made at midnight (Hefner's working hours are very much his own) to go on with it.

'Welcome,' Hef had begun his speech on a podium decorated with blown-up soft-porn photographs of the 1992 Playmate of the Year, Corinna Harney, 'and I'm delighted by the turnout. It's a little difficult to hold a celebration like this, on a day like this, in the middle of so much tragedy and what's happening outside on the streets – but maybe it's appropriate that *Playboy* should be holding a celebration of beauty in a time of chaos.'

When Rome had burned during the great fire of AD 64, Nero had supposedly recited his own poetry, played the lyre and threw a party as he enjoyed the spectacle from his villa in the hills. That sixty-six-year-old Hugh Hefner – Ner to his closest pals – should have slipped out of his John Player Special black silk pyjamas into a flared *Saturday Night Fever* linen suit to host the thirty-second Playmate of the Year luncheon whilst LA went up in flames, was not, I reflected, very surprising. Hef – like so many of LA's celebrated denizens – has always been cheerily oblivious to the real world.

After lunch I sat waiting for my cab by the mansion's oak front door, casually flicking through the glossy pages of June's *Playboy*. It included a ten-page nude pictorial of Corinna from Las Vegas, whose Playmate of the Year title was 'an honor that comes with a lipstick red Lexus SC 300 and a check for $100,000'. In addition to her svelte twenty-year-old body, she had won because of her talent as a poet. 'Her fascination with the emotional power of poetry began in the second grade,' I read. 'Flying in an airplane over fluffy, white clouds, the shapes reminded her of a pet cat that had recently died, and she "just let my thoughts flow from my mind onto the page".'

When the Hefner underling informed me that LA's taxi companies had closed down, I explained my dilemma to him.

'I don't suppose anyone could give me a lift,' I said, glancing towards Hef's parked limousine, draped in a heavy cream dust-sheet. 'It's rather urgent.'

'Relax,' he said, pointing to what looked like two thirty-feet high oyster shells on the billiard-green lawn beside Hef 's tennis court. 'You can use Mr Hefner's study. The Playboy mansion's satellites can pick up any TV station in America – we can probably get you the BBC.'

'That won't be much use,' I replied.

'Sure it will.'

'You don't understand,' I said. 'The fact is I am the BBC.'

Or, at least, had been for the last twenty-four hours, when I was called on, in some desperation, as an emergency fill-in for the *BBC Breakfast News* and the *BBC Six O'Clock News*.

'Follow me,' he said.

I was led through the marble-floored great hall which resembled the lobby of a five-star Trust House Forté country hotel, with its 'medieval' staircase leading up to Hef 's mastersuite bedroom, equipped with four giant *Goldfinger* monitoring screens. A butler of sorts politely asked me if I would like a drink ('This place is run like a hotel oughta be run' Hef had once told Tom Wolfe from his whirring, seven-and-a-half-foot-wide revolving bed. 'It goes 24 hours a day.') I ordered a Pepsi.

The next room boasted a thirty-foot high movie screen (Hefner has a library of 4,000 films) that pulled down from the ceiling and several ten-foot-long leather sofas in Harvey Bristol cream leather. I noticed a special joy-stick implanted under the left arm-rest of Hef 's personal seat, so that he can adjust the focus without getting up. Several staff members, the Hefner underling told me, were employed full time simply recording up to fifteen hours (the mansion has twenty-eight video recorders) of television each day.

Walking through a heavily draped door, I entered Hef 's private panelled study. Its bookcases were lined with leather-bound editions of *Playboy* dating back to 1953, a backgammon board was set up to play and a twenty-six-inch TV set above the desk was showing pictures of a supermarket ablaze in West Hollywood. A framed *People* magazine, featuring Hef 's recent marriage on the cover, hung proudly on the wall. Above the imposing fireplace was a Holbein-style old portrait of Hugh M. Hefner posing in medieval costume as 'Renaissance Prince'.

Lying with her feet up watching the TV was a tall girl in a short turquoise mini-skirt.

'Howdy,' she drawled to me in a Texas accent. 'I'm Marlene.'

Pinned above her pointed breasts was a jumbo-sized badge which said 'Playmate 1976'. She was flipping over the TV channels – switching for a moment to scenes of the Beverly

Center shopping mall being evacuated – with a complicated-looking remote control. She got up and drifted in and out of the room.

Sitting down in Hef 's creaky leather desk-chair at his mahogany desk – overstocked with de luxe personalised notepads – I took out a sharp pencil from the tray and began scribbling down notes as the latest news about the riots was broadcast live on a gamut of stations. Appropriately for a businessman who seldom leaves his home, Hefner's mansion is a sophisticated global communications centre.

Hefner's armchair could not, in fact, have been a better place to have kept readers of *The Times* in Britain up to date with the deaths, fires and lootings that had followed the start of the riots at the junction of Florence and Normandie Avenues the night before. The study was also conveniently lined with a complete *Encyclopaedia Britannica*.

When a news flash announced that LA Mayor Tom Bradley had ordered a dawn-to-dusk curfew to be enforced throughout the entire city, I picked up Hef 's private telephone and dialled *The Times*'s US freephone number.

'Copy-takers, please,' I said.

I gave the girl my name with a Los Angeles date-line.

'Ready,' she said.

'Mayor Tom Bradley ordered a curfew throughout the city of Los Angeles after President Bush sent in 5,000 federal troops to restore calm. Stop. Violence raged well into the early hours yesterday leaving scenes resembling a battlefield. Stop. Motorists were dragged out of their cars and beaten to death . . . ' and so on.

Fifteen minutes or so later, I spoke to the foreign desk.

'Any queries?' I asked.

'No, William, that's just fine – be sure to keep us updated for the final edition.'

'Okay.'

And so it went on – with Marlene re-appearing shortly after I filed for the last edition.

'The house is blocked off,' she announced. 'We're going to

be staying here for a while.'

My reporting duties over, I strolled out into the fifteen-acre safari-style garden with its 'Love Grotto' waterfall and landscaped swimming pool. A number of peacocks and pink flamingoes basked on the springy grass lawn in the late afternoon sunshine. Hef 's outdoor 'zoo' was a little disappointing. It consisted of a large hutch of wild rabbits, a cage of pet monkeys and a thrashing pool of tropical goldfish.

His guests gone, Hef was sitting out on the front lawn with his wife, Kimberley, and various dogs, playing with his two small children. Loud rock music blared from a large portable stereo beside them. He had kicked off his shiny, Italian shoes and wore his pink shirt open. From a distance, his face had the rubbery smooth sheen of Play-Doh.

Indoors, Marlene was starting to panic. An emergency had arisen. She said she would drive me back to my house in Hollywood if I would accompany her on a 'rescue-mission' to get a friend of hers out of a West Hollywood street, which we could see on the TV was mostly engulfed by flames. She grabbed me by the hand and led me outside. Opening the boot of her shiny silver Datsun sports car, she pulled out a dangerous looking – and extremely sharp – sword.

'I've been carrying it around with me for the last twenty-four hours – just in case,' she said, jumping in the driver's seat and turning up the volume on the Guns N' Roses tape in her stereo. As we waved goodbye to the Hefner family, still sitting on the lawn, I noticed a bodyguard lurking visibly in the bushes behind them. Marlene screeched down the gravelly drive, swinging past the mansion's security cameras onto Charing Cross Road.

In front of us, the traffic in Beverly Hills was grid-locked, with some cars resorting to driving along the pavement. There was a great deal of honking and hooting of horns. Turning down the Guns N' Roses, Marlene placed her hand on my leg.

'Okay, let's use our brains,' she said, squeezing my thigh.

I changed Axl Rose for the local radio. A few minutes later

an emergency warning was broadcast.

'Drivers are advised not to drive along Foothill Boulevard. There are reports of rocks being thrown at cars. We are reminding motorists that there is a curfew in Hollywood from 7p.m. If you have no business there you will be arrested.'

I twiddled the radio and got another local station.

'Do not exit on the 710 freeway. People have tried coming through the barriers. You will be arrested. Why anyone should want to go into South-Central LA tonight, we do not know. Get it First. Get it Fast. Traffic every ten minutes, only on KFWB, News 98.'

After about an hour, as the light began to fade and the early evening sky swirled with inky purple-blue clouds, we swung into north Hollywood just as the curfew hour approached.

Smoke was billowing from buildings, teenagers scurried off down back-alleys loaded with sneaker boxes and children walked around the streets hunting for souvenirs. Frederick's of Hollywood, the famous lingerie shop, had been badly looted. The next day it was reported that somebody had removed a gold brassière that once belonged to Madonna.

But Marlene's friend was nowhere to be found.

'William,' she said, sounding frightened and looking me in the eyes. 'What if we don't get out of here?'

'I'll look after you,' I said. 'Don't you worry.'

INTRODUCTION

A Mirror to Caliban

IN 1947 EVELYN WAUGH HAD his agent arrange a free six-week holiday in Los Angeles (paid $2,000 a week and put up at the Hotel Bel-Air) with the excuse of discussing the possible filming of *Scoop*. On his return he wrote an article describing the Hollywood community as living like monks in a desert oasis, their lives revolving around a few shrines, half a dozen immense studios, a few hotels and restaurants, 'their sacred texts being their own publicity and the local gossip columns'.

Today, LA remains its own greatest fan. The accounts of my various adventures and encounters are attempts at demythification. Firstly, and most importantly, of America's celebrity circus – the booming global influence of which I cannot be alone in viewing as comically absurd. The book holds up a mirror to the warped diamond of modern fame and the darker side of the Hollywood publicity system.

In my view the media are as star-struck – *gobsmacked* – as the masses who camp out all night to get a seat in the stands on Oscar night. The popular idea that the movies represent the most democratic and avant-garde of new art forms is probably LA's most disingenuous myth. It has become a commonplace to hear that Los Angeles is a metaphor for the future, *the* city of the twenty-first century – just as Paris, Rome and London have stood as symbols of social and artistic energy in past centuries. In my experience, however, Hollywood is more feudal than futuristic. This book hurls a few javelins into the fruity and crazy caboodle that is modern Tinseltown.

Tina Brown called *Vanity Fair*, where she aspired to turn the cult of celebrity into an art form, the 'great high–low show'. She was referring to what is, I think, likely to become the most interesting cultural issue of the end of the century: the place of mass culture in the critical statusphere. These pages aim to add raw fuel to this debate – by which I mean front-line reportage and observation from Hollywood rather than from the offices of trendy Philadelphia academics or Groucho Club media pundits. The book is something of a cross-cultural roller-coast ride.

My second theme is with the demythification of LA. Since coming out to LA in September 1991, California's Illyrian image has been turned – literally burnt – to cinders. The notion of it being an adult playground for the beautiful, the frontier town of the American Dream, a wacky trampoline for the *Zeitgeist*, is now sadly out of date – the once Eden-like image is in need of some extensive plastic surgery. Despite the peace which followed the 1993 Rodney King verdicts, the new LAPD police chief, Willie Williams, went on television to frankly warn Angelenos that they had better get used to crisis – because in the future that is what living in LA is going to be all about.

This is not any sort of all-embracing attempt to be a book about Los Angeles. To do so, after living in LA for less than two years, would be presumptuous. As a journalist, I make no apologies for the eclectic mix. Part of the fascination with the United States lies in the scale of the antilogies skewering the land from coast to coast. After two years that the *Los Angeles Times* described as the 'most tumultuous' in the city's history, the old cliché of LA as America's cultural melting pot is redundant. These days it feels increasingly like an urban pressure cooker whose lid could blow off again at any moment.

The evening it did – the first night of the riots – an angry gang of black youths threw lumps of concrete through my car window. My view of LA remains fractured and splintered –

indeed, as if looking through a broken windscreen. You cannot really help this if you are a correspondent or expatriate living abroad. In Salman Rushdie's essay, *Imaginary Homelands*, on the predicament of living away from one's own country, he wrote: 'Meaning is a shaky edifice we build out of scraps, dogmas, childhood injuries, newspaper articles, chance remarks, old films, small victories, people hated, people loved; perhaps it is because our sense of what is the case is constructed from such inadequate materials that we defend it so fiercely. . .'

Inadequate materials. That pretty well sums up what it is like to be a journalist abroad – hopelessly chaotic cutting files, barely readable faxes, insufficient wires, unreturned phone calls. Lost receipts. Vast telephone bills. Unfiled expenses. Piles of glanced-at newspapers. Early morning deadlines.

That warm evening of 29 April 1992, when I drove down into the bowels of South-Central – past the lights of Dodger Stadium glowing across the 101 Hollywood Freeway to my left, swinging right under a graffiti-scrawled railway bridge onto Normandie Avenue – only one thing seemed certain. I had set off with the blind self-assurance of an Englishman who didn't know what the hell he was letting himself in for.

In a way, that is what this book is all about.

1

Dancing with Madonna

AS MADONNA'S STRETCH BLACK MERCEDES swept past the paparazzi caged outside the gates of the Hotel du Cap d'Antibes and began to descend Boulevard John F. Kennedy towards Cannes, I lurched into first gear and tucked my navy Peugeot 305 neatly behind the last limousine in the convoy. The police-escorted cavalcade, with their hazard lights flashing, was bound for the Palm Beach Club Casino where Madonna was throwing a $500,000 party the night before the Cannes Film Festival première of her film *Truth or Dare*. My invite had obviously been lost in the post.

Hundreds of feet below the snaking cliff road, with the yellow fairy-lights of Monte Carlo flickering across the bay below, lay the craggy rocks where photographers with lenses the size of baby elephant trunks had sunbathed all day whilst waiting for Madonna to emerge on the terrace of her £1,400 a night sea-facing lily-white suite. It was now cool and the cyan evening sky was studded with zircon stars. After a minute or two, as her party of four limousines and several pairs of police on BMW motorcycles started to squeal around the tight bends of the winding coastal road at around 50mph, I switched on my own hazard warning lights. I am not a skilled driver and as we cut through the crowds lining the streets of Juan-les Pins like a high-speed funeral cortège I managed to keep up only after a *gendarme* whistled me through a red traffic light. I had hired a Peugeot 305 because it closely resembled an unmarked French police car.

With all journalists – so I had been told – strictly barred from Madonna's party, my plan was to masquerade as a member of her personal entourage. In the wild, flash-gun frenzy of her arrival, as her bodyguards tried to control the scrum of shutter-crazy, dinner-jacketed paparazzi and TV cameras surging towards her limousine door, I planned to jump out of my official-looking Peugeot – dressed in a dark suit – and slip into the Palm Beach Club along with her VIP party.

There was a perfectly good reason for this desperation. Far from being any sort of jet-set international showbiz reporter, I was, in fact, on holiday in the South of France – writing a travel article. Back in London, I was employed as a lowly twenty-four-year-old trainee news reporter for *The Times*. My desk was located so close to the newsroom back door that when it opened on a windy day my notes would blow out of the door into an adjacent building-site. Knowing no shorthand, ignorant of British libel laws and able to type with only two fingers, it was not a job to which I was wholly suited. On my first day in Wapping, a chain-smoking Fleet Street veteran on the newsdesk handed me a coffee-stained, bulging copy of the new (and 'strictly confidential') *Times* Style Guide, written by editor Simon Jenkins. Reporters were required to stick to it rigidly. 'Read that,' he said gruffly. 'That's all you need to know.'

My first regular assignment had been to trawl each day through the office's incomplete library of United Kingdom telephone directories, which were strewn chaotically about the newsroom, checking up on the exact address and initials of the winners of the Times Portfolio Plus lottery – an up-market version of the *Sun*'s Bingo. My early journalistic contributions to the paper ran along the lines of 'There were no valid claims for yesterday's Portfolio Plus prize. The £2,000 will be added to today's game.' My Gulf War had been especially inglorious – being frequently sent off to march with anti-war protestors at midnight, holding an office 'peace' candle and disguised in an anorak.

By the time I took my holiday on the Côte d'Azur, I had

worked in the newsroom for a little less than a year and – with the exception of the time I conveniently happened to be driving past Victoria Station when a large IRA bomb exploded, and returned to the newsroom with my notebook smeared in blood – had yet to distinguish myself.

Dangerously low on funds, my holiday on the Riviera had only been made possible by promising to write a travel piece on the newly refurbished Bel-Air Cap Ferrat, in St-Jean Cap Ferrat, near Nice. Robin Young, the paper's food and wine critic, who sat a yard or so away from me in the office, had tipped me off that the new owners of the hotel were looking for some up-market publicity after its Wilson, Gregory & Aeberhard interior-designed £15 million face-lift. Booked in for three (complimentary) nights at this pharaonically expensive luxury palace – where the Russian Imperial family and the Duke of Connaught used to spend the winter, and the likes of Tina Turner, Roger Moore and Ivana Trump did now – I was spending a few nights prior to my arrival in an ultra-cheap *pension* on the northern outskirts of Cannes. Thanks to a somewhat spurious letter of assignment signed by Rebecca Nicolson, then deputy editor of *The Times Saturday Review*, I had no difficulty in getting a press pass which enabled me to see all the festival films for free.

When I phoned up the Bel-Air Cap Ferrat from my bed and breakfast to confirm when I was arriving, I was told I had a message. 'Call *Times* foreign desk – urgent' it read and gave News International's toll-free number from France.

'It's William Cash speaking – I'm calling from France.'

'Yes, thank's for calling,' a voice replied. 'Where are you?'

'In Cannes.'

'Look, we know you're on holiday,' I was told. 'But there's starting to be a lot of stuff in all the papers over here about Madonna. Apparently she's arriving in Cannes tomorrow – Saturday – and we were hoping you might do a piece for us. You know, get close to her – if you can. Plenty of colour.'

With Madonna, even before her arrival at Nice airport, generating a level of hype not seen in Cannes since 1955, when Brigitte Bardot walked down La Croisette in velvet trousers and an off-the-shoulder sweater, accompanied by a huge mastiff, I swiftly agreed.

Usually *The Times* covered the Cannes Film Festival with daily reports from the newspaper's film critic – for years David Robinson, succeeded by Geoff Brown – often accompanied by a feature writer or Cannes diarist (such as Griff Rhys-Jones) who provided the festival gossip, atmosphere and celebrity-fluff. In 1991, for some reason, *The Times* had no guest diarist, feature writer, or other correspondent, in Cannes.

Later that evening, I looked in at the European Pavilion – a ritzy Agincourt-style drinks tent stuck behind the Palais des Festivals, set in a crazy-paving marine garden surrounded by mini palm trees and flood-lit sprinklers, which doubled up as unofficial headquarters for British journalists and film executives. Held down by a few blue nylon ropes, the tent had nearly taken off and blown into the sea during the previous night's heavy storm. The air was still damp and clouds hung in the early evening sky like dirty tea-towels. Crossing the wooden gangway, I recognised the lanky figure of *Sunday Telegraph* hack Nicholas Farrell.

The British tabloids had, predictably, already descended on Cannes *en masse*. That the *Sunday Telegraph*, of all papers, had flown Farrell over for less than forty-eight hours just to stalk Madonna gave a pretty clear idea of the scale of media interest that was building up for her visit. To pursue Madonna from Nice airport, he had hired a fuel-injected, mango-coloured Talbot Samba convertible.

I woke the next morning with bright streaks of peach-white sunshine pouring through the curtains of my *pension* window. A cheery, Californian disc jockey on my radio said that it looked as if Madonna was bringing some LA weather with her to Cannes. The temperature was expected to peak at 83 degrees. Instead of wasting time hanging around at Nice airport, where hundreds of paparazzi were already camped out, I decided to drive up to the Hotel du Cap and wait for her there. I had made a 1p.m. lunch reservation at its Eden Rock restaurant under the name of Mr Jak King – executive director of the British Columbia and Yukon Council of Film Unions – who had left a pile of his thermographed visiting cards for people to pick up in the American Pavilion.

By the time I arrived, motorcyle police had erected a pen of metal wire-mesh barriers in which a mob of leather-jacketed, sun-burnt and tattooed photographers squeezed, heaved and jockeyed for a space closest to the hotel's twenty-foot high wrought-iron gates. A great barrel-chested Italian, who had three cameras slung around his hairy neck and looked as if he had just eaten a roasted boar, sat on a half-squashed black aluminium camera case. He was smoking a cigarette and reading *Penthouse*.

As I crunched up the pinky-grey gravel path to the main entrance, past two springy lawns manicured like giant billiard tables, a hotel guard in white gloves and a sable uniform stood to attention by a Venetian archway of clipped yew hedge. Beside him was a clipboard with hotel residents' names and what resembled a squash-league ladder with several visiting cards placed in the wooden grooves.

'Excuse me, sir,' he said. 'Are you a resident of the hotel?'

'I'm here for lunch.'

Digging into my wallet, I presented my newly acquired visiting card. After checking his tippex-splodged list, he slotted my card into the ladder board and ushered me through into the gleaming white marble lobby, with its deep cream sofas, gilt-mirrors and yellow damask silk cushions. The midday sun burned high in the cloudless sky. Not much was happening. The odd helicopter whirred loudly overhead, WASPy looking couples squeaked across the lobby holding tennis rackets. A Venezuelan woman in Onassis sunglasses rustled the pages of her *International Herald Tribune*. Robert De Niro jogged up from the swimming pool in a baggy grey track suit. Dark patches of sweat ran across his chest and under his armpits.

Shortly after 12.30p.m. I strolled down to the busy pool terrace restaurant. I ordered a club sandwich and a coffee that arrived in a silver pot so heavy that it stayed hot for nearly an hour. Then, just outside the entrance to the Eden Rock, there was a sudden fever of activity as a small army of staff encircled the entrance to a large villa which contained a number of VIP sea-facing suites. Squeezing past the ring of security guards in walkie-talkie heaven, I succeeded in standing hidden in a flower bed by the villa's smoked-glass doors. Several other journalists – none of them British – were already camouflaged behind a thorny eucalpytus bush: a busty blonde German with dull, Coca-Cola eyes and a leopard-spot swim-suit who worked for *Stern*; a suave man with a Leica in a sea-cotton shirt from *Nice-Matin* and a photographer from *Paris-Match* in a billowy, lime-coloured suit. Standing just inside the doorway was a barefooted pony-tailed giant wrapped in a chunky Hotel du Cap swimming robe.

A few minutes later, four black limousines pulled up sharply outside the entrance. The photographers crouched like sprinters on a starting block. A large minder opened a door and – instead of Madonna – what appeared to be an American football player stepped out in a pair of strawberry red bermuda shorts. It was, in fact, Arnold Schwarzenegger – in town to promote *Terminator 2* and his Planet Hollywood restaurant chain. Although he grinned widely at the cameras, nobody moved. Nobody cared.

The next hour was dull and cramped. Pulling out my small radio from my briefcase I heard through a tangled ear-piece that Madonna had – apparently – now arrived at the airport. There were unconfirmed reports that she had been strip-searched down to the inside of her dumb-bells. Shortly afterwards, Madonna's financial manager, a burly man in preppie glasses and a saggy Armani suit, arrived, along with her New York press agent, Liz Rosenberg, a schoolmarmish, self-important woman in her mid-forties who issued various sharp orders to hotel staff.

At that moment, a stream of police motorcycles roared up with their blue siren-lights flashing. Behind them a convoy of five stretch Mercedes limousines, the last with smoked black windows, swung down the immaculate drive and screeched to a halt amidst a cloud of dusty gravel. Doors and boots automatically clunked open. A dozen luggage boys moved in with the speed of a Formula One pit-stop team. Suddenly, the man in the towelling robe ingeniously produced a television camera from under his legs and started to film manically. He turned out to be from France's Channel 5. The rest of us leapt out of the eucalyptus bush.

A dark-haired Madonna eased herself out of the back seat. She was wearing purple leopard-spot leggings and was clutching a bouquet of orange roses. As she stood in front of me for about thirty seconds, I was surprised at how very scraggy and very small she was. Around her were her trainer, her dietician, her brother and a squad of bodyguards.

'What the fuck is all this!' she scowled, looking at us. 'I said *no* press at the hotel.'

'Get these people out of here now!' ordered Rosenberg.

Two bodyguards marched purposefully towards us. It was time to leave.

The next morning, after Madonna had gone jogging around the Cap d'Antibes (her bodyguards brawled with several pedestrians and left a cyclist lying on the road with a buckled wheel) I decided to pay a visit to the Majestic Hotel office suite of Dennis Davidson and Associates public relations to investigate the possibility of an official meeting with Madonna. I had been told she was doing a number of 'selected' interviews. The ground floor of the Majestic Hotel resembled a scene from a giant children's cartoon pop-up book. Gargantuan 3-D laminated cut-outs of forthcoming sci-fi and action films sprung out of the walls. Lines of baggy-suited executives sat in rows of soft leather armchairs inside tinted glass cubicles.

The DDA suite was on the second floor. My meeting lasted roughly two minutes. The man I spoke to looked like a nightclub disc jockey, with a spiky fringe and a brash, cock-sure manner. He wore a Blond Ambition tour tee-shirt. I disliked him on sight.

'You want to interview Madonna?' he asked in a guffaw of sarcastic laughter.

'That's right. I understand she's doing some British press.'

'You're a bit late,' he sniffed. 'Interview requests had to be in two weeks ago, so that journalists could be vetted. Her schedule has been drawn up – and it's full.'

'Vetted?'

'We need to have seen your work,' he said. 'We want to know which stars you've interviewed before. Madonna doesn't just see anyone.'

My rather thin cuttings-file, with my name tippexed on the spine, was pasted up with such stories as the Crufts dog show, the campaign to ban smoking on buses and the remodelling of the Post Office Tower. It was lying on the floor under my desk in *The Times* newsroom. I decided to switch the subject.

'What about her *Truth or Dare* party?' I asked. 'Are any press being allowed?'

'Sorry,' he said, showing me the door. 'Absolutely no press. It's a private party.'

Securing an invitation to the party – *the* party of 1991 Cannes Film Festival – made the procedure for getting inside the Royal Enclosure at Ascot look about as easy as buying two matinée movie tickets at the Fulham Road ABC. Invitations had been traded as part of high-finance Cannes film package-deals, stolen, forged and bootlegged – touts in the lobby of the Carlton Hotel were reported to be asking $1,000 a ticket.

As Madonna's convoy – hazard lights still flashing – continued to speed along the empty and twisting coastal road towards Cannes, I felt as if I was chained to the back of a high-speed roller-coaster. Whilst the limousine ahead of me hugged the road's hair-pin bends like a Scalextric racing car, I skidded and screeched around each bend, narrowly missing the cliff edge on several occasions. Accelerating up to 60mph after Nice, centrifugal forces took on new meaning as a blur of rocky banks, mountain barriers and dark tunnels flashed past me. Finally, near the bottom of the *corniche*, I somehow lost Madonna at a series of traffic lights.

In the event, however, I got into her *Truth or Dare* party without difficulty. Walking through the throng of fans, paparazzi and TV cameras outside the neo-Palladian entrance of the Palm Beach Club, I was mistaken for a VIP by *Entertainment Tonight* – America's most popular show-business news programme – and given a ten-minute interview about Madonna. I think they may have confused me with British actor Rupert Everett – a close friend of Madonna – who I had seen standing around in a pair of slippers looking lost. After the interview, I just followed the crowd.

The party was in the Palm Beach Club's Mogambo Club – a nightclub at the end of a gleaming black-and-white marble corridor, next to the casino's chic *salons privés*. It had been decorated for the evening like a tropical jungle and exotic aviary. Champagne and dainty little *hors d'oeuvres* were being served by semi-nude Jean Paul Gaultier muscle-men models dressed in matching flourescent green sandals and flamingo feather wigs, looking like a couple of extra-large dusters glued to their heads. Instead of a loin cloth, each had a kind of kinky leather jock-strap – as worn by the gay dancers on Madonna's Blond Ambition tour.

The outside dance floor, overlooking the Bay of Cannes, resembled a giant floodlit boxing ring, surrounded by little garden fête-like white VIP pavilions dotted around land-scaped water pools. The various bars had a choice of five malt whiskies and were over-stocked with enough cocktails to keep Harry's Bar in New York supplied for a year. Linen-covered banquet tables were piled with silver plates of chocolate strawberries, plump glacier fruits, fun-sized eclairs and itsy-bitsy crackers smothered in *foie gras* and caviar, and a row of silver platters the size of whirlpool baths heaped with giant shrimps, oysters and lobster claws.

It wasn't long before I spotted Baz Bamigboye, the giant panda-like showbiz editor of the *Daily Mail* and Piers Morgan of the *Sun* huddled together on a sofa by an outdoor fountain. Tina Turner and Robin Givens (former wife of

Mike Tyson) were sitting opposite. Bamigboye, dressed in a navy suit and flashy lime-and-silver tie, had apparently succeeded in getting into the club by claiming he was the son of Nigerian Prince Mogambo, who owned the nightclub. He had had a box of bogus Prince Mogambo business cards printed. Morgan, I think, was rather badly disguised as a waiter. A number of other tabloid hacks also skulked around, along with Radio 1 disc jockey Simon Bates who walked around on his own all evening.

Not being a regular of international showbiz parties, the impression from my debut was that despite the organisers' efforts to create a Bacchic carnival, nobody seemed to be particularly enjoying themselves. Apart from a few dozen household celebrity names, the vast majority of the guests (presumably film industry executives) looked bored and, like Bates, wandered around self-consciously before leaving on their own. And another odd thing. Celebrities such as Eddie Murphy sat inside their private pavilions like medieval Oriental suzerains, surrounded by their bodyguards, and never came out. I peeked inside his tent and he was sitting crouched on the floor wearing sunglasses. It was pitch black outside.

Madonna herself was enclosed in a roped-off super-VIP area close to the disco, chatting with Rupert Everett. The likes of Dennis Hopper, director Alan Parker and Roman Polanski, the Cannes Jury chairman, sat at nearby tables, trying hard not to keep glancing at her. As she talked, she touched up her blubbery lips with Chanel scarlet-red lipstick. Wearing a shiny sequinned black top, fish-net stockings and hot pants, her sleeked hair looked as if she had just used a can of black treacle for shampoo. About a hundred film executives, as well as dozens of Hollywood sub-celebrities, and micro-celebrities, were gawping at her, craning their necks and ogling on tip-toe to get a glimpse, like a bus-load of Japanese tourists at London Zoo.

Without warning, Madonna's bodyguards forcefully parted the crowd of oglers as Miss Ciccone, dragging along a pony-tailed local dancer, suddenly took to the dance-floor.

Encircled by minders, she began to strut and groove wildly, moving her sinewy and pumped-up arms like a well-synchronised piston engine. Having taken off her top, her sharply pointed black brassière stuck out like a pair of dangerous looking torpedo tips. A few moments later Roman Polanski joined her, after which she seemed to dance on her own. Seeing my chance, I was surprised to be let through by her bodyguards into the ring. As I did so, Madonna glanced at me with a look that said: 'Okay, you lanky English smart ass, show me your stuff.'

I suddenly had an overwhelming desire to be John Travolta. Unfortunately, I have never been a very good dancer. Whilst she twisted and turned herself inside out, with sweat glistening down her back like warm cooking oil, I did my best to keep up. Suddenly somebody handed her a small red rose, which she quickly stuffed into her cleavage. Her designer stubble armpits at close quarters was not a sight of beauty but as she grooved and twisted on I did admire her animal energy. As I shook around in front of her, Madonna gyrated and dervished so hard that one of her earrings fell to the floor. In a flash, Baz Bamigboye – who was also now swaying beside Madonna – quickly threw himself to the floor like an eager Tongan pearl diver, scrambling under the dark sea of legs and heels until he finally emerged triumphantly clutching a dinky little silver earring. It looked as if it could have come out of a Christmas cracker.

'Where do you want me to put it?' he shouted above the blasting music.

Before she had time to reply, a bodyguard snatched it away.

As the music got louder and louder, and with gluey sweat now streaming down Madonna's body, her precision-engineered dancing began to take on a dangerous new aspect. With her body's joints swivelling together like those of a finely calibrated robotic doll, she began inter-coiling her back with a newly appeared French dancer. They resembled a pair of randy toads scratching their rumps against the roots of a tree. Politely known as the 'lambada', it was, basically, a form of sex on the dance-floor. Sensing that I was well out of my depth, I beat a retreat. Taking a final look at her studded ice-cream cone brassière, I concluded that if Madonna's dancing was anything to judge by, going anywhere near her bedroom was probably a highly hazardous activity.

I squeezed out of the throbbing dance-floor and wandered over to the nearest bar to get a much-needed drink, where I met a late-twenties-looking green-eyed Californian blonde in a cream Valentino suit. I can't recall exactly how we began talking but her name was Beverly. She was a producer in LA with her own film company and lived in the Hollywood Hills. She said she was in Cannes to sort out the distribution of her new film. After we chatted for about an hour, she handed me her heavily embossed business card – President, Rhinoceros Films – scribbled her Cannes number on the back (she had rented a penthouse apartment overlooking the sea) and said she had to go. The friend she had come with – a female Hollywood director – had a car waiting.

'We can drop you somewhere if you like,' she said.

I took them up on their offer. There was a late-night party at the Majestic. It was now about midnight and Madonna's party was beginning to thin out. She had left some time ago.

Ten minutes later I was being chauffeured down La Croisette in the back of a navy stretch Mercedes with tinted windows, walnut interior and all-black leather seats. Although I tried slumping back on the rear sofa-sized seat in an effort to look as if I was used to being limoed around London's West End, it was, in fact, the first time I had ever been in such a vehicle.

At 10.45p.m. the next evening I was standing in steamy drizzle on the top of red-carpeted steps of the Palais des Festivals waiting for Madonna to arrive for the *Truth or Dare* première. I was quickly losing interest in her. A boppy selection of her greatest hits – including *Holiday* about four times – blared out of small speakers fixed to the wall. It was impossible to move. I was surrounded by a local crowd of thousands, along with several hundred elbowing and pushing paparazzi, kept in order by a three-officer solid line of trench-coated *gendarmerie* armed with machine guns and rubber truncheons.

When the Material Girl finally did arrive, wearing a candy-pink satin wrap, the paparazzi simply stampeded through the police line like a rampaging mob of wart-hogs. As she got about half way up the red-carpeted steps, only a few feet from where I was standing, Madonna turned to face the frenzied whir of motor-drives and electronic flash-guns and dropped her pink coverup to reveal her Gaultier designed underwear: white armour-plated brassière and matching 1930s-style tight corset. The publicity stunt over – it had taken three months to plan – Madonna was ushered towards the Grand Auditorium Lumière where she received a nasty surprise.

Instead of this pompadour pleasure dome being packed, with 1,500 guests luxuriating in their purple velvet bucket seats, the auditorium was, in fact, only about a third full. Despite *Truth or Dare* being one of the most over-hyped moves in Cannes history – the film was delivered to the festival chained to security guards – its world première audience, ridiculously, resembled that of a Tuesday afternoon matinée of a soon-to-be-taken-off 'B' movie. Thanks to some crass security handling, the entrance doors were closed long before Madonna actually arrived – resulting in over half of those with actual tickets, such as myself, being left outside in the spitting rain whilst the crowd and photographers slunk away. Frankly, I no longer cared. My Madonna mission over, I now intended to enjoy the remainder of my holiday on the Riviera.

Dinner with Beverly the next night went well – very well, in fact. We went to Mesclun, tucked away behind the Carlton hotel on the Rue St Antoine and sat at a cosy little table eating mussels and *fillet de rouget*. Afterwards we stopped off for a late drink at the Petit Carlton bar, with its noisy crowd of lager-slurping tabloid hacks spilling onto the street like drunken weekend football fans. When I invited her to have dinner, again, the following evening in Cap Ferrat, she agreed. The Hotel Bel-Air was thirty-five snaking kilometres east of Cannes. She did not have a car.

We began an affair at the hotel over the next few days. I was glad to be away from Cannes – where the faces of so many at the festival wore the defensive and wounded expressions of people who had spent too many years having their ideas misunderstood and ambitions stalled.

The hotel – with only fifty-nine rooms – resembled a sumptuous private villa whose *Architectural Digest*-featured black and white Italian marble lobby made the Hotel du Cap seem about as glamorous as a Midwestern Motel Six. The lobby, framed by two fifteenth-century urns containing topiary trees clipped like spear heads, was dominated by a huge gilt round table with carved golden dolphin legs sitting on a Louis XIV carpet.

My room overlooked both the Mediterranean and the hotel's fourteen-acre rolling park of wild broom, orange, myrtle and thyme set amidst sub-tropical gorges and pine trees. The huge white marble bath, with gleaming gold taps and a water-resistant telephone, would not have looked out of place in a James Bond film. The biggest novelty of all, however, came on my first visit to the lavatory. The moment any pressure was applied to the seat an electronic device was activated which piped melodious musak out of a hidden speaker. That the room was not costing me 6,000 francs a night – a fact I did not mention to Beverly – merely added to such pleasures.

On the last night, I crashed my car in Cannes. The next morning, Beverly hired a car and announced she would drive me back to London herself. She didn't think much of my driving, and she had two weeks free before her next movie went into development.

After a few days staying in my London flat, followed by a weekend in Gloucestershire, Beverly flew back to her deals and power-lunching in LA – whilst I returned to my desk by the newsroom back-door. Being realistic, I doubted I would ever see her again.

2

West from Wapping

ABOUT A MONTH AFTER RETURNING from Cannes, and a few days after *The Silence of the Lambs* opened in London, an airmail envelope arrived on my desk postmarked San Quentin, California. Inside was a neatly typed letter from Douglas Daniel Clark (address: Death Row, San Quentin Prison, California) politely submitting an unsolicited article on serial killers to *The Times*. He wanted no payment, and asked only that we send him a copy of the relevant issue if the piece was published 'as I cannot obtain your fine journal at my present address'.

The letter was not a hoax. Although Clark never bragged to police of killing more than sixty people like Donald Leroy Evans, or of chopping up and cannabalising his victims like Jeffrey Dahmer, a phone call to Colin Wilson, author of *The Encyclopaedia of Modern Murder*, informed me that Clark was otherwise known as 'The Sunset Slayer' – being one of America's most notorious convicted serial killers in recent criminal history. Another call to Don Lindsey, assistant to the warden of San Quentin prison, outside San Francisco, confirmed that forty-three-year-old Clark was currently awaiting the gas chamber (although the last execution in California had been nearly a quarter of a century ago) for the murder in 1980 of six young prostitutes whom he picked up on West Hollywood's Sunset Strip and shot in the head whilst they had oral sex with him. Clark subsequently confirmed to the officer who visited the cell that he had submitted an article to *The Times*.

Whilst many murderers send notes to the police (Jack the Ripper) or newspaper editors (Son of Sam), revealing the urge to be 'somebody' in their macabre quest for recognition, the submission of a cogent article to *The Times* was believed to be unique. Colin Wilson could think of no convicted mass murderer in modern history who had offered to write feature or editorial articles for a national newspaper before. The only precedent was Moors Murderer Ian Brady, who wrote to the letters page of the *Daily Mirror*.

Clark's 900-word article, entitled 'A Fatal Attraction', was fluently written – typed with double-spacing, on cheap white paper – and argued that an increase in the number of state executions would lead to an epidemic of serial killings since many mass killers, such as Ted Bundy, viewed the prospect of the electric chair as the biggest thrill of all. 'Death,' wrote Clark, 'is the object, not a dreaded consequence to the killers' minds.' Being marked 'Attention: *Times Editorial*' in large black-ink lettering, the letter ended up on my desk after being handed to me by Graham Paterson, *The Times*' op-ed editor (i.e. comment page), to whom I had recently been assigned. With the record-breaking British box-office success of *The Silence of the Lambs* inducing a glut of news and 'Inside the criminal mind' articles comparing Dr Lecter with Dahmer – the *Daily Telegraph* went so far as to note architectural differences between their cells – Paterson told me to try calling up the 'Sunset Slayer'. 'See if you can talk to him,' I was told. 'He's in an American prison – he's probably got his own phone.'

I put a number of calls about this through to the warden's office at San Quentin. Clark was, I soon discovered, something of a serial killer celebrity, having been profiled at some length in *Vanity Fair*. The magazine reported, for example, how he was well educated, had a high IQ and regularly played bridge with three other death-row inmates. Such was his personal magnetism, indeed, that seven years before he had been married inside San Quentin prison to a legal researcher convinced of his innocence. They did not know each other before he was arrested. 'We got married in the room next to the gas chamber,' his wife told me from her Arizona home, 'I guess it wasn't too romantic.'

His lawyer in Los Angeles, Verna Wefald, explained that her client had a fascinating although stubborn personality and that she was hoping to have the verdict on him overturned, claiming that important evidence was witheld at his original trial. Clark always maintained his innocence. Representing himself, he had told the jury: 'I don't march to the same drummer you do. If we were all like me, Sodom and Gomorrah might look like a nice place to stay.'

About a week after receiving Clark's letter and article, I got back to my desk after a late lunch to find a yellow memo sticker on my telephone.

'Somebody called for you,' I was informed by Ray Clancy, the ruthlessly efficient Glaswegian reporter who sat next to me. 'I wrote it down.'

Her scrawled message simply read: 'Doug called.'

Calling up the warden's office at San Quentin I received some inauspicious news.

'Mr Cash, we're real sorry,' I was told. 'We did allow inmate Clark to call you before morning exercise.'

'But he didn't get through. I never spoke to him.'

'He got through to somebody.'

'Would you be kind enough to let him call me again – later?'

'I'm afraid we can't do that. It would be against the regulations.'

'Why?'

'He's used up his telephone calls.'

'I don't understand.'

'Clark is permitted to make one telephone call a month.'

Instead of speaking to the 'Sunset Slayer' long-distance, I began a lengthy correspondence with him. Within a month or so the drawer of my desk was bulging with several thick airmail envelopes, each meticulously typed with his death-row address in the top-right corner. When his typewriter broke down, he wrote me a ten-page letter in black biro, in a stylish, clear hand. His spelling and grammar were perfect.

The letter ended by saying he would 'write again soon' with another article that he had recently written on the 'copycat' phenomenon, which is 'awesomely popular in the USA'. In the last letter I received, he wrote: 'If you want to visit me, I can probably arrange it. San Quentin is a quaint little seaside town. The prison overlooks the San Francisco Bay. You mentioned that you also played bridge. I could organise a four with some friends if you like.'

I began to think about this unusual invitation from the 'Sunset Slayer' – and a possible summer holiday in California, combined with seeing Beverly again. She had written regularly – long letters in loopy handwriting on onion-skin paper – asking me to stay in her house up in the Hollywood Hills.

Not long after, at a drinks party, I got chatting with *The Times*' foreign editor, Martin Ivens. Although I sat only about twenty yards from the foreign desk, with its bank of telephones and array of international time-zone clocks, we had hardly ever spoken. Often, returning from lunch by the newsroom back door, he would shuffle hurriedly past my desk in mid-conversation with a foreign desk colleague or senior editor. I had once been seconded to the foreign desk for a day during a snow blizzard to help man the phones and had caused chaos as I began trying to field simultaneous calls from correspondents in New York, Japan, Moscow and Johannesburg. Despite the fact that all trainees were meant to work for a few months on the foreign desk I was never asked back after that débâcle.

'William,' Ivens said. 'I think you're meant to spend some time working for me.'

'Yes,' I said awkwardly. 'I'm meant to. But I don't have to do it.'

'Frankly I don't think working on the foreign desk would be a very good idea,' he said. 'Don't take it personally or anything. I just don't think it would work. You're not an office person. In fact you're a huge liability.'

'You're right,' I said dourly. 'I'm not much good with computers.'

'But you could write for me instead.'

'Write?'

'The foreign pages always need plenty of colour stories. Think about it.'

Getting out of Britain seemed a good idea. In my last year at Cambridge, I remember sitting in the Magdalene College Parlour, enveloped in a candlelit haze, listening to an after-dinner talk by Anthony Sampson, author of *The Anatomy of Britain*. 'If I have any advice to give you,' he said, looking at us down the long table, strewn with coffee-cups, 'get a job as far away from London as is humanly possible. Apart from anything else, people will always think you are having a much better time than they are.'

When I later suggested to Martin Ivens that I go out to California in September – taking up the invitation of the 'Sunset Slayer' – I was a little surprised, I have to admit, at the apparent eagerness with which my idea was received. They clearly couldn't bear to have me in the office much longer. More to the point, I was extremely cheap.

Los Angeles seemed a good place to start out as a foreign correspondent. To begin with, *The Times* – like the BBC and ITN – simply had no correspondent on the West Coast of the United States. Coverage came from *The Times'* New York super-hack Charles Bremner, and the wire services, or *The Sunday Times*'s correspondent, Sam Kiley. Not that this especially troubled the foreign desk. With the exception of the *Daily Telegraph*, whose respected correspondent John Hiscock first came out to California in the early seventies, and the *Guardian*'s Christopher Reed who – rather oddly – lived practically in Death Valley, four hours' drive north-east of Los Angeles, neither did any of the other quality papers.

Traditionally, California was viewed on Fleet Street as something of a pasturing ground for fluffed-out hacks. It was considered, rather uncharitably perhaps, as a marshmallow beat – the soft-centre of American journalism. Whatever news came out of Tinseltown mostly appeared as tabloid showbiz gossip or as a light colour piece at the bottom of the foreign pages. Nobody took Los Angeles very seriously.

By mid 1991, that was beginning to change. Just two months before the 3 March video of Rodney King writhing on the ground as he was clubbed fifty-six times by four white LAPD officers was beamed to TV sets around the world, *The Economist* had dispatched the highly regarded twenty-eight-year-old John Micklethwait to open up a West Coast office based at the *Los Angeles Times.* Six months later *The Independent* decided to send out their former Gulf War reporter Phil Reeves to be their first LA correspondent. He was arriving in early autumn.

By September, *The Times* foreign desk machinery went into action. My passport was sent to the American Embassy in Grosvenor Square, returning stamped with a journalist's 'I' visa – valid until 1996. Like twenty-eight-year-old Peter Fleming, who had worked as a special correspondent for *The Times* in China in the thirties (writing up his experiences in *One's Company*), I was given a batch of very official looking '*To whom it may concern*' letters of introduction signed by Martin Ivens and embossed in purple-black ink with a pre-war looking *Times* stamp the size of a Privy Council seal. There was a letter to get accreditation with the LAPD, another for attempting to gain access to the cuttings library of the *Los Angeles Times.* 'William Cash is *The Times* of London's correspondent based in Los Angeles. Mr Cash is establishing a new office and has no press cuttings. I would be very grateful if you could give him access to your library on an occasional basis.'

Next stop was sorting out my contract in the upstairs executive office of the managing editor of *The Times*, Peter Roberts. Although the affable Mr Roberts always seemed to have a glowing smile on his face, in the case of my contract he had an especially good reason. The financial terms of my contract are, frankly, too embarrassing to disclose. But I was so grateful to be moving from the News International plant in Wapping to the Hollywood Hills in California that it didn't bother me. I was scheduled to arrive in Los Angeles a few days before Elizabeth Taylor's 'wedding of the century' to eighth husband Larry Fortensky. Beverly was to pick me up from the airport.

After my leaving party, at which I had been presented with, amongst other items, a jumbo-sized box of condoms marked 'For use in LA', I went along to say goodbye to the editor of *The Times*, Simon Jenkins. I had long admired his de Quincean style. It was around 7p.m. by the time I was ushered into his editor's office, the size of a large portacabin, with its nineteenth-century oil paintings of former *Times* editors hanging on the walls, a large mahogany bookcase and several split clumps of *The Times* lying around on a desk. After checking the proof of a leader he had just written, he poured out two large glasses of Scotch. 'I think you are going to the right place,' he said. 'LA seems to be turning into the South Africa of the Nineties. What happens there will be very interesting. I wish you luck.'

'And William,' he finally added. 'Be careful. LA is not Shropshire.'

3

Invitation to a Wedding

WHEN TWENTY-SIX-YEAR-OLD David Hockney first arrived in LA on a warm December evening in 1963, he knew absolutely nobody. Having bought his airplane ticket with the money earnt from his autobiographical series of sixteen *A Rake's Progress* prints – his twentieth-century update, set in New York, of William Hogarth's nineteenth-century cautionary tale of dissolute youth – he checked into a cheap motel in Santa Monica. Wanting a drink, he walked along the beach – looking for LA. 'I saw some lights and I thought, that must be it,' he wrote in 1976. 'I walked two miles, and when I got there all it was was a big gas station, so brightly lit I'd thought it was the city.'

I wasn't quite that naïve. I had been to Los Angeles once before – aged eighteen, in the summer of 1985, at the end of a work-around-the-world trip after leaving school. On my third day in LA, however, I had been robbed at knifepoint by a black teenager outside the Sunset Palms Motel on Sunset Boulevard. With no money, I had to fly on to New York immediately. Having spent most of my first day in LA on a tram doing the Universal Studios tour, and the second getting hopelessly lost in the Holmby Hills trying to follow the recorded directions to Rod Stewart's $10 million mansion on a 'Tour of the Movie Stars' Homes' cassette that you played in your car, my knowledge of the city was minimal.

On my return in 1991, I also knew nobody – with the exception of Beverly, whose position as a producer I was trusting would be my *entrée* into Hollywood's Roladexes, and the 'Sunset Slayer' up near San Francisco. Like Hockney, who had done some quite serious fantasising before he arrived in LA, I was rather hoping that California would be a 'sunny land of movie-studios and beautiful semi-naked people'. Staying – or rather *living* – with Beverly, high up in the hills, above the 101 Hollywood Freeway, I had some pretty high expectations of LA this time round. As Martin Amis has John Self admit in *Money*: 'California, Land of my dreams and my longing.'

It began, at least, like in the movies. Shuffling down a LAX escalator towards the baggage claim I stepped out into the electric-blue afternoon, feeling the heat whoomph into me as if walking into a sauna in a ski-suit. But the dream didn't last very long. About six minutes to be exact. For a highly successful Hollywood movie producer, Beverly did seem to have rather an unusual choice of car: a seriously smashed-up old Fiat that made a three-wheel Robin Reliant suddenly seem like a Saab turbo. Back in the early seventies, I suppose, it must have been a dinky little black sports convertible. But as I squashed myself into the passenger seat, rather anxiously noting that half the dashboard was missing, I felt as if the jaws of a scrap-yard crane were just about to clamp down on us. After about five minutes, the vehicle finally started – belching out oily black smoke – only to groan, whine and then shudder to a halt after ten yards.

'Are you a member of an emergency road rescue service?' I asked.

'It's just overheating,' she said, revving the motor. 'Nothing serious, William. Can you get out for a moment. I think I might need a push.'

About two hours later, we finally spluttered up a hill in north Hollywood. Her 'house' was not really a house – it was a hut. Perched at the top of a steep rocky path overlooking Universal Studios, you almost needed climbing boots to make it to the door. The studenty furniture was covered with dog-hairy white sheets. I have always liked dogs. But her two yapping mongrels were the most unpleasant animals that I had ever encountered. They had a nasty habit of scratching their bottoms on either your legs, or the legs of a chair, until their skin was pink raw. They were fed with what looked like dried cardboard. On a more practical note – such as reporting on Liz Taylor's wedding – I soon realised that I was completely *incommunicado* from not only LA, but the rest of the world. The TV didn't work properly – lacking even the basic CNN cable service – and the fax machine was broken. I had a telephone and my short-wave wireless.

It didn't take me long to work out that Beverly – nice as she was – was not exactly close to becoming the next Sherry Lansing of independent producers. She had, it should be said, produced one super low-budget 'D' horror film called something like *Sex and Sorcery 4*, which included lashings of clumsy sex, buckets of stage blood and had been released directly onto video. Apart from that – as far as I could make out – all other 'projects' were either 'in development', 'seeking finance', 'temporarily on hold' or 'generating interest'. Beverly was, in fact, very representative of a certain type of 'producer' – and I came to meet plenty of them in LA – who gave out the quiet impression they were practically running a studio when, in reality, there was about as much chance of any of their films being made as Liz Taylor inviting the *National Enquirer* to be her official 'Liz n' Larry' wedding photographer.

* * *

Meanwhile, inside an ivory-silk tent pitched on the front lawn of pop star Michael Jackson's 2,700 acre Neverland Valley ranch, an hour's drive north of LA just outside Santa Barbara, the props, stage and silver forks were being set for what was being billed by the American media as fifty-nine-year-old Elizabeth Taylor's biggest role since she floated down the Nile to the sound of trumpets on a golden barge in *Cleopatra* – her fairyland 'wedding of the century' that Sunday

(6 October) to Larry Fortensky, a Mr Nobody with permed goldilock sideburns, a waddly Gary Glitter walk and a dubious past. Not that this comparison bode very well for her nuptial extravaganza. The Egyptian 'epic' in which she had co-starred in 1963 with Richard Burton, had not only been the most expensive film ever made, but also one of the most mismanaged, over-hyped and absurd movies in cinema history.

But to the world media, the $1.5 million *marriage-à-la-mode*, with supporting cast that was supposed to include two former American presidents and half of Hollywood's *hoi oligoi*, seemed like a fantasy come true. Liz n' Larry met at the Betty Ford Centre in 1988. For thirty-nine-year-old lorry driver Larry to be arrested for drunk-driving, be ordered by a Californian court to enrol in a rehabilitation centre and end up being proposed to over a hamburger by a co-patient, who also just *happens* to be one of the richest and most famous film stars in the world . . . such things are only meant to happen in bad TV movies.

After hiring a car, I soared up an empty Golden State freeway early on the day of the wedding. Turning off near Santa Barbara, I took a narrow track which cut through the bare desert landscape of the Santa Ynez Valley. Winding between two camel-hump hillsides of scorched grass, the dusty three-mile road leading from the western town of Los Olivos – population 250 – to Michael Jackson's ranch looked as if it would normally be deserted around midday on a sulphur-blue Sunday morning.

But when I drove past the castellated lodge and gates of Jackson's Neverland fantasy estate, the track did – indeed – resemble what looked exactly like the set for a multi-million-dollar TV mini-series. Pulled up on the side of the road were dozens of caravans and TV satellite trucks, each with their own whirring generators and transmitters like fifteen-foot high porcelain saucers.

Poking my head inside a large caravan, parked up on the dusty verge like a giant beached Portaloo, I was met by a sweating man in a lumberjack shirt and jeans who resembled a hippy motorcycle mechanic. He had greasy-looking wavy brown hair, dark-ale-brown eyes and introduced himself as Barry Levine, chief correspondent of the American Tabloid the *Star*. Once he had established that I was not a spy for his two main tabloid rivals, the *Globe* and the *National Enquirer*, he invited me to sit down in his trailer's springless zebra-striped sofa-bunk. He fished out two cans of Coca-Cola bobbing in the ice-slushy cool-box. Inside the caravan the chaotic mess (a bank of TV monitors, CB radio equipment, bundles of manky sleeping bags, crates of beer and cigarette boxes) made the inside of the Merry Prankster's 1939 Day-glo schoolbus after their 1964 American roadtrip suddenly seem as Ajax-clean as a Tokyo subway train.

I asked him how big a story this wedding really was.

'HOW BIG?' he exclaimed, slurping his Coke down his front, 'We're going to hog wild on coverage. I've covered all the BIG stories – from Christina Onassis' death in Buenos Aires to Mike Tyson's visit to Moscow – and this is by far the biggest event of the decade. You see this—'

He pointed to a bank of TV monitoring screens.

'You know why we're using these?'

'No.'

'Liz is not a schmuck,' he grunted, wiping his brow. 'She's a pro at publicity. She has been clever. What makes this wedding such a bitch to cover is that every detail we possibly wanted to know was let out a month ago. We've known the story for a whole month already!'

There was a crackling noise on one of his CB radio receivers. 'Come in mission control, come in Barry . . . some security goons have jumped me in the bushes. I'm riding in the back of a van. I can't see where we are going . . . are you there Barry? I think they're just gonna throw us out at the gates. They've ripped out my film. Can you send someone to pick us up?'

'Shit!' said Barry. 'We started off with twenty reporters. Now we're down to about six. This whole stupid event is starting to piss me off. I mean if Liz had really wanted a "private" wedding she could have sneaked off to Las Vegas, or simply had a ceremony in a Beverly Hills church and given a fifteen-minute press conference afterwards. But she'll regret it. When we send the choppers up, she'll wish she had invited the whole goddamn bunch of us to sit in the front row.'

Levine clicked down on his CB radio. 'Okay, guys we're sending someone over.'

The Neverland grounds (which included an amusement park and zoo) were guarded by the American Secret Service (for Ronald Reagan, who was a no-show due to 'pressing business') and a cadre of Santa Barbara County Police patrolling inside the ranch on horseback and circling the neighbouring hills to check that nobody was trying to slip in from the neighbouring Los Padres National Forest. In addition, there was also Michael Jackson's own team of mercenary personal guards *and* a sixty-strong force of security troops handpicked by six-foot Moshe 'The Brute' Alon – Miss Taylor's full-time personal bodyguard, reported to be a former Israeli Mossad commander. His 'Professional Security Consultants' installed, for example, a metal detection device at the entrance. But despite spending a rumoured $100,000 stringing up a circle of helium Mylar balloons around the estate, which he hoped would deter helicopters from flying below 250 feet, by about 3p.m. the sky above the ranch resembled a scene from *Apocalypse Now*. A roaring armada of fifteen Vietnam-style media helicopters whirred a dozen or so feet above the balloons like a swarm of giant black wasps on heat.

This buzzing nest included several helicopters commandeered by British reporters who had flown over to LA just for the wedding. Squashed for six hours inside the cockpit of one tiny little helicopter, for example, was the *Daily Mail*'s Baz Bamigboye clenching a pair of ultra-powerful zoom binoculars. He was, however, virtually unable to see any of the ceremony. After whirring around in what felt like the inside of a tumble dryer, he started to feel unwell. When his attempt to file copy to London from his cellular phone failed, Baz resorted to hammering on the door of a local farm and bribing the farmer with $50 to let him use his telephone. 'I'll never go in a helicopter again,' he assured me later. 'I had the fright of my life that day because the photographer had taken the door off.'

Whizzing around the clear blue sky with Bamigboye, having left his private hangar at Santa Monica airport that morning whilst I was breezing up the Golden State Highway, was Phil Ramey, the infamous paparazzo and celebrity stalker who is widely credited with being the first photographer to chain himself regularly to the outside of a helicopter. Or rather *his* helicopter. So successful had Ramey become at snooping from the air that he hadn't just hired a helicopter for the afternoon, he was using his own $1 million customised French-made helicopter. It was equipped with a million candlepower laser beam and a microwave device that enabled him to wire photographs anywhere in the world from the back-seat – whilst in mid-air. Described by *American Photo* as 'the most dreaded paparazzo in Hollywood', Ramey's asking prices for Liz Taylor wedding photos made him dreaded equally by photo editors and celebrity guests. On assignment for both the *Daily Mail* and *Globe*, he had spent two days practising in the sky above the ranch, working out aerial vantage points and hovering above the previous day's wedding dress rehearsal.

Ramey earns over $500,000 a year. 'All photo editors are whores,' he told me later. 'None of them wouldn't buy a $10,000 picture for fifty bucks if they had the chance. What passes for paparazzi these days is usually just a bunch of jerks hanging around outside a restaurant. To be good, you have to get in and burn celebrities – right at their tables, or from the sky.'

In another helicopter was paparazzo Kip Rano. Originally from Hendon, north London, he now drives around LA in an old gold Rolls Royce. For the wedding, he drove out to Neverland in a jeep fitted with a custom-made rack for transporting his specially adapted set of professional astronomical telescope lenses. They all fitted snugly in a series of coffin-like cases custom built by an LA cabinet maker.

The media lapped up the bait offered to them. As a carefully calculated publicity stunt, Taylor's plan seemed to work perfectly. As the blazing afternoon wore on, the media resorted to increasingly desperate – and dangerous – measures to catch a glimpse of her most extravagant and expensive wedding yet. A pair of tabloid photographers, reportedly disguised as kangaroos, were arrested at 3.30p.m. close to the gardenia-bedecked gazebo in which the ceremony was scheduled to start at 5p.m. Other would-be photo-snipers who were escorted off the premises were reported to include a man in a Michael Jackson mask.

Earlier, the *Star*'s surprise *coup de grâce*, masterminded by Barry Levine, went disastrously wrong when the Zeppelin-like seven-storey hot-air balloon with which they intended to block out the view of the wedding for their tabloid rivals in helicopters failed to take-off as planned. They spent thousands of dollars persuading a local Santa Ynez wine-maker to allow them to turn part of his vineyard into a camouflaged launching pad. But Levine's hopes of obtaining world exclusive pictures were swiftly dashed when their Baron Münchausen craft, equipped with two photographers and several telephoto lenses the size of four-ton cannons, exploded after lifting only six feet off a patch of scorched grape scrub.

'It was the wrong fuel!' ranted Levine by way of an explanation. 'We were sabotaged. This is the stupidest, most ridiculous event I have ever covered,' he cursed as he slammed shut his trailer door.

Meanwhile, back at the ranch, final preparations were getting underway for Liz's great comeback role in Elizabeth Taylor VIII – the movie. That morning, whilst florist David Jones had decorated the gazebo, the bride-to-be, Miss Taylor, 'came out in her night-gown to watch,' he said later. 'She was like a little girl at her first party.' Later that afternoon, when she first heard the helicopters, she stepped outside and wailed into the sky: 'You bastards!'

Guests had been asked to arrive *no later* than 4.30p.m. Limos – with the exception of Nancy Reagan's – were searched at the lodge for cameras. Each guest had to present an invitation, vehicle pass and personal ID. The official wedding photographer was Herb Ritts, who was donating an undisclosed *part* of the multi-million dollar world syndicated sale proceeds to Aids research. Following a tip that an invited guest was going to try and snap a photograph with a camera hidden inside a cigarette lighter, all smoker guests – such as David Hockney – were required to turn over their cigarette lighters in exchange for cheap plastic Bics.

As with most Hollywood 'events', the actual guest list bore little relation to the names of those widely advertised as going to be present. The cast who did attend were a strange mix of old Hollywood, gay Hollywood, New Age Hollywood, medical Hollywood and rebuilt Hollywood, along with a posse of maverick stars, a legion of sub-celebrities – such as hairdresser José Eber – your average bus-load of non-entities and the respective Taylor and Fortensky family clans. The latter refused to be limoed to the service, preferring to arrive in their own cars.

By the late afternoon those ready to sit on the white wooden fold-up chairs on Michael Jackson's lawn included: Fox chairman Barry Diller with date Diane von Furstenberg (quote: 'You could just look in their eyes and tell Liz was very happy.'), billionaire record mogul David Geffen, actress Brooke Shields, *Rolling Stone* publisher Jann Wenner, Quincy Jones, Merv Griffin and Eva Gabor, Gregory and Veronique Peck (quote: 'Larry is very attentive; he takes care of her and is very loving.'), billionaires Marvin and Barbara Davis, film director Franco Zeffirelli and Californian plastic body surgeon Dr Steve Hoeflin (whose clients include Michael Jackson and Ivana Trump). And, of course, there was host Michael 'The Gloved One' himself, dressed in a high-collar designer black Darth Vader track-suit outfit, with what looked like a sheriff 's badge sewn onto his breast pocket, and silver cowboy boots. He kept his black gloves on all day.

Barred from the *Star*'s trailer, whilst they sulked inside trying to come up with a contingency plan, I moved over to the headquarters of the *National Enquirer*. Their trailer was a bit less shambolic, with several senior editors and reporters hunched over a set of video monitors, twiddling lots of knobs. This time, however, there was at least a fuzzy image to look at. Peering closer, the black-and-white screen flickered and crackled like a TV set without an aerial.

'I think I can see something,' muttered a man in an LA Raiders cap.

'There's the signal. He's jumping,' said another.

'There's no picture. I can't see the picture.'

Suddenly there was a loud cheer from the crowd of gawkers, celebrity tourists, locals and hundred-strong pack of reporters gathered around the Neverland gates. Following the *National Enquirer* team outside, I could see the figure of a dare-devil parachutist pulling frantically on his toggles as he glided dangerously close to the frenziedly spinning sea of helicopter blades above the ranch. His two-minute descent, from which he looked down on a private lake, was watched in bewilderment by the crowd and a posse of police. As his rhubarb-and-blue striped chute disappeared from view, there was a second loud burst of applause.

The parachutist, whose flight the *Enquirer* seemed to have been tracking, turned out to be a thirty-four-year-old LA photographer Scott Harris, a manic fan of Elizabeth Taylor, who was attempting to capture her wedding for posterity with a camera that he had Sellotaped to his crash helmet. The special camera was supposed to transmit live images of the wedding back to two caravans on the ground but it failed to work properly. Harris, an experienced sky diver, had landed just fifteen yards from Liz Taylor in the middle of the wedding ceremony.

Before he had a chance to unzip his jumpsuit to present Liz Taylor with the bunch of silk red roses he had carried with him, he was handcuffed by a dozen security guards and led away for two hours of 'questioning' by Moshe 'The Brute' Alon.

The ceremony increasingly seemed to belong in a Tom Sharpe novel. As the helicopters continued to roar overhead, drowning out the possibility of hearing any of the actual service – let alone the grand piano and violin quartet – love-guru Marianne Williamson grabbed a cordless microphone in an attempt to get heard. But the noise still prevented any part of the exchange of vows being understandable. Added to the fact that they couldn't hear, many guests became extremely nervous about the possibility of a mid-air crash between two helicopters, with the wreckage bombing – and killing – the seated guests. Not long before the parachutist had decided to drop in, another photographer in an ultra-light single-seater plane had flown over the Neverland Valley, Dick Dastardly style, but had ended crash-landing after a close encounter with a rotary blade.

Larry Fortensky, with his 'himbo' haircut and dressed in a luxury-cruise waiter's white dinner jacket, was particularly anxious about a helicopter collision. By the time he pledged 'From this day forward you shall not walk alone. My heart will be your shelter, and my arms will be your home,' he was described as trembling and looking pale. 'I was very concerned,' he later confided to New York columnist Liz Smith, the only journalist invited to the wedding. 'I was afraid there might be an accident. I didn't even want to look at them, and I tried not to. But then I just put them out of my mind.'

Many guests felt that the occasion comprehensively failed to live up to its hype. The *National Enquirer* had trumpeted it as 'the wedding to end all weddings'; its rival the *Globe* published a special three-page 'Wedding Extravaganza' colour souvenir pull-out for the 'showbiz wedding of the decade'. Invited guests, however, didn't get so much as a box of souvenir matches to take home. Moreover, the service started an hour and a half late, with guests refused a drink until around 7p.m. After the ceremony, as the Dom Perignon flowed and Mrs

Taylor-Fortensky (as she now wished to be called) cut into her $1,400 five-tier chocolate mousse cake, guests were left to wander around the grounds on their own. Barry Diller and Diane von Furstenberg, for example, went off to bounce up and down on Michael Jackson's giant trampoline. Nobody quite knew what they were meant to do.

David Hockney, whose framed Liz n' Larry wedding invitation now proudly hangs in the downstairs lavatory of his Hollywood Hills house, said the afternoon was one of the most peculiar he could ever remember. 'I was so disappointed by the whole thing,' he told me later. 'In my mind I had built up Jackson's house as this absolutely marvelous fantasy land. And it didn't seem fun at all. It was like a hotel, with pictures of children hung up all over the place.'

The most surreal moment in the Wodehousean pantomime had been when the renowned Italian soprano Aprile Millo stood up to sing *Ave Maria* as the helicopters whined above like angry hornets. 'Anyway, I love singing, so I was at least looking forward to this opera singer they had flown over,' Hockney added ruefully. 'But in the event it was impossible to hear a single note. It was completely absurd. She sang with her fingers stuck in her ears.'

According to Liz Smith, the *après*-wedding party, which began with the twelve-piece orchestra playing Stevie Wonder's *Overjoyed*, ended early – at around 10.30p.m. When she asked host Michael Jackson at the end if the whole occasion had got a bit out of hand, he replied softly: 'I would do anything for Elizabeth. I truly love her. We're so much alike you know. She and I, we're exactly alike. It's hard being a child star and having to grow up.'

* * *

But it wasn't quite over yet. The next morning, whilst reading the Metro section of the *Los Angeles Times*, my attention was caught by a full-page black-and-white advertisement, superimposed with a large photograph of Liz

Taylor. In large bold lettering across the top of the page it declared 'You're invited to meet Elizabeth Taylor.' Underneath her demure-looking photograph, dominated by a diamond earring the size of a small chandelier, I read on: 'Have tea with Elizabeth Taylor, Thursday at Del Amo at 3p.m.'

It continued: 'Purchase a limited edition, one ounce parfum, numbered and decorated with Elizabeth Taylor's signature, for $300, and you will be among the select guests to have tea with Elizabeth Taylor.' There was a number to call. Figuring that there was nothing to stop me from buying the scent, and simply swapping it for something else later – or getting my money back – I made a reservation over the phone. I was told to report at 4p.m. that Thursday to the lingerie department of Robinson's department store (the John Lewis of LA) in Torrance.

I duly drove out on a sultry afternoon to this dreary middle-class suburb forty minutes' drive south of LA. After I walked through the empty shopping mall into the Robinson's lingerie department, there was Liz Taylor – rather oddly – spending the fourth day of her honeymoon in a department store rounding off her US Tour to promote her newest fragrance. In the approach to her wedding there had been some media speculation over the coincidence that Miss Taylor just *happened* to choose to get married at exactly the same time that she was also launching her new perfume. White Diamonds is described as 'a rich sensual floral fragrance that intrigues with living Amazon lily, Egyptian tuberose, Turkish rose, jasmine . . .'

Wearing a strawberry-print dress, she sat up on a make-shift stage under a legion of boom poles and the glare of TV cameras fiddling with her new diamond ring. (How much it had cost, of course, all rather depends on how much Liz had wanted to spend.) Hundreds of frenzied middle-aged housewives heaved and pushed around her, hopelessly waving their plastic instamatics above the rows of frilly pink-lace underwear. After giving her lingerie department press conference, those 'invited' to take 'private tea' with Miss Taylor were led in an elevator to the third floor. Standing near the furniture department, we were then each handed our personally signed one-ounce $300 bottle (whose few teaspoonfuls of ethyl, alcohol, water and fragrance had cost Elizabeth Arden around $4 to make) and led into an 'executive' suite.

Each guest – there must have been nearly one hundred of us – was allowed a strictly timed *twenty-second* conversation with Miss Taylor as she circulated around the tables, each piled high with salmon toasties, Scottish shortbread and glazed chocolate strawberries. Waiters in dinner jackets glided around serving iced tea from silver jugs. In a discreet corner, a tall blonde woman melodiously plucked away on a golden harp.

The sixty-eight-year-old woman seated on my left wore a purple velvet zip-up suit and had recently had a major face-lift. Her skin was creased like fine tissue paper. She told me that she had come along not because of Liz Taylor – 'She was a lousy Cleopatra' – but because she was addicted to buying perfume. She had a collection of about two hundred bottles at home. 'Any item I don't care for,' she said, spilling her tea on the table-cloth, 'I use as flyspray, deodorant or air-freshner.'

Opposite me was a 'retired' Hollywood actress who confessed that she would never be able to bring herself to open the champagne-gold packaged box. 'I'm going to keep it beside the photograph of my mother on my dressing table,' she said with a sigh. 'She loved Liz, and looked quite like her – once.'

Finally Elizabeth Taylor came round to our table. I wanted to get a very good look at her. For someone who was nearly sixty, she didn't look bad at all. She had a deep tan, a surprisingly squeaky voice and a pair of over-made-up blue-grey eyes that stared right through you as she talked. The white-china teeth flashed brightly. We spoke for fifteen seconds. Her bodyguard, Moshe, glared at me like a deranged pyschopath and led her on.

Liz Taylor's talent, I reflected, really has very little to do with being a movie actress and a lot with generating publicity – the one drug that she is not cured of. Publicity, it seems, works like neat Benzedrine on her ego.

Like Madonna, her real achievement has been to get herself written about as a *news*, rather than as a showbiz or gossip, story. She knows that survival on the high-tightrope of the celebrity circus has nothing to do with actual success – Taylor's last starring role in a hit movie was *Who's Afraid of Virginia Woolf?*, nearly a quarter of a century ago – and everything to do with what you can *get away with*.

The Liz n' Larry nuptials were not really a marriage at all – rather it was Liz Taylor casting herself to star in her own comeback fantasy movie. But then, as Tom Wolfe suggests in *The Electric Kool-Aid Acid Test*, America has always been like living inside a drive-in movie theatre. And in Tinseltown, where the edges between reality and fantasy are especially blurred, to produce a film with such a star and supporting cast for *just* $1.5 million must rank as a real achievement. Normally you would have difficulty shooting a 'D' movie for that.

4

Sofa so Good

FOR MY FIRST FEW WEEKS in LA, my 'office' had been Beverly's small kitchen table at which I sat over my Panasonic lap-top on a wooden stool. While I worked, her dogs – called 'Marilyn' and 'Marg' – did their usual rump-scratching exercises on either my leg or the stool. Every breakfast, lunch and supper, I had to clear my desk of all notes, papers and clutter. Our relationship was becoming strained, and it soon became obvious that I was going to have to move out.

I bought a $7.95 manual called the *LA Survival Guide* whose blurb boasted it would show how to get settled and take *control* of my life in Los Angeles. 'Your primary concerns are getting a place to live and getting a car,' I read. 'You must have a car in Los Angeles. It's not a question of choice, but of necessity. Also many people will judge you by the car you drive. So buying a good car is extremely important to your survival in LA.'

In 1963, it took David Hockney only a few days to get himself organised. On his second day in LA, having no idea how to drive, he bought a bicycle. Lazing on his motel bed in Santa Monica in the late afternoon, smoking a rolled cigarette and reading John Rechy's *City of Night*, the novel's descriptions of the sleazy hot night-life of Pershing Square soon became too much for the twenty-six-year-old painter. He unfolded his tourist map on his bed and saw that Wilshire Boulevard began in Santa Monica and ran all the way to

Pershing Square in downtown LA. To reach the exotic gay bars and clubs that he had fantasised about for so long, all he had to do was keep on a single street. He couldn't possibly get lost and judging by his map downtown didn't seem very far. And so Hockney, flushed with randy excitement, stepped out into the fading afternoon light, and began to cycle . . .

After about three hours of furious peddling, he stopped off for a much needed drink. He was sweating a lot. When Hockney pulled out his map to see how he was getting on, he received an unpleasant shock. He had not yet got as far as Beverly Hills. When he asked how much further it was to downtown LA, and pointed to his small bicycle, the barman looked at him strangely. 'You've about another twelve miles,' he was told. 'You might make it by morning.' When Hockney finally arrived, it was so late that Pershing Square was deserted. 'So I just cycled back,' he wrote later, 'and I thought, this just won't do, this bicycle is useless. I shall have to get a car somehow.'

Within less than a week, Hockney had passed his Californian driving test, bought a Ford Falcon for $1,000, found a little studio in Venice which overlooked the sea, driven to Las Vegas, won some money *and* started painting. 'And I thought,' he wrote later, 'it's just how I imagined it would be.'

My move to LA turned out to be somewhat less auspicious. For a start, buying a car: 'You should plan on having a rental car for at least two weeks,' my *LA Survival Guide* assured me. 'This will give you time to find, purchase and register a vehicle without being rushed.'

Rushed? I wouldn't say I exactly rushed out to buy a car. In fact, it took me just over a *year*. A mixture of work, ignorance about how to get a Californian license and a complete lack of any knowledge or interest in cars, meant that I hired over *thirty-five* vehicles from Hertz before I got round to looking for a car. In the event, I simply bought the first one I went to see – a black Golf GTi. In LA, it was quickly pointed out to me, this was a 'woman's car'.

Next came the Californian driving test. I would admit to being an exceedingly bad driver. I do not know the exact reason for this. Ever since passing my British driving test on the fifth attempt, I have been a serious danger to other motorists, cyclists, pedestrians and anybody who has the misfortune to be sitting in the passenger seat. When I worked in Wapping, I was twice breath-tested on my way *to* work as my driving was deemed suspicious.

Like *Times* columnist Bernard Levin – who cannot drive and gets lost in his own flat – I suffer acutely from what he calls 'direction-blindness'. When friends give him a lift, for example, and usher him towards the car, he will regularly make for the driver's side, to the amazement of the driver. He cannot remember, without peering inside it, which side of a car the steering-wheel is. After two years in Los Angeles, I still frequently forget that I have a left-hand drive, and open the passenger side door by mistake. As regards directions to anywhere in LA, I tend to navigate by architectural landmarks – such as Tower Records on Sunset – rather than cross-streets. On freeways, I can never work out whether I am going north or south, east or west.

I had been told that it was almost impossible to fail the Californian driving exam. It certainly seemed a very casual procedure. After queuing up for about half an hour at the DMV on Cole Avenue, north Hollywood, behind a ragged trail of Mexicans, blacks and goaty-looking high school teenagers in baseball boots. I paid the small fee and was told to read off a few large letters from what appeared to be a primary school spelling board. I wasn't sure whether this was a sight or literacy test. I was then led into a small room with peeling walls that resembled a civil service examination hall. I was shown to a wooden desk and handed a double-sided list of twenty-three multiple choice questions. I was permitted to make up to seven errors. Most questions seemed ridiculously obvious.

Q: If you get angry or upset, you should:

a. Go for a drive to forget your problems
b. 'Cool off ' before driving
c. Control your emotions when driving.

I ticked 'c'. The answer was 'b'.

Q: To help avoid being hit from the rear by another driver when preparing to turn, you should:

a. Keep parking lights on at all times
b. Signal at least 100 feet before you turn
c. Check your rear-mirror often.

I ticked 'c'. The answer was 'b'.

I failed the test.

After studying the Californian Highway Code booklet for half an hour I took the test again. Once more, I failed. I was now allowed one more attempt. If I failed another time – which *was* virtually impossible since by a process of elimination I now knew the answers to two out of three choices on all the questions – I would have to pay again and come back the next day. To make absolutely sure, however, I sat at the back of the room – in a cubicle fitted with headphones for those who couldn't read English – and double-checked my answers in a smuggled-in Highway code booklet. This time I passed. Just.

Next came the driving bit. After waiting in a queue of Student Driver cars for about half an hour, a middle-aged woman with thick, wide-rimmed glasses and a clipboard came and sat down in my passenger seat. We lurched off and turned right, right again – failing to stop properly at a 'Yield' sign – and then pulled up in a quiet tree-lined north Hollywood residential street. I was told to reverse about ten yards. This I did – squealing loudly up against the curb. We then continued for a few hundred yards – failing to give way to a van on my right at a junction – and then swung back into the DMV. It took about nine minutes.

'Well, Mr Cash,' sighed my examiner. 'How long have you been driving?'

'Nearly ten years.'

'I would advise you take some instruction. At the moment, your driving simply isn't up to the required state standard. I don't think you saw it – but you nearly killed someone back there. Nearly ran a man over.'

'Oh, dear,' I said. 'I'm sorry.'

'But I'm gonna pass you anyway,' she added, squirling her signature to an official-looking piece of paper. 'One, because you've passed the British driving test. Which ain't easy. And two, I just love your English accent. It's, like, so cute.'

And that was it.

Within three weeks of arriving in LA, my relationship with Beverly was over. The final straw had been when the phone suddenly started to ring – late at night – almost incessantly. When I answered it, the receiver always went dead. On one occasion, however, at about 11.30p.m. a man's voice mumbled:

'I'm calling about the ad.'

'What ad?' I said. 'I don't know what you're talking about.'

'The Swedish massage ad. Is Beverly there?'

'Massage ad?'

'Yeah. In this week's *LA Weekly*. I've got it here. How much for an hour?'

'What exactly does it say?'

'Foxy Californian blonde, late 20s, gives sensuous full-body Swedish massage. Total relaxation guaranteed. Outcall only. Call Beverly on . . .'

He gave the number.

'There's been some sort of mistake,' I said and slammed the phone down.

When I asked Beverly to explain what was going on, she burst into tears and told me that she had been getting a series of calls from strange men, all wanting a Swedish massage. She had never placed any ad in *LA Weekly* (the *Time Out* of LA) and suspected – correctly, as it turned out – that it was a prank by her jealous ex-boyfriend who was, apparently, furious that I was living with her. So upset did she become, in fact, that she decided to leave LA for a long weekend. I was left in the house with her two dogs, *sans* TV (cable still cut off), *sans* fax (still broken), *sans* communication.

The number of phone calls started to rapidly increase. They started at about 10a.m. and came about every half an hour. There were all types of callers, from drunk teenagers to croaky geriatrics. By about 6p.m. the phone rang every fifteen minutes. I soon got so fed up with answering the calls, or screening them on the answermachine – I would say that Beverly was 'no longer in business' and slam the phone down – that I unplugged all the telephone sockets. I was now completely cut off.

When, a day or two later, I plugged the sockets back in, I got an unpleasant surprise. The phone rang almost immediately.

'William – is that you?' asked a distant voice. 'It's the foreign desk.'

'Speaking.'

'Where the hell have you been? We've been trying to reach you for the last 24 hours. There's a huge firestorm up in Oakland, outside San Francisco – dozens of people are dead. We want you up there, by the flames – eye-witness stuff.'

'I've had a communication problem,' I said awkwardly. 'I'll get up there straight away.'

* * *

Whilst I had been scanning the Sunday newspaper rental ads for a modest apartment for myself, my eye had been caught by a large box ad that kept being placed by Asher Dann & Associates, Canon Drive – one of the most exclusive real-estate agents in Beverly Hills – advertising a number of multi-million dollar mansions discounted by up to 50 per cent. One address, in particular, intrigued me, as I recognised it as that of British rock star Rod Stewart – whose imposing, gated Mediterranean mansion had been one of the few houses I had located on my Movie Stars' Homes self-drive tour back in 1985.

Since the 15,000 square foot mansion, in the same street as the homes of Barbra Streisand and Gregory Peck, had originally been put on the market for $14.5 million in 1990 – with viewing 'strictly by appointment' – I was surprised to see it being touted a year later for a mere $7.8 million in the *Los Angeles Times* classifieds. When I phoned up Asher Dann – claiming to be a prospective buyer – I was assured that this new asking price was very much 'open to offer'. According to the brochure I requested, the two-storey house, which Stewart had owned for fifteen years, was designed in 1926 by architect George Washington Smith. It boasted a master-suite with two fireplaces large enough to roast a pair of giant oxen, three family bedrooms, three maids' rooms, a ballroom with a ceiling the height of two double-decker buses, a minstrel gallery, a paddle tennis court and a mini-lake sized pool.

There were, I soon discovered, several good reasons for this bargain. California's real-estate industry, which boomed in the 1980s, had been severely hit by the state's deep recession. In 1992, unemployment in California reached a record 9.7 per cent – compared with an average of around 7 per cent across America as a whole. Eight out of ten new businesses folded within twelve months. The beleaguered and debt-ridden Californian economy left a legion of ruined property developers who swarmed over to LA in the early to mid-eighties. By 1993, commercial property in California had crashed in value by around 50 per cent from three years before, and residential property prices – especially up in the multi-million dollar end – had slumped by 35–50 per cent.

I decided to see what other bargains were available. Instead of relying on an outdated $5 Map of the Stars' Homes I was given a Grand Tour of Beverly Hills sitting in the brand-new open-top pale yellow Rolls Royce Corniche of Bruce Nelson.

For anybody with serious *cash* to spend on a mansion in the nineties, Nelson is the ideal guide to the Los Angeles property jungle. A fifty-eight-year-old native of Beverly Hills whom you might mistake for being the senior partner of a Washington law firm, he doesn't have a conventional office. Doesn't need one. Not these days. Not when your average real-estate agent's salary is around $24,000 but he has a bad year if he earns less than a $1 million in commissions. He simply meets his clients at his own $3 million red-brick mansion, tucked away in Beverly Hills up a discreet tree-lined street off Wilshire Boulevard.

The heavily studded oak door was opened by a man-servant. I was led into a finely furnished drawing room that looked as if it belonged in the centre-spread of *House & Garden*. As I might have expected from a man who had just sold a house to Vidal Sassoon for $5 million and was about to be showing Madonna a $20 million *two-bedroom* home in Bel-Air, his own house contained a Chagall bronze and two Picassos.

It was a hot and cloudless Los Angeles afternoon. After the electronic hood of his Rolls Royce ('a little $150,000 gift I treated myself to') has whirred smoothly back, Nelson lights up a cigar, eases the automatic gear into 'Drive' and we purr up the hill towards the 'Platinum Triangle' – the local name given to the choicest areas of Bel-Air, Holmby Hills and Beverly Hills.

Nelson chuckled loudly behind the wheel at the mention of Rod Stewart's house. I had been told that the reason Stewart was selling the house was because he wanted to build a new 'English' home on a $4 million lot in Beverly Park, with new neighbours such as Aids spokesman and basketball player Magic Johnson.

'It's a classic example of a celebrity wildly over-pricing their property,' he said gleefully. 'Some celebrities think that the fact they are well known adds value to their house. That's rubbish.'

Stewart's house, he continued, was worth about $6.5

million (which is exactly what it was eventually sold for). Some of the rooms, I had heard, were like dark caves.

'The real reason Stewart is moving,' Nelson went on, as his Rolls Royce began to climb steeply up the road, 'is because his new wife simply refuses to live in his old wife's house. Rod, I'm sure, would most likely dearly love to stay.'

We arrived at a house several times more expensive than Rod Stewart's. The gleaming car glided slowly through a set of wrought iron gates into the courtyard of an enormous French château. 'Celebrities often don't have nearly as much money as people think,' said Nelson. 'They're not exactly poor, but they are not usually the people who live in the really big houses. Most of the real wealth in Los Angeles belongs to businessmen, not movie stars.'

We got out of the Rolls and crunched along the pink gravel to the front door. The house has no name. 'It doesn't need one,' said Nelson.

Perched like a Disneyland castle above the Beverly Hills Hotel, the 28,000 square foot mansion was used for filming the final *Dynasty* series. The bronze bannister on the staircase alone cost $400,000. After Disney chairman Michael Eisner first came to the house, he was so overwhelmed that he took the mansion over for a Disney Special. Nelson then rattled off some of the past owners of the site – Elton John, *Gone With the Wind* producer David Selznick and silent film-star John Gilbert.

'But with a house like this, it's the property that's the real celebrity,' Nelson continued as he punched a series of combinations on the security buzzer. The original asking price was $39 million. Just four months later, Nelson dropped it to $29 million, and a year later it was still on the market at $24 million – which would still make it, says Nelson, one of the most expensive private houses to be sold in United States history. He already had two people – sorry princesses – wanting a 'little holiday house in LA'. If they don't like it, he had another château down the road for $25 million.

What was even more extraordinary, perhaps, is that every

brick, tile and walnut balustrade of the château was *brand new*. After inheriting the historic house, the first thing the owner did was to bulldoze it to the ground. The new mansion, which looks from the outside like a giant dolls house, took five years to build – which involved removing half of a nearby mountain (25,000 dumper-truck trips) to 'improve' the view.

This once fashionable Hollywood trend – 'tear down' – was started by the astronomically rich television producer Aaron Spelling, creator of such shows as *Dynasty*, *Charlie's Angels* and *Beverly Hills 90210*. After buying the beautiful old five-acre Bing Crosby home – through Nelson – for $10 million, Spelling proceeded to raze it to the ground and build himself a $20 million bespoke French palace reminiscent of Versailles (56,000 square feet), half the size of the House of Lords. Dozens of others followed – demolishing often beautiful old houses and replacing them with architectural monstrosities.

'Nobody is tearing houses down these days,' said Nelson. 'The banks simply aren't giving the loans.'

The real-estate trend for the nineties is called 'repair'. What began as a craze for building dream homes in the eighties has turned bitterly sour, with the dramatic crash in property prices leaving a number of half-finished mansions scarring the rolling Bel-Air landscape to the *Angst* of long-term residents. Many of the houses that have at least been completed, such as the Spelling house, have been widely ridiculed. As Dominick Dunne noted in his waspish *Vanity Fair* account of LA's teardown mania: 'Probably not since Ludwig of Bavaria brought his country to the verge of bankruptcy with the extravagance of his palace-building has a residence been so publicly criticised as the Spelling house. Television newscasters have hovered over it, pointing out to their viewers that it was being built for a family of only four.'

As I stepped inside the marble-floored hall of what was probably the second most expensive house in America, I have to say I was acutely disappointed. I felt as if I had walked into a giant Berni Inn Steak House. No amount of bad taste was spared. The interior was decorated in a ghastly mock-Gothic with absurd stained glass windows and several new Persian rugs that made the gloomy entrance hall resemble a cross between Gleneagles and the Nile Hilton. Everything was overdone, oversized and overexpensive. The dining room resembled the Selfridge's glass and furniture department, the master-bedroom suite a deluxe Barratt showhome, the front staircase looked as if it had been borrowed from Harrods and the ballroom modelled on the Golden Nugget Casino in Las Vegas.

Not knowing quite what to say, I kept silent – and smiled. There was, in fact, nothing to say. The house – sorry château – was a $39 million monument to bad taste.

'The nineties are a very different period,' Nelson told me as we ended the tour. 'If you had been a client I never would have taken out the Rolls. When *everyone* was making money it was fun to drive but now we are in a bad recession and people are hurting. You don't want to give a bad impression. You don't see many of these sort of cars around today. They are too conspicuous. I use a new Cadillac for my clients. I just drive the Rolls in the evening.'

* * *

Meanwhile, my own plans for finding a place to live in LA were not going well. I had now moved out of Beverly's bedroom and was being charged $30 a night to sleep on her foamy sitting-room sofa, upholstered in the sort of beige fabric you find on furry dice.

I would have gone to a $29-a-night Hollywood motel – but didn't want to risk losing my computer and luggage (in what was used mainly as a pay-by-the-hour brothel.)

Finding somewhere to live in LA is a daunting task. The first step was to fathom out the peculiar terminology used in the 'For Rent' classified ads. A quick glance through the *Los Angeles Times* rental section made a Michelin guide seem about as complicated as a Macdonald's menu. A typical example would be:

> Los Feliz, Old World Charm, gtd Dplx, 2 + 1 + den, pool, in 'Grdn Eden' grnds, parquet flr, Blow out VU & sun-deck, Form Din Rm, 'Pipe' stv, H.Tub, cozy yd, W/D, small pet ok. Perfect Writer's Retreat. Very posh! Very Private! Very You! $1800/mo.

Of course, this might as well have been written in Chinese. I could, however, read a dollar sign – and what I did know was that if I took anything above about $800 a month I probably wouldn't be able to afford to eat. I wasn't too bothered about not living in 'Garden of Eden grounds' and certainly didn't want a 'Hot Tub'. Since I had no furniture, knew nobody, and couldn't cook, there didn't seem much point in having a 'formal dining room'. So long as it wasn't bare concrete, I didn't mind what sort of floor I had. My needs were, in fact, fairly basic. I just wanted one bedroom, with a 'den' – i.e. study – preferably with a view ('VU'), a sitting room, bathroom and a small kitchen.

I had no idea even where to begin to look. I knew a lot of British people lived by the ocean in Santa Monica – which seemed a particularly good reason for avoiding it. Beverly Hills was too expensive. West LA was too trendy, and had too many students. Hollywood was too touristy (and too dangerous). The only other areas I had really heard of were Pasadena – a bit too like Wimbledon – and the Valley, which was the Essex of LA. This left the Hollywood Hills; or to be more exact with my budget, the 'foothills'.

I must have gone to see about two dozen studios, duplexes, triplexes, fourplexes, lofts, bungalows, condos, apartments, guesthouses, huts, converted garages and so on. It was a depressing experience. Most of the Hollywood apartment buildings were built in the fifites and resembled the run-down Salvation Army hostels around London's King's Cross.

Heaving open a heavy iron-grid door, you would find a heap of unopened mail lying scattered on the floor. Plastic bags full of rotten orange skins and milk cartons would be piled up in a corner. A shady-looking manager with greasy hair would lead you up some concrete stairs into a poky apartment with peeling grey walls and an overhead fan that was lit by a naked 40 watt bulb. It could have been Jakarta.

Most of the 'guesthouses' I went to see were about the size of a shop window. One I was offered for $600 a month, at a Spanish mini-mansion on Outpost Drive, was clearly used as a swimming pool changing-room. It was a single room with a tiled floor and shower. Inside the door was a rack of Speedo briefs and an extra-large turquoise bikini. When I asked about this, I was told by the fifty-something blubbery blonde wife of the owner: 'Don't worry dear – we won't get in your way. We don't use the pool much. The kids only come over in the summer. It's just a place to change. We're like in and outta here in five minutes.'

If nothing else, the eclectic range of places I looked at was educational. At a duplex I went to look at in the Hollywood Heights, the door was opened by an unshaven man in Armani darkglasses, a towelling robe and Leo Sayer hair. When he took off his sunglassees for a second, he had to quickly cover his eyes with his hands to hide them from the bright morning sun. Leading me inside to find the upstairs key, the spacious house – which smelt fetid – was in pitch darkness, except for a luminous green IBM computer screen on the dining room table. Beside it were several cartons of half-eaten Chinese food and a six pack of Grolsch beer.

'I'm Jason,' the man said. 'Excuse the mess. I'm late with a script. I don't mean to sound stupid but can you tell me what day it is?'

I told him.

'Can you believe that?' he said rummaging around in a drawer. 'I haven't been outside for a week.'

Finally, whilst attempting a short-cut from Hollywood to the 101 Freeway, I drove up a residential street and saw an orange 'For Rent' sign stuck up on a freshly painted house with a Spanish door. A balding Australian called 'Bob' showed me inside. The small groundfloor apartment, a few hundred yards above the Hollywood Freeway on Vine Street, had two windowless bedrooms, a 'den' which overlooked a washing-line, a new hardwood floor and a stand-up kitchen. By now I was desperate. I talked him down to $800 a month.

'Who lives next door?' I asked before signing.

'An artist,' I was assured. 'He's nice.'

'What about the Freeway noise?' I asked. 'It's really quite loud. Could you put up some sound-proofing?'

'You'll get used to it,' he said. 'It's kind of therapeutic. Just think of it as the ocean-roar.'

I signed the contract. The following day I moved in my luggage (two large suitcases). My small Vine Street apartment was, in fact, only a hundred yards away from the grungy Alto Nido Apartment House, above Hollywood and Ivar, in which the broke screenhack Joe Gillis had lived in Billy Wilder's classic 1950 Hollywood satire, *Sunset Boulevard*. I consoled myself with the fact that whereas Gillis had only a 'one-room affair', with a rusted Murphy bed that pulled out of the wall, I had three rooms.

But it was hardly *Lifestyles of the Rich and Famous*. Whereas Gillis' unpaid for bedsit at least had a 'couple of worn-out plush chairs and a Spanish style, wrought-iron standing lamp', a 'chest of drawers', 'portable phonograph' and a few 'reproductions of characterless paintings' on the walls, I simply had no furniture. All I possessed was an old double-mattress, which I lay on the floor of my windowless bedroom, a large desk which I bought off the landlord for $90, an ex-rental swivel-chair and a broken director's chair which Beverly had given me. I also purchased a fax machine, a TV set, a table light, a restaurant-sized Krupps coffee-machine (I had been advised that one's status in LA was largely defined by the size of one's coffee machine), six cereal bowls and two mugs. That was it.

Whilst Gillis was three months behind on his 1946 yellow

Plymouth convertible, I was paying Hertz $170 a week for a mid-sized white Chevrolet. But now, at least, I had a car and somewhere to live. 'Once these things are taken care of,' I was assured by my *LA Survival Guide*, 'you can concentrate on the finer things in life.'

If only.

I heard the first quivering twang of bass guitar at about 11p.m. on my second night. It was a cruel, wild, screeching sound – 200 watts of electric bass groaning through my bedroom wall like a bad Alice Cooper imitation played at maximum volume. On the wrong record speed. The deafening wail could only be described as a form of otological torture – the sort of evil whine that would have even your average hardened Van Halen headbanger blocking his ears.

When I confronted the 'artist' in the morning, he informed me that he was a rock 'songwriter' who often worked late hours. He was in his late twenties with tattooed muscular forearms and a bushy pony-tail. Peering inside his small apartment, which he shared with his wife and brother, I noticed two giant stage speakers, with woofers the size of two low-profile car-tyres. A number of electric guitars were propped up against the wall.

'Could you keep the volume down at night?' I asked. 'I have to work late as well.'

'I can't do nothing 'bout the volume,' he told me. 'I'm a professional musician. It's what pays the bills. You have to play rock *loud*.'

It went on like this. Because of London deadlines – 9a.m. in LA is 5p.m. in London – I would often work late at night, wearing a large pair of headphones to muffle the grim wail.

My next immediate difficulty was not having any proper cuttings or access to the basic news wire services – such as AP. Reuters, UPI etc. In the event of a major breaking story, this could prove extremely awkward. As it was, my 'library' consisted of three cardboard boxes (news, entertainment, other) into which I heaped clippings each day. My letter of introduction got me nowhere with the *Los Angeles Times*.

They were extremely polite but simply pointed out that they had no cuttings library. All their research was accessed from computer data-banks and they were charged for each search.

As my three cardboard boxes rapidly began to overflow, and I became increasingly worried about my lack of access to wires, I came up with an idea that turned out to be nothing less than a masterplan.

Towering like a giant twenty-third-century space-station above Sunset Boulevard and the 101 Hollywood Freeway were Fox Television Studios, owned by Rupert Murdoch – who also owned News International, and hence, *The Times*. After sending a short note to the news editor at Fox, inquiring about the possibility of using their wires in the event of a breaking story, I was invited to drop by at his office.

I had never been to a Hollywood studio before. Passing under a large electronic barrier controlled by a team of uniformed guards, I followed the short driveway, past a landscaped tropical garden and fountain pool, into a labyrinthine concrete car-park. In the main lot, in which were parked a number of satellite TV trucks and a fleet of Fox News jeeps, was a gargantuan statue of a silver robot, a forty-foot high cross between the Tin Man from *The Wizard of Oz* and the morphic cyborg from *Terminator 2*. On the base was written in large bold letters: 'All Power to the Minds that Created the Medium.'

I was guided down a series of corridors, past several huge open sound-stages the size of aircraft hangars – where such shows as *In Living Color* and the hugely popular TV dating game, *Studs*, were made – until I came to the Fox News Room. Like CNN, ITN or any other major news station, the open-plan office was crammed with several dozen TV monitors, VDU computer screens and the usual clacking of printers, wire service machines and so on. Reporters and editors bustled about.

I was ushered into the news director's smart executive office. He was a rugged forty-something with curly brown hair and designer glasses. He got straight to the point.

'So Mr Cash,' he began 'you've recently arrived from London and have no access to wires.'

'That's right.'

'I don't have any objection to you coming in here,' he said, 'so long as you don't get in our way.'

'That's wonderful.'

'Where are you working? Where's your office?'

'Frankly, my . . . er . . . office situation is not very satisfactory at the moment. I haven't really got one, in fact.'

'Well, if you're interested,' he continued, 'we've got some spare office space around the back. Nobody's using it – it's just empty. You could use that if you wanted. Come and go as you like.'

A week later, I was handed a security key and led by a secretary along the corridor where the TV studio dressing-rooms were. About half-way along, opposite one of the make-up rooms, I was shown inside a plush executive suite that had more square feet than my whole apartment.

'Here we are Mr Cash,' said the blonde secretary, 'I hope this suits you. It's the old personnel department. There's plenty of space.'

'Splendid.'

'When is your secretary moving in? – I'd like to meet her.'

'Secretary?' I gulped. 'I don't actually have a secretary.'

'Not a lot happens on this corridor,' she went on. 'Mr Murdoch's daughter has just started work a few doors down. I expect you'll meet her – she's very nice.'

'I'm sure she is.'

Sadly, we never met.

Although this new set-up was ideal from a work point of view it was also a little embarrassing. People kept asking me when my staff were to join me. I gently deflected such questions.

My office was so large – to be honest it was almost the same size as the editor's office of *The Times* in London – that furnishing it proved tricky. After buying a huge executive office desk, swivel chair, coffee-table and filing cabinet it still felt empty – so I added a 'credenza', television set and a sofa. With immediate access to wires and an extremely efficient mailroom it couldn't have worked out better.

The office sofa came in especially handy over the following months. The wail from the bass guitar of my neighbour drove me out of Vine Street after about eight weeks. When the noise was especially bad – by now he had turned his flat into a recording studio – I would work late at the office and then sleep on my sofa. It was extremely comfortable. For about a fortnight, when my neighbour was auditioning for a drummer, I pretty well lived at Fox TV studios. Nobody seemed to mind. I ate my breakfast in the canteen and shaved in the bathroom at the end of the corridor. Occasionally, if no one was around, I would watch a late-night movie in the Fox TV library a few doors down from me. As I left the office at about 9a.m. a security guard would say:

'Working late Mr Cash?'

'London deadlines,' I replied.

5

LA Lust

'TO HELP US WITH THE match-making process,' began the love-heart framed contestant form, 'we need you to tell us what you're looking for in the opposite sex. PLEASE BE AS SPECIFIC AS POSSIBLE.'

The LA 'interview' office of *Love Connection*, America's longest-running TV dating-show, which so far boasts twenty-seven marriages, is reached up a dark and paint-splattered concrete stairway above the Collar & Leash Discount pet store in West Hollywood. Hanging from the ceiling is a selection of kinky-looking silver chains and heavily studded leather straps that look as if they belong in a sex shop.

After pressing the grimy buzzer for 'Eric Lieber Productions' ('that's the name we use when we call you at work to avoid any embarrassment'), I was met by a fat woman with frizzy red hair who slapped on a jumbo-sized name badge, led me into what resembled a police station waiting room and told me to fill out the questionnaire. A small pencil was fastened by string to my wooden clipboard.

A dozen other would-be 'contestants' were sitting on steel chairs, hunched over their forms in deep thought. An old Zenith television set was playing grainy, video re-runs of the show in one corner. 'This next hour should be thought of as an audition,' I read. 'We're looking for outgoing, energetic people who like to KISS AND TELL!'

Some questions were easy enough. *Do you kiss on a first date? (If no, why not).* I wasted no time in scrawling 'yes'. (I was doing this for a piece. I didn't want to risk immediate disqualification.) *What is your job?* I claimed to be writing a book on Hollywood pop stars. *What is the best advice you have been given for going on a date?* More tricky. I quoted Quentin Crisp: 'If at first you don't succeed, failure may be your style.'

'Loren', a lanky idiot in his late twenties with a degree in 'media psychology' came on to referee an 'open discussion' to decide which of us might get the chance to risk humiliation in front of millions on national TV. 'If any of you are already married, you had better leave now,' he crooned. 'Some people think we offer a free dating service. We don't.'

What the 'real-life romance' chat-up shows do offer, however, is a chance for the masses to live vicariously through the sex-lives of contestants. When it isn't safe to be promiscuous anymore, the American appetite for sexual voyeurism appears insatiable. Since 1991, four new date-confession shows have been launched from Hollywood – including one which featured real life single male millionaire participants.

Love Connection – a hard-core version of LWT's *Blind Date*, known in LA as 'Lust Connection' – is so successful in America that two shows are broadcast every night, at 7p.m. and 12.30a.m. Fox TV's rival dating-show *Studs* (beamed by Rupert Murdoch via SKY to predictable success in Britain) regularly attracts more viewers in Washington than all the network newscasts.

But the idea that these 'relationship' shows have anything to do with 'romance' in the nineties is risible. Their popular success is a sordid platter of smutty scriptwriting – 'I was in ecstasy when he gave me his creamy pudding' – that only works because in LA, lonely-heart capital of the world, people will do *anything* to get on TV. The behind-the-scenes reality is rooted in sleaze and rabid sexual desperation.

Sitting to my right in the 'interview' room was Melora, from the suburb of Encino, a spotty Valley Girl in an over-sized blue windsheeter who had experienced difficulties filling in the form. When asked by Loren to describe her 'ideal' man, she sobbed out that she had never been on a proper date before. She left in tears, accompanied by her father.

Next was bearded Don, a gas engineer from Van Nuys, dressed in a camouflage anorak and size twelve cowboy boots. He liked barbeques and watching videos. Having left his third wife, he said he wanted to go on *Love Connection* because he was bored with singles-bars and 'fancied some of the recent girls on the show'.

Next was my turn.

'So, William, tell us about your worst ever date,' smirked Loren.

'Ah,' I spluttered awkwardly. 'Well . . . there was the time this girl . . . er . . . fell off my motorbike.'

Expansion on the incident resulted in making it through the first round. If selected – it worked as in Tokyo brothels, only in reverse, with girls choosing their dates after viewing a selection of male contestant videos – I would be given $75 to spend on the evening; I would be liable for 'any additional costs'.

I reported back above the Collar & Leash Discount store the next evening to make my video in a poky backroom with a shaggy, burnt-omelette carpet and old 'B' movie posters Sellotaped to the peeling walls. As the lens of a home-video camera was pointed in my face, a plump New York producer interviewed me for fifteen minutes, mainly about the Princess of Wales. 'I just love your Royals,' she said. 'I mean Diana is so beautiful, and like, so elegant.'

I said I was looking for more of the Playmatey type.

'Well,' gulped the producer. 'We're going to fix you up with a wonderful girl. Just wonderful, William.'

Afterwards, I was made to sign a seven-page release agreement declaring that I was not 'a candidate for public office' at the 1992 election, that I was not a professional actor or comedian and that I would not make any 'unauthorised mentions or plugs' in return for payment. To do so, I was warned, was a federal offence 'punishable by imprisonment'.

Three months later, I got the phone call. I had been chosen by Andrea, a bi-lingual twenty-five-year-old Californian stockbroker. She invited me to her house in Santa Monica at

8p.m. the next night.

She was very tall – tight cream riding breeches – with mocha-brown eyes and a long swirl of ice-cream blonde hair, making her regularly attractive in a bubbly *Blue Peter* sort of way. She poured out two glasses of chardonnay. I drank mine down rapidly.

Now I know what you want to know. And I'm not going to go into lewd details. Let it suffice to say that although it wasn't exactly *Fatal Attraction*, the evening was not without incident. After some initial success, my advances were flatly turned down. She *didn't* on a first date.

The next afternoon I got a call from Tim, the show's Australian scriptwriter. For about an hour he grilled me about the minutiae of the date, demanding a frame-by-frame replay of its conclusion.

'Okay, so you guys are back at her place after dinner. You kiss her goodnight?'

'Yes.'

'Is this a peck on the cheek or is it a. . . ?'

'Something like that.'

'Okay, William. I need to know. Is this a goodnight kiss you give your sister or your girlfriend? I mean, are you guys just kissing because it's time to go – or did it lead to something?'

'Ask her,' I said.

The show was recorded at 5p.m. in front of a studio audience of 500 at KTLA Channel 5 on Sunset Boulevard, in the middle of the worst storms in Los Angeles for fifty years. The studio roof leaked badly. Plastic dustbins were lined up along the make-up corridor. The waiting rooms – His n' Hers – were furnished with cheap sofas and chipboard tables. A scrawny, unshaven producer came in to check the suitability of our outfits. We were forbidden to move.

The $75 liaisons of the other contestants locked up with me were hardly 'romantic': a young business executive whose date was violently sick all over him during a rough crossing on the scenic ferry ride he had organised, a thirty-something TV addict in a knitted banana yellow and turquoise sweater whose evening ended with a 'quickie' in the back of his Ford Bronco pick-up.

Worst of all was a loud-mouthed sixty-five-year-old called Gene, in a beige golfing jacket and slacks, who boasted for two hours of how he had repeated sex with his date – a sixty-year-old woman with an artificial hip – within half an hour of meeting her. They already had a local $29 motel booked for afterwards.

During most of the show I sat perched on a rickety stool behind a black curtain, with my heavily made-up face displayed *Newsnight*-style on a large monitor to the left of the set. Andrea sat on a scarlet sofa quizzed by the Jeremy Beadle-like host Chuck Woolery. Finally, I was led out onto the stage like a circus clown.

At this point the audience pressed on the electronic buttons by their seats to rate our 'contestant compatibility'. If it was high enough we would win an 'ultimate dream-fantasy prize'. Our score of 34 per cent – completely fixed – meant that we missed out.

'What exactly is the dream fantasy prize?' I asked the producer immediately afterwards. Unlike LWT's *Blind Date*, there is no post-show party. You simply picked up your bag and left.

'Another seventy-five bucks,' he grunted.

'That's not very generous.'

'Yeah – but think about it. Now you're famous.'

I was walking back to my car along Sunset Boulevard in the torrential rain when Andrea came running out.

'Hey, William,' she panted as she clutched my arm. 'I feel like a movie,' she said squeezing my hand. 'Do you want to go see *Basic Instinct*?'

I had already seen it. So, I thought, had she.

'Sure.'

After the movie she invited me back to her house in Santa Monica for a coffee. My research over, I realised I should – in the tradition of such reporting – make my excuses and leave.

But where would I go? I was homeless. After moving out of Vine Street, I was living on a night-by-night basis in $29-a-night motels.

I stayed about three weeks. Not on the sofa.

* * *

'So that's fixed,' I said down the phone. 'Thursday lunch. One o'clock at Le Dôme – I'll book a table.'

'No,' said Jackie Collins. '*I'll* book the table.'

Jackie Collins has her own table at Le Dôme on Sunset Boulevard. Past the oval-shaped bar, into the main Art Deco dining room, discreetly tucked away on the left behind a frosted-glass panel. The fifty-something author of *American Star* – 'Jackie Collins's most explosive, exciting book yet. A riveting love story for the nineties which will take you on a wild and wonderful trip and keep you guessing until the unforgettable roller-coaster-style climax. Feel the sizzle! Feel the burn!' – of which 750,000 (the first print run, that is) hardback copies were about to go on sale around the United States, was exactly on time. She was wearing a sharply cut black pin-stripe suit, with a white waistcoat and designer dark glasses, gold earrings and a few diamonds.

'It's my favourite table,' she breezed in her mid-Atlantic drawl. 'You get to see everybody. You see who's here.'

'Who is here?' I asked. I have always had a problem with Hollywood celebrities. I don't know who most of them are.

'Today isn't a hot-lunch day,' Jackie Collins replied after glancing around quickly. 'No table's creating any real heat. David Giler, the screenwriter, is here. Dick Donner just left.'

I knew the names. I had no idea what they looked like.

'I'm bad at recognising people,' I said. 'I only know the big names.'

'Dick *is* a big name. He directed *Superman* and *Lethal Weapon*. We said "hello". First rule of power-lunching in LA. You always have to say "hello".'

'What are the other rules?'

'An acid-tongue. The right table. The right people,' she continued. 'I was invited to lunch at CBS the other day. Five guys and me. Five heads of department. They were trying to impress me so they had this private chef. That's another rule. Your office must have its own chef. You mustn't over do it, though. I once took a power-lunch with a big-time Hollywood producer who had a hair-cut whilst we were eating. I wasn't impressed. Wasn't impressed at all. What a jerk!'

Jackie Collins is every blockbuster publisher's wet-dream. No book of hers has been out of print since 1969, when her first book, *The World is Full of Married Men*, was published. With 170 million sales of her books in more than thirty countries she continues to reign as the *femme terrible* of the airport bestseller lists. But in real life she hardly seemed much like the Ice-Bitch Jackie of her latest jacket photograph, tinged in gold sepia with a black panther statuette in the foreground. There was something very likeable about Ms Collins. She was fun and sparky. Better looking than her sister. Less brittle. Less pawky. Her brand of in-your-face vulgar chic seemed to have mellowed considerably from the Jackie Collins publicity shots *circa* 1979, which I seemed to remember featured her spread-eagled on a leopard-spot rug, surrounded by huge floor-cushions. As a fifteen-year-old, I thought that she was a porn star.

Following the death of her husband, Oscar Lerman, in March 1992, she was adjusting to being unattached. In an interview with *Hello!* not long after her husband's death, she admitted that she did not relish the prospect of the Hollywood singles scene. As with power-lunching in LA, a strict etiquette applied to the Bel Air and Holmby Hills dinner-party circuit. 'I'm sure there are certain women who will not want me around, because this is the Hollywood rule,' she said. 'You're fine when you're a couple. But when you're a single woman you're a threat. I've seen it happen a million and one times. I quite expect that.'

That had been six months before. I asked the author of *The World is Full of Divorced Women* how it was going. I found it rather difficult to imagine Ms Collins – as a vast number of other LA women are doing – paying up to $50,000 for the services of an up-market video match-making service, or sitting alone on a high bar-stool in a Westwood singles bar.

'I got married when I was twenty-four so being free is kind of interesting,' she said, taking a sip of mineral water. 'The power of freedom is so heavy its almost intoxicating. I have so many friends and three great daughters. I go out with groups of people. I'm enjoying it because I can do just what I want. If I want to go to Rome after lunch, I (for a moment I thought she said 'we') could get straight into my car and drive to the airport. I write in long-hand, so I can work anywhere in the world. I love to travel. The thought of dating is absolutely appalling. Sitting with somebody making conversation. *Absolutely* not!'

Jackie's enduring marriage was something of an anomaly in LA. By the loin-crazy seventies it was practically unthinkable that any self-respecting rock or movie star, or avant-garde SoHo Boho artist, would be *married*, let alone be faithful.

Artists have, of course, always liked to be different. The difference between then and 1993, it seems, is that when an artist – if that is the right word – made a personal commitment, even if the signature on the wedding registrar was soaked in lust, you at least felt some romantic integrity to lurk behind the pose. Sure, plenty of mistakes were made. But your marriage, at least, remained off-limits to the image-makers.

That appears to have changed. In Hollywood, at least, everyone seems to be racing to get down the aisle – Tom Cruise, Warren Beatty, Anjelica Huston, Whitney Houston, Cindy Crawford are just a few recent examples, and, unlikeliest of all, perhaps, Hugh Hefner (of whom more later). To claim that this is all because of Aids is to blindly miss the point. Hollywood is afflicted with another, seemingly incurable, virus: pre-packaged and self-serving publicity. What is so depressing about flicking through so many recent glossy magazines – from *People* to *Vanity Fair* – which love to drool over newly wed 'celeb couples' is the realisation that many of the recent betrothals are not real marriages at all.

Often they are little more than a publicity stunt designed to remind the world that such-and-such an ex-star still exists. With a few exceptions, they often appear to be Designer Marriages, serving little conventional purpose other than being mutually convenient business partnerships, invariably signed and sealed with a pre-nuptial contract complex enough to bewilder any Wall Street corporate accountant.

One of the problems of lunching in LA is the problem of being in a restaurant with a well-known studio executive, producer or agent – or anyone resembling one. If a waiter recognises a top producer – as producer, Ms Collins gets to cast her own TV mini-series – or even *thinks* you might be important, he tends to start performing the day's specials, spending several minutes auditioning for what they think may lead to a possible acting part. I remember once having dinner with an executive producer of a TV comedy show, and after we paid the bill the waiter handed over his business card, saying: 'My agent's number is on the back.'

Ms Collins ordered lobster bisque and a chicken and mushroom salad. I had asparagus and grilled liver. No wine. Evian mineral water. She kept on her chic tortoise-shell sunglasses throughout lunch. Her wrinkle-free and lightly freckled skin was the texture of over-ripe peach. Her dark brown hair was thick and glossy. The tan was perfectly even – like a well made *crème caramel*. Although twice my age, she was in considerably better condition than myself. Exactly *how* old Jackie actually was, I did not think propitous to bring up. In 1992 *Hello!* stated that 'feisty' Jackie was fifty-two. According to *Who's Who*, however, her sister Joan was to turn sixty on 23 May 1993. Jackie Collins – not listed in *Who's Who* – is two years younger. By my calculations, at least, she was fifty-eight.

Jackie Collins moved to California from London in the early eighties. Having lived in LA as a teenager, hanging out on Santa Monica beach, cruising up the Pacific Coast Highway, making out with boys at drive-in movie theatres on warm summer nights, she says she knows the city as well – if not better

– than London. 'I'm guilty of living in Beverly Hills,' she said unapologetically. 'I don't like the hills. I like the flats.'

'Aren't the flats rather suburban?' I asked.

'I just love it. It's really great. Because it *is* suburban. You can walk out of your house and walk down the street to the shops. I guess it's an English thing. Walking.'

'How much walking do you actually do?'

She paused. And winced.

'Okay then . . . none really,' she said. 'But it's nice to know I *could*. I do walk around my house. That's enough walking for anyone.'

'People seem to have this rather clichéd idea that you live an incredibly luxurious and glamorous life. Is it really anything like that?'

'It is actually,' she said. 'It's just like that. It's basically all true. I like to drive – so I'd usually only take a limo for a book signing or something like that. There are screenings in the big houses. Sure. I never go to the movies anymore because somebody is always showing the latest film. I don't have a screening room myself. I have a video-screening room. I'm a television freak. Everything I miss, I get taped. You should see my library.'

I nodded.

'What is a glamorous life anyway?' she went on. 'Is it one day you're in the supermarket and the next your at a major Hollywood party – seated between, say, Billy Wilder and Sidney Poitier? I guess it is. I love it. When I grew up in London I used to watch these guys' movies. I'm like a sponge. I love to listen to these people talking about Jack Lemmon, Marilyn Monroe or Greta Garbo. I love to hear what they have to say.'

'I've found a lot of the celebrities I've met rather disappointing,' I said dourly. 'Many actors, in particular, seem to have absolutely nothing to say for themselves.'

'I know. I know. You're actually right. Actors can be terrible. They get very defensive. They surround themselves with sycophants and people who will laugh at their jokes. They always have their entourage around them in a restaurant – protecting them. Keeping them cut off from the real world.

It's pathetic to watch.'

Ms Collins craned her neck around hurriedly to ensure nobody she knew was in ear-shot.

'They will always shove you out of the way to get to the mirror first,' she added, practically breathing down my neck. 'It's always me, me, me – they only want to talk about themselves, their own careers, what's happening to them. But millions of women still want to sleep with them – although they are never happy with the woman they *are* sleeping with. They're always looking for the next one who will make them a complete person.'

She sat back.

'So some women don't mind sleeping with a moron, so long as he's a famous moron?'

'That's right. I have this expression that everybody is a star-fuck. And they are. I've never seen anything like it. And you know who the worst star-fucks are?'

I shook my head.

'No,' she went on. 'It's the stars. They're the worst of all. Sex is incestuous in this town. You go to a big Hollywood party and you see the star-fuck shuffle. You will see the stars looking around to see where the other stars are seated – so they can sit with them. Because they can't sit with ordinary mortals. It's hilarious.'

'That's always been my fascination with celebrity sex. Famous people who sleep around are never happy with the woman they have because they never know why she's there. Is she there because he's famous? Or because she really loves him? It's the women in this town who really have the power. The women control the men. The women make the social decisions. He wants the freedom to go out and be whoever he has to be. So she soon has the money under control, the career under control – until he meets a sexy little make-up artist on a late-night shoot. . .'

'But hasn't the LA sex scene changed a lot in the nineties?' I said. 'I can't believe it's really much like you describe it in your books.'

'It hasn't changed at all,' Jackie replied tartly. 'I've surveyed this whole thing. My conclusion is that people in this town still sleep around a lot. I do know a few men who are incredible studs who are too frightened to sleep with a woman at the moment. They are paranoid. But they are the rare exceptions.'

'What about this lesbian chic?'

'I think lesbianism is on the rise – pardon the expression – because women are so dissatisfied with their relationships with LA men. I guess it started with *Basic Instinct*. Why is Sharon Stone such a big star today?'

'Because she has no competition,' I said.

'She certainly has no real competition. But the real reason is that she has the two essential qualities that make a movie star: likeability and fuckability. Being sexy isn't sufficient. I loved her in *Basic Instinct*. But I wish she hadn't flashed her crotch because to me that took away. If she was going to flash it, why didn't we get Michael Douglas flashing his balls? How come he's allowed to flash his balls in Europe but not in America? It's not good enough, William. It's not good enough!'

I asked if she knew any LA power-lesbians. Or whether she suspected some women were just faking it?

Apart from a few lesbian actresses who lived openly together, Ms Collins admitted that none of her more powerful friends – if they were lesbian – had come out of the closet. She once had an advance from one of Prince's girlfriends in the lady's room of a restaurant.

'I didn't know how to handle it,' she said grinning. 'I mean you always know how to handle men. I've been handling men all my life. I suppose I was rather flattered. You know – another day in the life of.'

'I have a nice, steady, quiet fame,' she went on. 'My name is very well known but I don't get recognised wherever I go. Publishers treat me very nicely. But I'm a woman who can walk away from any deal. That is the ultimate power. I can get whatever I want because I can just walk away. If a producer says "Hi Jackie – we're going to change this, hope you don't mind", I say, "That's fine, guys, here's your money back, and I'm walking away from this." I don't write what I think the public wants, or what a publisher tells me to – I write what *I* want.'

Ms Collins has an uncharitable view of the literary *arrivistes* who have tried to gatecrash the Hollywood circuit. 'I've seen writers come here who want to write about Hollywood and they get it all wrong,' she sniffed. 'They don't know anybody. They haven't been to any of the parties. They haven't been to any of the mansions. They might have been to Spago once – waited at the bar for half an hour and got the wrong table. And when you read about it, you're in hysterics because they have got it all wrong.'

'What about Julia Phillips?' I asked.

She lunged her fork sharply into a slice of tomato.

'I don't think she's ever mentioned quite frankly,' Jackie said without looking up. 'She's been forgotten. Nobody talks about her.'

The author of *You'll Never Eat Lunch in this Town Again* was reported to be breaking her literary silence with an essay in *Harper's* about what she contends is LA's 'power-trend' of the nineties: lesbian chic. But the article never appeared, apparently because it was too long. 'There's a very glamorous set coming up and they're not taking anything from anybody,' Phillips maintains. 'They have a wide power-base in Hollywood. From the young and the beautiful to the moustache-on-upper-lip-in-black-leather-jackets crowd.'

Their rise to power, she contends, mirrors that of the trendy and elite posse of gay men who ascended to power in Hollywood during the seventies and eighties. With one important exception. Whilst the powerful gay or bisexual men – whose number included studio chiefs – consolidated their power by establishing a network to help each other up the slippery pole, the hundred-odd women interviewed admitted that no real jobs-for-the-girls mafia existed. They unanimously told Phillips: 'No, because women are bitchy to one another.'

Lesbianism certainly seems to be no longer taboo in LA; you can forget the frumpy clichés of lesbians in bad Eton crop haircuts, lace up army boots and dungarees. Lesbianism is suddenly quite socially acceptable. Hard, erotic, lesbianism is viewed as the Radical Chic of nineties LA, which makes the trend very different from the avant-garde coterie of Hollywood's underground lesbian circle in its Golden Age. Aldous Huxley's wife, Maria, shared her husband's taste for beautiful American girls.

That lesbianism should go mainstream in LA is hardly surprising. Female political trends tend to lag at least ten years behind their male counterparts. As a result, just as it became practically hip to be gay in the early eighties – gay being synonymous with creativity and good taste – with many men allegedly claiming they were gay as a way of getting on in Hollywood – so many perfectly straight women are hinting that they are lesbian, or at least bisexual, as a way of appearing different, sexy and in control. What has certainly surprised me about the trend is the number of women I have met in LA who have casually volunteered – almost boasted – of the fact that they have had a lesbian experience recently. One appeal of lesbianism, of course, has to do with safety. The film community has three times the national average of Aids-related deaths.

'So you're not worried about Phillips' new book?' I continued.

'Wasn't she with that publishing firm that went bust? I never hear her name mentioned.'

But whilst Jackie Collins's publishers may, in the interests of boosting sales, boast that a book like *Hollywood Husbands* is 'a dangerously close-to-the-truth novel which kept everyone guessing as to the identities of the true-life Hollywood husbands', her fictional arrows have always been – with a few sharply pointed exceptions – rubber rather than arsenic-tipped. This is hardly surprising. Her position as chronicler-in-chief of the Lifestyles-of-the-Rich-and-Randy A-list posse in Malibu or Beverly Hills has come about because, as she says herself, she is a fully paid up Hollywood Club member. Included in her *American Star* publicity-kit – a glossy cardboard zebra-stripe folder with velcro patches – is a blown-up quote from *Newsday*, October 1992. 'When Collins writes,' it proclaims, 'Hollywood listens . . . Not since Jacqueline Susann has a writer of bestselling Hollywood scorchers been so embraced by the town she dishes.'

'A lot of people don't get in,' she said. 'They don't make it in the Club. It's a very closed circuit.' Ms Collins lunches out several times a week and, she says, she can usually get the table she wants at ten minutes' notice. 'I do know everybody,' she added with a sweet-bitch smile.

I asked Ms Collins about the LA literary life. Did writers hang-out together? Were there Hollywood literary salons as in London and New York?

'I'm friends with Sidney Sheldon, Billy Wilder, Michael Caine – loved his book – Dominick Dunne is a very nice man, you'd like him. The interesting thing about Hollywood is that there are all these famous people who *pretend* to be writers – and then have somebody else write the book for them. And then go on television shows and say how it was such a cathartic experience, that it was so wonderful – and you think "wait a minute", you didn't pick up a goddamn pen. There are all these writers in LA who don't write – it's ridiculous. I find it rather insulting. But it's just hype. You can't kid the public.'

'So how did you get into the Club?'

'Through Michael Caine. When I first moved to LA Michael and his wife were quite incredible. He introduced me to all their friends. It's not easy getting in. But when you're in, you're in.'

'What about your sister, Joan – how does she like LA?'

'Ah,' she said crisply. 'She lives in Europe now. But I wouldn't like to answer for her. I assume she likes France more, but I never like to say what she thinks.'

Jackie Collins cannot now think of living anywhere else other than LA. 'It's a terrific place. It's bizarrely terrific, you know what I mean? Kind of isn't real life, but is. You can park somewhere and have a machine gun stuck in your face. Which actually happened to me. You can be in a crazed earthquake. I think it's a very adventurous place.'

As we sat drinking our double-decaf espressos, a casually dressed man who looked to be in his forties walked past our table.

'We're off. Nice to see you again, Jackie,' he said.

'Goodbye. See ya.'

'That's David Giler,' she said as he strolled off. 'He's a good screenwriter. Very good.'

'What's he written?' I asked.

'You think I can remember?'

* * *

Armistead Maupin – whom Christopher Isherwood acclaimed as the Dickens of the West Coast – thought he was a rich man when he was handed a fountain pen by a Warner's executive to sign away the film rights of his *Tales of the City* sequence of novels. He was telling this story over a green salad by the swimming pool of the Sunset Marquis hotel, on Sunset, just down the block from Le Dome.

'There's gonna be just one small change,' volunteered the studio producer as Maupin pulled off the cap.

'What's that?'

'The gay and lesbian characters – they've gotta go.'

Maupin refused to sign.

'It was absurd,' he added. 'It was like telling Dickens to cut out all his poor people.'

Dressed in foamy white sneakers, pale brown corduroys and a sea-cotton shirt, he was lounging back in a plastic chair by the hotel swimming pool. With his marmalade moustache, chunky Yogi bear six-foot frame and strong blue eyes, he looked like a cross between an overweight Robert Redford and Ian Botham.

After some time passed, Maupin went on, he received

another phonecall inviting him to the home of the producer to meet another scriptwriter of *Tales* for the screen. They had a new idea. 'We had a lovely dinner. He seemed to be charming and have no problems with my homosexuality – that is, until halfway through dessert.'

'I really loved *Tales of the City*; I think it's absolutely brilliant; I've been doing some thinking – and I've got one small suggestion: what if that gay gynaecologist is made to be a serial killer."

Maupin put down his fork and stared at him in disbelief.

That the contract for a twelve-part Channel 4 TV series was finally drawn up – fourteen years after *Tales of the City* first appeared as a daily fictional column in the *San Francisco Chronicle* – with the British production company Working Title (*My Beautiful Laundrette, Caravaggio*) was hardly surprising. Such scripts seem to be read and handled by the Hollywood studios as if rubber-stamped with a leprosy warning.

Although frequently hailed as *the* chronicler of gay life, it is a label (although he is gay himself) Maupin resents.

'I always wince at that term', he said with a sigh, 'as it seems to imply that gay people are not part of the mainstream of life. The whole point is that gay people are an integral part of day-to-day life. More than half my characters are heterosexual – and that's what sets me apart from many other gay writers. It always annoys me when the term "subculture" turns up.'

Maupin was the first author in America to write extensively about Aids as a subject. Witnessing the spectre of the disease changing the face of San Francisco, his achievement was to deal with the subject with a sense of balance, avoiding the temptation to turn the disease into an issue that swamps the rest of life. The disease has so far killed twenty of his friends, including Rock Hudson. His own lover and business manager, Terry Anderson – who was sitting next to him – tested positive for HIV six years ago.

'I think San Francisco was probably better equipped to deal with Aids than any place on earth. We are a very tolerant city – the homophobia isn't as bad as other places. But I wouldn't say I have stopped wanting to write about the city because I see it as an end to an era. Many of the issues I deal with in *Tales of the City* continue in my own life. With Terry antibody positive, we continue to live with that, just as the character Michael does.'

He castigates Hollywood for failing to face up to Aids as a subject, while making such a public show of concern at the glut of $500-a-head Aids charity galas. Maupin has a point. On Valentine's night 1992 I attended a Bacchic Aids charity party in a mansion high up in the Hollywood Hills, thrown by the fashionable Aids charity Project Angel Food, hosted by New Age love guru Marianne Williamson. There was a seventies disco, with dancers writhing over the parquet floor, and balloons shaped like sausages were strung up across the floodlit swimming pool. Late in the evening, I came across a semi-naked couple necking in the bushes. When I asked the organiser how many Aids events the charity had recently hosted, her answer was: 'There are never enough parties.'

Under the patronage of Liz Taylor, Madonna and Bette Midler, Aids has become the charity *du jour* in LA. Every week, the stretch-limos line up outside the Beverly Hilton and the diamond-swathed Aids Angels spring out for yet another dinner. When the American Foundation for Aids Research presented Madonna with its Award of Courage in 1991, it described her as 'the bravest person in the world'. The dinner at the Beverly Wilshire included a jewellery auction and a performance by Barry Manilow.

'Hollywood is so used to patting itself on the back and calling itself liberal when it isn't,' said Maupin. 'What good does it do to throw these huge Aids bashes at which every star is present and yet never televise it for the American public? And why not? Because they are desperately afraid of tainting their own careers by being associated with homosexuality.'

'Aids forces you to take every moment and live it to the full,' Maupin, who has tested negative, says. 'It forces you to eliminate pettiness and adds a colouration to life that wasn't there before. None of us can make the assumptions that our parents did, that we have decades ahead of us.'

6

To Live and Die in LA

'THEY WORSHIP DEATH HERE. THEY don't worship money they worship death,' wrote Raymond Chandler. It took less than a month of living in LA to understand exactly what Chandler meant by this.

That the remembrance service for *Star Trek* creator Gene Roddenberry should have been held on All Saints' Day at the Forest Lawn Memorial Park was not inappropriate. Death has always been taken seriously in the City of Angels. But judging by the scale of commotion in LA that followed the newsflashes announcing that he had 'passed his final frontier' (fade out back to regular programmes with *Star Trek* theme) after a heart attack in Santa Monica, you might have thought the Pope had just produced Siamese twins. 'Few ideas in the annals of motion picture and television history have inspired more passion and allegiance on the part of an audience as has *Star Trek*,' quickly declared Paramount Pictures chairman Brandon Tartikoff. Leonard Nimoy, alias the goblin-eared Mr Spock, said (through his agent): 'He had an extraordinary vision about mankind and the potential of mankind's future.'

The 2p.m. Memorial Service for the blue-eyed former LAPD officer who boldly went where no writer–producer went before – rescuing genre-bound science-fiction from its 1960s voyage to oblivion – was one of the more extraordinary afternoons of my life. It was so surreal that it made the bizarre obsequies at Whispering Glades in Evelyn Waugh's *The Loved One* suddenly seem about as sober-minded as your average

Scottish Presbyterian sexton's monthly newsletter.

The ceremony took place at Forest Lawn's Hollywood Hills cemetery located next to Warner Bros and Disney's sprawling movie studios in Burbank. It was the sort of glaringly hot LA day where you saw people driving around in their swim wear – or underpants – and if you had forgotten your sunglasses, you stopped off in a gas-station and bought a pair for $10. Sunroofs were down, radios blasted out Michael Bolton and the lead-free exhaust from the car in front of you dissolved into the bleached blue sky like a canister of disco-smoke.

Turning right at Forest Lawn Drive, the scorched hillside suddenly seemed to grow a thick head of tufty green hair. The mortuary, with its manicured car-park and adjoining flower-shop ('Artificial flowers are not permitted') closely resembled a mock-Tudor clubhouse. Dressed in regulation dinner-jackets, sunglasses and white gloves, a legion of Forest Lawn staff directed traffic along a gently winding drive that rolled past an icing-sugar church and swept up a steep hill towards the 'Hall of Liberty'.

As I walked up the hillside, a crocodile of several hundred Trekkies, many decked out in full Klingon battle-suits – suddenly appeared on the crest of the hill – like a scene from *Planet of the Apes*. The Trekkies, for some reason, were not allowed inside. Many were crying. They lined up in an orderly line along the clipped yew hedges, clutching photographs of the *Star Trek* cast which they wanted autographed. VIP guests, cast members, Roddenberry's friends and family and non-Trekkie members of the public swarmed along a red carpet into the service, passing the usual wild circus of TV cameras, boom poles and reporters' microphones.

This being Forest Lawn, there were no tombstones to be seen. A huge thirty-foot high engraved granite slab by the glass doors detailed the Builders' dream, surrounded by acres of rolling green fairways pock-marked with shiny brass plaques ('memorial tablets').

Traditional cemetries were 'wrong', declared Forest

Lawn's founder, Dr Hubert Eaton, in 1917, 'because they depict an end, not a beginning. They have consequently become unsightly stoneyards, places that do nothing for humanity save a practical act, and that not well.'

The Hall of Liberty was not so much a hall as a luxury cinema auditorium. As if at a gala première, several front rows of ergonomically designed bucket seats were taped off for 'Cast Only'. *Star Trek* theme music was piped out of several wall speakers. On the podium was a large framed poster of Roddenberry, wearing a sky-blue V-neck jersery, his glassy blue eyes smiling. The Christmas card programme depicted three herons in a pond under a shower of sprinkler-jets.

'Nice card,' said the elderly Roddenberry in-law I was sitting next to.

'Oh, yes. Very nice,' I replied.

'I guess they chose it because Gene was called the "Great Bird" by his fans. Did you know that?'

'No, I didn't.'

'Gene loved his fans,' he sighed. 'He would've liked this card. Nice touch.'

After Captain Kirk (William Shatner), Mr Spock (Leonard Nimoy) and the cast of *Star Trek: The Next Generation* had settled in their seats, the lights dimmed and the service began with a rendition of Paul McCartney's *Yesterday* – an odd choice, perhaps, to honour the elder statesman of science-fiction. The Beatles, apparently, were Gene's favourite band.

Then came the tributes.

The grey-haired Ray Bradbury, a close friend of Roddenberry's and another elder statesman of science-fiction, said: 'A man who has a following this large will go on to the end of the century – and beyond. At the centre of *Star Trek* was the problem of the universe itself. Who knows where it will end?'

Former *Star Trek* crew member Whoopi Goldberg was also profound: 'Gene helped change the entire face of the world. He wanted to make the world a better place.'

Hollywood, I thought, was good at tributes.

This was all very appropriate. *Star Trek* may have a mass

audience of tens of millions, but it has also been the subject of 150 books and some finely tuned intellectual attention. The book *Meaning in Star Trek*, for instance, was written to illustrate that 'the Starship Enterprise (after which NASA named its first space shuttle) explores not simply outer space, but also the inner reaches of the human psyche'. Roddenberry happily went along with all this psycho-babble. 'We did try to raise some interesting issues,' he once said. 'What does it mean to be "human", for instance?'

Indeed. Whilst pop cultural armchair pundits concede that some of the episodes were truly terrible – although, they will say, touching in a ridiculous sort of way – the best ones had a 'sense of mythic imagery' offering a collection of multi-ethnic, inter-galactic, democratic and humanistic parables that offered a 'modern mythology for a secular age' – i.e. a religion. Roddenberry, indeed, wrote a 'bible' for writers to follow. '*Star Trek*'s message,' I read in one obituary, 'was that power without humanity, intellect without compassion, are uncivilised.'

I was never much of a *Star Trek* watcher. But each time Roddenberry's beaming smile clicked up on the screen, there was something there that embodied that happy–crazy optimism that snuggles deeply somewhere in the Californian psyche. That passionate, childish, determined, sincere, enduring – almost endearingly absurd – belief in *hope* as an elixir of the human condition.

The service ended very oddly. A man stepped up on the stage and announced that Gene loved to reel. Scottish reel, that is. There was suddenly a loud wail of Scottish bagpipes – followed by a band in full tartan kilts reeling on the stage for about fifteen minutes. They did an Eightsome, a Gay Gordon's and – I think – the Duke of Perth. After this unlikely celebration of Scottish culture, the service ended – reverting to the *Star Trek* theme as the several-hundred-strong congregation filed out into the afternoon sunshine to the waiting cameras. A drinks party reception followed outside during which a squadron of US airforce fighter jets roared overhead as a salute.

For dozens of fans, the event was manna from Zorgon. 'I've been a Trekkie for over ten years,' one rotund woman in a body-hugging *Star Trek* suit that was two sizes too small told me. 'I've never seen so many of the cast together before. It's like a wonderful college reunion.'

Her fellow Trekkies shuffled around with their photographs and autograph books. Many seemed to be rather greedy – 'Can you sign here, here and here?' This, I later discovered, was not so much because they were especial *Star Trek* fans but because an autographed photo of Mr Spock or Captain Kirk can fetch up to $150. 'More, in fact,' I was assured by one signature hunter, 'if it's got at an event like Roddenberry's funeral. Collectors will pay hundreds.'

Not all the Trekkies were quite so mercenary. For many, their objective was simply to get photographed with as many *Star Trek* cast members as possible. The please-can-I-have-a-photograph-with-you crowd were a mixed bunch. Cast members such as Patrick Stewart – he was fairly difficult to miss as his gnomish head is as bald as a brown boiled egg – happily obliged. An occupational hazard of being a *Star Trek* crew member, they smiled cheerily into the blazing sun.

I drove away from Forest Lawn with that relieved feeling of leaving a second-rate horror movie.

* * *

The Californian necropolis of Whispering Glades was, of course, inspired by Forest Lawn Cemetery. But the Forest Lawn that Waugh called a 'Tivoli Garden for the Dead' was not the Hollywood Hills cemetery park where the Roddenberry Memorial Service had been held. He had been referring to their grander Glendale cemetery a few miles down the freeway.

Ever since Waugh flayed Forest Lawn in *The Loved One* ('a purely fanciful tale, a little nightmare produced by the unaccustomed high living of a brief visit to Hollywood') the mortuary has been the subject of plentiful stereomythical ridiculing. The 1960 film version of Waugh's novel was directed by Tony Richardson – who became a fixture of Hollywood's British colony when he moved out to California. Aged sixty-five, he died from Aids in Los Angeles on 14 November 1991 – just two months after I arrived.

There was no remembrance service for Richardson – certainly not at Forest Lawn. When I called up the executive offices to inquire whether Richardson's ashes were, by some macabre irony, being laid to rest in Glendale I was gruffly informed that 'it wouldn't be appropriate to comment'.

I made a call to the Director's Guild to discover whether they were planning any sort of tribute to Tony Richardson. A major Hollywood memorial service had been organised for Frank Capra.

'Richardson?' a voice drawled. 'That Brit guy who just died from Aids?'

'That's right,' I said.

'Na – I don't think we would be doing anything. I'll check, but I just . . . well . . . I just don't think we would.'

To mark the twenty-fifth anniversary – which passed almost unnoticed – of the death of the founder of Forest Lawn, Dr Hubert Eaton, I decided to take an afternoon tour of Forest Lawn in Glendale, the Disneyland of American cemeteries (Walt Disney does, in fact, 'rest' there – along with the likes of Errol Flynn, W.C. Fields, Humphrey Bogart, Jean Harlow and Clark Gable). It would also be, I decided, a mini-tribute to Tony Richardson.

Dr Hubert Eaton, upon whom Waugh based the Dreamer in *The Loved One*, died on 20 September 1966 – just a few months after Waugh himself was found dead on the floor of his downstairs lavatory in Somerset. Originally from Missouri, Eaton graduated with a degree in chemistry from William Jewell College. The son of a clergyman, he worked for ten years as a research chemist, metallurgist and general manager of a smelting company before realising the business potential of the mortuary trade. On becoming general manager of Forest Lawn in 1917, he declared: 'I shall endeavor to build Forest Lawn as different, as unlike other cemeteries as sunshine is unlike darkness, as eternal life is unlike death.'

Forest Lawn today seems cryogenically frozen in time. You sense this from the moment you swing in through the entrance gates. According to my 'Points of Interest at Forest Lawn' guide these were the largest wrought-iron gates in the world, standing twenty-five feet high and eighty feet wide. Designed in English Renaissance style and decorated – for some unfathomable reason – with the gilded coats of arms of English and Scottish aristocratic families, they were larger than the gates at the old Imperial Palace in Istanbul. Each gate weighed 5,000 pounds. 'Yet,' I was assured, 'they are so perfectly balanced that they may be opened or closed with the finger tips.'

I was stopped at a lodge.

'Good afternoon, Sir – are you attending a service or just looking at cemetery property?' I was asked by a uniformed guard.

'I'm looking at property,' I said, and was sent on my way.

Along a short drive set in green parkland, I came to the Administration Building. Parking my car on the gravel, it looked to me like an expensive Ascot health farm. The Tudor manor, inspired by Compton Wynyates, the Warwickshire seat of the Earls of Northampton, had been aged with a special substance, I read on, 'to give it the softening touch of time' and the effect of 'seeming to have been transported intact from the sixteenth century'.

Pushing open the heavily studded mock-Elizabethan oak door leading into the dark oak-panelled Great Hall – the mortuary reception area – I was welcomed by a large-spectacled woman, with a body that looked like a deflated bouncing ball, sitting behind a table that would not have been out of place on the set of *Camelot*.

'How can I be of assistance to you, Sir?'

'I'm looking for the casket room,' I said.

'Through the doors on your right.'

A form of sublime musak was piped out of speakers hidden up in the 'weathered' oak beams and the stained glass windows depicting the Knights of the Round Table. 'Here time has been turned back to the sixteenth century,' I was again reminded by my guide. Despite the fact that it was over 85 degrees outside, without a cloud in the deep azure sky, a fire was blazing in the huge stone chimneyplace. Above a chest was an 'ancestral' oil portrait of Dr Hubert Eaton by Arthur Cahill – 'internationally known for his portraits of leaders in business and the professions'. I was also told to note a stand-up globe – described as 'yellow and cracked with age'. That it depicted several countries that were yet to be discovered by the sixteenth century did not surprise me.

I passed a series of small private telephone kiosks. That was where the business end of things took place. Passing along a thickly carpeted corridor, I opened a heavy door and entered a chamber straight from the pages of *Alice in Wonderland*. All along the walls, pink and seemingly padded, was a selection of dozens of open caskets, all in different colours – silver, brown, blue, black – each with quilted lining and a cardboard price tag, ranging from around $350 to $10,000. The huge room was quite empty.

Upstairs, the deep pile carpet was thicker still. I was left to stroll freely around the maze of corridors, along which were the open doors of various 'Slumber Rooms'. Each resembled an expensive hotel suite decorated to be a mini-botanical garden. I walked into one. A small ante-room with a chintz sofa led into the master viewing suite, with an open casket lying on a bed. There were few mourners about. The casket I peered into contained an elderly woman's body with eye-balls like ice-blue marbles and her face painted to make her appear healthier (and happier) in death than in life.

Tucked away behind the Administration Building, close to the incinerating furnaces, was the 'Little Church of the Flowers' – a replica of the medieval village church at Stoke

Poges, Berkshire, which inspired Thomas Gray's 'Elegy Written in a Country Churchyard'. It was built to about three-quarters scale, with its façade having a plastic feel to it, like those, hollow, moulded rubber churches you found glued to a green papier-mâché hill on a 1950s sixth-form school train set. If I kicked it, I didn't expect to hurt my foot. Its 'weathered stone' walls looked squishy.

Like its Hollywood Hills sister cemetery, Forest Lawn, Glendale resembled a suburban golf course. This time, however, it had a hoity-toity Royal Championship feel to it. Further up the drive was an even more peculiar church, the Wee Kirk o' the Heather – a replica of a ruined chapel in Dumfriesshire in which Annie Laurie's love story is told on the stained glass windows. Again, from the outside it looked like an addition to a Hornby landscape, with its scaly stone walls like varnished rhinocerous hide. Inside it was gloomy, empty and air-conditioned.

A life-sized replica of Michelangelo's David was set in a private courtyard – the Court of David – with more elevator musak piped out of a series of small speakers nestling in the branches of a nearby tree. Unlike the replica of the statue in the Palazzo della Signoria in Florence, splattered with pigeon droppings, this David looked as if he has just stepped out of a bath of strong bleach. Behind him in a walled garden stood another statue, with a plastic button to press. On doing so, a booming recorded voice informed me to wait and I would hear 'The Story of the Meaning of Life'. I departed hurriedly.

Forest Lawn, it seems, remains primarily concerned with the quest for immortality through financial means. This was apparent from its 'Facts about Funerals' guide, 'prepared by Forest Lawn to help you and your family consider what you and they want when – not if – the time comes'. It was an odd booklet, like a glossy American holiday brochure to Britain, with chocolate-box pictures of immaculate lawns, the mock-Tudor manor, a private lake with swans and a village church. 'You wouldn't consider buying a car without informing yourself, shopping, and comparing,' I read. 'So why do so many families fail to take that simple, important step when it comes to the once-in-a-lifetime purchase of a funeral?'

A few pages on, the booklet began to resemble an estate-agent's brochure. Under the heading 'What kind of cemetery property?' was a list of 'several important advantages' of buying a plot in advance. The reasons included: 'It avoids emotional overspending just after a death takes place' and 'It enables the buyer to choose pre-developed cemetery property at a substantial saving.' Easy-credit terms, of course, were available.

Cremation, my booklet said, was a cost-effective alternative to a casket burial – 'the price for internment space or niche is usually less than that of a comparable full-sized interment space or mausoleum crypt.' The practice had become increasingly popular since the mid-seventies, with one in three Californians now choosing incineration. The utmost care was given to providing the most professional service. 'Cremation involves burning the body and the casket at nearly the same temperature as is used for firing china,' I read. 'Afterwards, bone fragments weighing about six pounds are separated and retained.'

Or at least were meant to be.

In exactly the same week as the twenty-fifth anniversary of the death of Dr Hubert Eaton, a gruesome behind-the-scenes picture of Forest Lawn emerged in a Glendale Superior Court that revealed the murky other side of Dr Eaton's Paradise.

An investigation was launched after the ashes of a Las Vegas woman called Susan Lescoe were found lying along the Glendale Freeway. She was cremated in Las Vegas and her remains were delivered by her family to Forest Lawn-Glendale in a cardboard box marked with her name. Although Forest Lawn officials insist that the box was transferred to a sealed urn to their crematorium, the cardboard box and torn bag of human ashes were later found by two highway workers on the freeway near the cemetery.

Forest Lawn was unable to explain exactly how they got there.

At about the same time, another inquiry was opened into the practices of Forest lawn, after a former employee, Shawn E. Allison, who quit working at the cemetery in August 1991, alleged in a sworn testimony running to over 100 pages that it was 'an occurrence of every day' for Forest Lawn to leave any not fully cremated bodies in the machine for the next case.

Shawn Allison's job at Forest Lawn-Glendale included loading and unloading bodies in the incinerating furnaces. He worked at Forest Lawn for a year and had received favourable job evaluation reports. In his sworn testimony, which the *Los Angeles Times* obtained, Allison alleged that:

i. Ashes that overspilled from the urns bought by relatives or friends were regularly shovelled into dust-bin bags, or dropped in a grave. Forest Lawn policy requires that unused ashes be returned to families. 'Nearly all the people that we cremated went into these bags because there was always spillage from the machine,' he said.

ii. Bone scraps and remains of human bodies that fell from the furnace were flushed down a floor drain in the crematorium. On finding 'bone fragments sticking out above the drain' he was ordered to wash them away with a fire hose.

iii. Bodies that had been partially cremated were mixed with bodies awaiting cremation.

iv. Employees mismatched identification tags and destroyed records in the furnaces.

The case was quietly settled out of court.

'Be happy,' Dr Eaton advised the bereaved in his *Credo*, 'because they for whom you mourn are happy – far happier than ever before.' In Glendale's Vesperland, an inscription reads ' . . . Happy because Forest Lawn has eradicated the old customs of Death and depicts Life not Death'.

Dream on, Hubert.

* * *

The news, however, is better for bereaved pet lovers. Following my visit to the Los Angeles Pet Memorial Park in the San Fernando Valley, I can – happily – report that the cemetery on which Waugh based the Happier Hunting Ground is flourishing today.

Located in Calabasas, a middle-class suburb very like Croydon half an hour's drive along the 101 freeway north of Los Angeles, the Los Angeles Pet Memorial Park had been going for sixteen years when Waugh visited Hollywood in 1947.

The plot of *Sunset Boulevard* – written just after *The Loved One* – turns on the fact that the unemployed screenhack Joe Gillis is mistaken by ex-silent movie queen Norma Desmond (Gloria Swanson) as having been sent from the pet mortuary to pick up her dead chimpanzee.

Norma: I've made up my mind we'll bury him in the garden. Any city laws against that?
Gillis: I wouldn't know.
Norma: I don't care anyway. I want the coffin to be white. And I want it specially lined with satin. White or deep pink.

Burying your pet in the garden was, in fact, punishable by a heavy fine. California's most famous pet cemetery was founded by a group of businessmen in 1931 after a city ordinance was passed forbidding burial of any animal within the city limits, even on private property. Prior to its existence, bereaved pet lovers were encouraged to hand over the furry cadavers of their beloved ones to a city rubbish disposal truck. This dumped the dead animals at a plant that turned them into manure.

Today, if a little jaded, a little in need of a new lawn mower, and more urgently in need of a coat of paint in the executive office, the cemetery probably remains the most popular resting place for pets in California. Saying 'office', in fact, isn't exactly accurate. After bumping along a desert track to the entrance, I pulled up in what looked like a trailer and camper park. I was met by Ms Mary Bayer, a slender forty-something woman in cowboy boots, who wanted to know the nature of my business. Her office was a large old caravan.

'I'm a tourist from England,' I said. 'I'm also an animal lover.'

'Come this way,' she said. 'Please respect my mourners.'

I was handed a 'Celebrity Pet List', a xerox copy of an article and guide to the cemetery that appeared in *Pets* magazine in August 1940, and was led out into a large, rather badly cut, lawn. Sloping down a hill to one side, with part of it shadowed by trees, it resembled a school 3rd XI cricket pitch. As at Forest Lawn, the grass was studded with small plaques dotted with bright red and yellow floral garlands.

She left me by the side of the cemetery.

'You need a strong heart to look at some of these,' I was warned. 'So much love here.'

The grass was absurdly springy. Since it had been raining, I squelched across the wet lawn leaving large footprints. Not wanting to draw attention to myself, I tried to avoid stepping on the grass at all by using my long legs to hop from one brass memorial tablet to the other, as if crossing a stony Scottish stream.

Many of the plaque inscriptions were absurd: 'If greatness is unselfish love, you reached the pinnacle. We feel so empty without you. Your family – the Johnsons; 'Sweet Little Dukie-Doo. Mommy loves you'; 'Winnie – Please Wait for us'; 'Till we meet in heaven'. On the ridge of the hill, under a large oak tree, was a stone monument to Tawny, a lion who died in 1940 – 'His adored tomcat pal sleeps beside him'.

When Norma Desmond warns Gillis not to give her a 'fancy price just because I'm rich' it was a pointed reference to the absurdly high cost of having a pet 'decently' buried in LA in the thirties and forties. The founders of the Los Angeles Pet Memorial Park, which is set in ten lush acres, built a sophisticated crematorium, mausoleum, columbarium, morticians' workshop and mortuary, along with purchasing a luxury pet hearse and building cottages for two caretakers and gardeners.

The service offered by the cemetery aimed to be in every smallest detail as professional as at Forest Lawn, offering either cremation, burial or embalming. The cost of burials even fifty years ago often stretched to over $1,000.

The cemetery quickly became a commercial success, with many of Hollywood's most famous citizens choosing the park as the final resting place for their pets. In real life, for example, Gloria Swanson had her cat buried there. Valentino's dog, Kabar, was buried at the cemetery with 'the tenderest care'; as was Hopalong Cassidy's horse and animals belonging to Charlie Chaplin, Humphrey Bogart, Lauren Bacall, Bing Crosby, Randolph Hearst, Alfred Hitchcock and Mickey Rooney.

Many owners have gone so far as expressing the wish to be buried with their beloved ones. A sixty-nine-year-old woman typically wrote: 'I am asking if it will be possible that I may be buried with my two pet poodle dogs. You bury large dogs and horses, why not me? I have three lots in a cemetery all paid for and a six-foot monument already up, but I really want to rest with my two faithful friends on earth, my little poodle dogs, Bobbie and Betty.' Such requests are not granted. What is allowed, however, is for the cremated ashes of an owner to be sprinkled over the burial site of a beloved pet. This is a frequent occurence.

Those who have difficulty coping with the death of their beloved can seek Professional Pet Bereavement Counselling with Stephanie Schatz, president of the Royal Pet Mortuary Inc. Her clients regularly pay $500–1,000 for 'counselling' and limousine escort to the funeral. Recently, her pet mortuary – which is operated from a bedroom in her Marina Del Ray apartment in LA – received a special order for a coffin to be made for a 'much loved' pet black rat. It was laid to rest draped in ermine and purple silk. 'It was like an emperor's funeral,' Ms Schatz told me.

In 1983, however, the cemetery faced the bulldozer, when a pair of get-rich-quick property developers made a substantial offer to purchase the fifty-eight-year-old park. In a move that not even Tom Sharpe could have invented, 700 outraged pet lovers hastily joined together to form an alliance called SOPHIE – Save Our Pets' History in Eternity – which declared that it would stop at nothing to prevent any violation of sacred pet ground.

The cemetery, in which 40,000 animals happily slumbered, had been bequeathed by its original founders to the Los Angeles chapter of the Prevention of Cruelty to Animals, upon which it had become something of a financial drain. Because the society's 'interest and expertise', as it put it, was only with *living* animals it decided to sell the cemetery to reduce costs. The belligerent feuding between the pet lovers and property developers lasted for three years. After dozens of boot sales and other fund-raising devices, the group finally raised $100,000 to buy the cemetery. They also got a state law implemented which protected the cemetery's legal status in perpetuity. 'Send money, not tears,' Mary Bayer urged pet lovers wishing to show their support.

After the victory 200 SOPHIE members held a picnic celebration on the cemetery lawn, with lemonade punch and homemade cakes iced with pink and yellow roses. At the tea-party Ms Bayer announced that one of the cemetery's first priorities was to build a chapel. 'These are kind of what our dreams are,' she said. 'You know, sometimes I lay in bed and dream about this place.'

7

The Mousetrap

As UNCLE WALT'S FAVOURITE TUNE, 'Zip A Dee Doo Dah', drifted over the candyfloss-pink turrets of Euro-Disney's Magic Kingdom before the start of its gala opening on 12 April 1992, one person who wasn't humming along was Edoardo Leoncavallo, originally hired as a senior architect on the $4.4 billion project. When Disney chairman Michael Eisner, Kylie Minogue, Eddie Murphy, members of the French Government and 7,000 other VIP guests grooved to the wail of pop singer Cher's 'Shoop Shoop Song' at the gala party, the fifty-six-year-old former Disney executive was in the Los Angeles Superior Court suing his former company after being dismissed from Euro-Disney in Paris, he claims, because he sported a moustache – a subversion strictly forbidden by Disney's 'Appearance Guide'.

According to Disney's detailed ten-page personal grooming and behavioural guide, Disney employees – whether in America, Japan or France – are also required to 'wear proper undergarments while working' and have 'fingernails which do not exceed seven millimetres'. Women should wear little make-up, preferably just mascara. They should not be fat or large-breasted. Bracelets, necklaces and more than one ring on each finger is prohibited. Tattoos and dyed hair are forbidden, as is chewing gum, smoking or eating in public view, or being caught in a photograph with any 'guest' holding an alcoholic drink. Earrings must be no bigger than a five pence piece. Despite the fact that only an estimated 55 per cent of American adults, 35 per cent of French and less than 30 per cent of Japanese regularly buy deodorant, the wearing of anti-perspirant is compulsory due to the close contact with guests.

Since it was this Snowy White image (Mickey is a *clean* mouse, a Disney Human Resources official assured me) that Disney executives repeatedly used to defend themselves from the scabrous accusations of American cultural imperialism in the countdown to the opening of Euro-Disney, I paid a visit to the original Disneyland in Anaheim, California, to research an article on the 'Disney Spirit' expected of the 12,000 new staff – sorry, cast members – joining Uncle Walt's Empire at Marnée-la-Vallee, twenty-four kilometres from Paris.

Danger was probably the last thing on my mind when, on the hazy blue morning of 27 February, six weeks before the Euro-Disney turnstiles opened, I drove thirty miles down the Santa Ana Freeway and bought a one-day ticket to Disneyland. I had never been before and I wanted to know if Disneyland, which boasts of being the 'Happiest Place on Earth', was any fun.

So seriously, indeed, does Disney take the responsibility of ensuring that its 'guests' (customers don't exist) are happy at Disneyland that a special Disney university exists to 'educate' – not brainwash – staff in corporate doctrine. 'Courtesy to guests is fundamental,' declared Dave Kanally, director of the university, shortly before the opening of Euro-Disney. 'Everything that the guests see is perfectly clean and impeccable. Every cast member's first job is to welcome our guests in a friendly way.'

But, as I discovered on my first visit to Disneyland, a flip side exists to Disney's popular image of fun, friendliness and cleanliness. Disney's empire today seems to bring with it a dark new world of authoritarian intolerance.

Having intended to spend most of the day researching the 'Disney Spirit', I arrived at Disneyland at about 11a.m. I spoke – or rather tried to speak – to a considerable number of Disney staff. Almost without exception, it was like trying to talk to mutants. I asked a question. There was a big wide smile and I was referred to 'Disney Human Resources' or 'Information'. 'Live characters,' I was curtly informed by a Disney spokesman, 'do not talk to guests because it breaks the magic.'

'At Disneyland,' declared my glossy guide, 'you'll laugh till you scream on more than fifty-five attractions.' I can't pretend the rides were much fun. I spent most of the day queuing up beside grey-haired couples in track-suits. After a forty-minute wait for an 'incredible galactic journey' on George Lucas's 'Star Tours', I was disappointed to find it about as thrilling as a four-minute journey from Tooting to Balham on the Northern Line. The only attraction that had no queue was called 'It's a Small World' in Fantasyland. This involved stepping into a small plastic boat which was pulled at about two miles per hour through a series of dusty cardboard sets full of bouncing dolls in national folk costumes endlessly singing 'It's a small world after all!' in shrill voices. Ten years before, a guest diarist on the *New Republic* had referred to the (as yet unchanged) ride as 'what hell must be like'.

In comparison to what happened to me later that afternoon however, 'It's a Small World' seemed like a mini-paradise.

When I paid $27.50 for a one-day passport ('Disneyland is dedicated to the ideals, the dreams and the hard facts that have created America' stated Walt Disney on Disneyland's 1955 dedication plaque), I did not expect my souvenirs to consist of a pair of bruised wrists, and a polaroid snap taken inside Anaheim jail. Or, for that matter, that I would *myself* be coerced into a form of Disney parade, and exhibited in manacles in view of Disney staff and various members of Hollywood *haut monde*.

It happened like this. The day I went to Disneyland turned out to be the day that Elizabeth Taylor was throwing a private sixtieth birthday party for herself at the theme park. It was not an event that my paper had expressed any interest in. I had, to be honest, no idea it was even happening that night. The preparations for the estimated $500,000 party had been confidential. Taking over Main Street, Fantasy Land, Tomorrowland and Videopolis for the night, Liz Taylor invited 1,000 guests to join her in celebrating an event that most sixty-year-old women might prefer to forget.

'Adult Children Only Please' proclaimed the invitation. Dressed in black leather, Liz n' Larry were to arrive at Disneyland at around 10p.m. Following the media helicopter invasion of her wedding five months before, the air-space over Disneyland had been cleared by the FAA for the evening. In Disney's baronial fiefdom of Orange County such things can be arranged.

At 6.05p.m., with the park awhirl with caterers, stage managers, ride engineers and Disnoids – Disney staff – I walked towards a cabin from which some exotic cooking smells were wafting into the evening sky. I simply wanted to inquire what was on the menu for the gathering of *tout* Tinseltown later that evening. It might make a two-line diary item. I was already on my way out of the park, following the rest of the crowd. It was just five minutes after the last public ride and nearly four hours before Liz n' Larry were due to arrive in an open horse-drawn carriage surrounded by Disney characters.

'Hello,' I shouted into the cabin.

There was no reply. Seeing a cloud of steam pouring through a window, I went round to the back door.

Suddenly, I was tackled by two Disney security guards who appeared to have leapt out of a bush. They seized my arms.

'You, there,' one shouted. 'Put your hands above your head and you won't get hurt.'

'What the hell are you doing?' I asked.

'You're under arrest,' one of the guards said, pointing a bright torch in my face.

'Got a gun?' the other Disney guard asked. 'Knife, concealed weapon?'

He began frisking me.

'No, I bloody well haven't,' I said angrily. 'There's been some sort of serious mistake. I'm just a tourist – look here, here's my ticket . . . my Disney passport.'

'You're under arrest for trespassing,' the other guard repeated, twisting my arm in a painful Chinese lock.

I was frogmarched down some steps and led back through Fantasyland.

'Disneyland is hosting a private party,' the guard continued, wrenching my arm as if he was tightening up a wheel hub. 'Scum like you weren't invited.'

I told them I worked for *The Times* of London and that I had been researching an article on Euro-Disney. I was hardly dressed like a gatecrasher. I was wearing a dark flannel suit and tie: I had a dinner engagement that evening in LA.

'Listen,' I said, my temper rising. 'How can I be trespassing when I've paid to get into Disneyland and there are still dozens of public still in the park.'

'They're leaving,' he replied. 'You were going to hide in the bushes.'

'Don't be so bloody ridiculous,' I snapped.

As we marched on, the guard kept saying: 'I'm taking this personally – personally you understand.'

'Where are you taking me?' I asked.

'I should remind you,' he said. 'That anything you say may be taken down in evidence and used against you.'

It was now 6.15p.m. Just fifteen minutes after the last ride. Instead of simply being asked to leave Disneyland, or – as I was expecting – being more or less politely escorted out of the park, I was led to the Disney police station, interrogated for an hour about what I was doing at Disneyland and then thrown in the back of a heavily armoured police van with my hands handcuffed tightly behind my back and left for three hours (imagine this happening at Alton Towers).

In the van, I was squashed next to another innocent member of the public – a freelance twenty-something male model called Christopher-Michael – who had had the misfortune of having fallen asleep that afternoon on the grass near the Pirates of the Caribbean. We were soon joined by Alan Zenger, a well-known tabloid paparazzo who was working for the *Star* (a picture of Liz Taylor on a flying

Dumbo was rumoured to be worth up to $50,000) and a medley of professional showbiz party gatecrashers, amateur photographers, Michael Jackson groupies and a further handful of Disneyland 'guests' who were rounded up before they made it to the gates. Soon, over twenty people were squeezed in – including a squad of five from the *National Enquirer*.

The van began to resemble a Black Hole of Calcutta on wheels. We each had less than a square foot of space and could not move. It was broilingly hot. Requests for water and to have our handcuffs loosened were all refused. After two hours, a Pavarotti-sized man with asthma – a dentist whose evening hobby was gatecrashing Hollywood premières and parties – started to wheeze and thrash violently.

He banged his head hard on the perspex window.

'I'm not breathing well,' he gasped out. 'I can feel an attack coming on. I have these attacks.'

'What sort of attacks?' I asked.

The man's face had turned a sickly grey. Blobs of sweat rolled down his balding head. His pupils were dilating as if he was on amphetamines.

'I'm feeling all dizzy and faint.'

He thrashed around a bit more, banging his head again on the glass.

A Disnoid eventually peered in through the security grill.

'This man's ill,' I said. 'He needs a doctor.'

A doctor was refused.

'Can you just loosen my handcuffs,' the man pleaded. 'They're cutting into my skin. I'm in agony – pleeeeease!'

The door was slammed shut.

When half a dozen new miscreants joined us, the bullet-proof doors were opened up and several of us were dragged out by members of the Disney police.

'You, you, you!' scowled a beefy guard, 'outta the van.'

Myself, in a dark suit, the stocky Alan Zenger, in casual trousers and an open shirt, and a female Jacko groupie, in a Michael Jackson world tour T-shirt, were told to stand by the front of the mobile prison – like three offenders in a medieval pillory. The van was parked in full view of Disney cast members, as well as other arrivals for the party. The evening's list of celebrity and sub-celebrity guests included Gregory Peck, Shirley Maclaine, Richard Gere, Cindy Crawford, Dione Warwick, Dame Edna Everage, Charles Bronson, *Dynasty* star John Forsythe, *Dallas* star Linda Gray and Beverly Hills hairstylist José Eber.

It was a deeply humiliating experience. Each time a new addition was thrown in the back of the van, we were paraded in the small courtyard by the Disney police station. As the birthday party got going, our tropical cattle-truck began to feel like one of the more popular attractions of the evening.

'This is the happiest place on earth!' Liz declared shortly before cutting her cake. 'Disneyland brings out the kid in me. I don't mind growing old, I just don't want to ever be forgotten.'

We weren't likely to forget.

'Tonight is the night of fantasy,' proclaimed the party programme. 'Here no one is grumpy and everyone is happy.' Whilst standing around the courtyard I could hear the wail of Barry Manilow singing live at the party. Because my hands were still handcuffed behind my back, it was imposible to block out the nauseating noise.

At around 11p.m., we were driven to Anaheim police station, where police rolled on prophylactic rubber gloves before ordering us to take off our socks, shoe-laces, ties, watches and sealing our personal effects in a plastic bag. We then stood in line as we were weighed, measured, photographed and finally fingerprinted – being handed a large tin of cold blue paraffin jelly to wipe off the ink.

Bail was set at $500. Clearly prepared for such an eventuality, the team from the *National Enquirer* were bailed out on $2,500 within half an hour. We were allowed to make one collect phone call to try to get somebody to bail us out. We were not, I was told, allowed to dial directory assistance. Nor to call abroad – so sending an SOS to *The Times* was out.

I could only seem to remember two LA telephone numbers: a less than fully employed English actor and John Micklethwait, who worked for *The Economist* in LA. Needing someone with quick access to $500 at 11.30p.m., I chose the latter.

I got his answer machine.

'This is John Micklethwait, I'm away in Washington until next week, please leave a message after the tone . . .'

I was not permitted to leave a message.

'Right, that's it,' said a muscular female police officer with a deep tan. 'You've had your call – come this way.'

Handing me a frayed grey blanket, she led me to a small cell. It had a steel lavatory, like on an aircraft, and a single steel bunk. The cell was completely bare – except for a cutting of a recent naked Playmate of the Month lying invitingly on the satin sheets of a king-sized double bed, Sellotaped to the wall by the bunk.

I was woken at around 6a.m. with a plastic mug of scalding coffee that had a soggy jam roll resting on the top. About an hour later, we were handcuffed in pairs and driven to court. Taking our shoes off again (LA prisons believe that not wearing shoes will seriously hinder any escape-attempt), I noticed that the baseball boot soles of a scrawny Mexican next to me had been cut out from an old Budweiser cardboard box and stapled to the canvas tops. Led in a clanking crocodile into the bowels of the courthouse, we were then herded into an over-crowded holding pen with an open lavatory at the back, used as a swimming pool by several dozen cockroaches. The thirty or so people already squeezed into the cage included a number of suspected rapists, murderers, armed robbers and at least half a dozen drug dealers. The pen 'regulars' were easy to identify. They had thick wadges of police station lavatory paper stuffed into their back pockets. I sat quietly in a corner with Alan Zenger and the male model.

We were in that filthy cage for most of the day. Because I was wearing a suit and tie, several of the inmates concluded that I must be an attorney.

A fat Mexican – a small-time drug pusher – with a shaven head kept hovering around me. He wanted advice on his case.

'I know you're an attorney – so please help me,' he kept saying. 'What am I gonna do? What should I do? What should I say in court? Please help me.'

To shut him up I told him to plead guilty. I gave the same advice to two other inmates.

A fight nearly broke out between two blacks over the ownership of an orange. At around 11a.m. we were each given a brown paper bag – or were meant to be – containing a rubbery sandwich and an orange. There were not enough bags to go round. The matter was settled when the older of the two men raised up his grimy white T-shirt to exhibit a ten-inch knife scar across his belly, branded on the skin like a railway track.

'Want one of these brother?' he boomed.

I talked to the man for a while. He was charged with running a brothel from the top floor of a local motel. In the seven hours in which we were kept under the courthouse, the only other disturbance came when a twenty-stone female inmate waddled past and suddenly flashed her football-sized breasts for our benefit.

Later that afternoon, nearly a day after being arrested by Disney, and still without having been allowed to make a phone call, I appeared in court and pleaded 'not-guilty' to the charge of trespassing. A jury trial date was set for the end of April. The charge carried a maximum sentence of six months in jail.

When I eventually got out of jail and got myself legal counsel from a well known Los Angeles criminal attorney, I was immediately warned of the dangers of facing a trial in Disney's personal fiefdom of Orange County. 'It's difficult for me to explain,' he told me. 'But facing a jury in Orange County, *against* Disney. That would be a mistake.'

'But I'm innocent,' I protested. 'I had a ticket. The ticket says nothing about having to leave Disneyland by a certain time – and it was only five minutes after the last ride. It's ridiculous. No jury could possibly convict me.'

'Believe me,' he said. 'Things are different in Orange County.'

I soon understood what he meant. Simply for being in Disneyland shortly after the last ride, photographer Alan Zenger – who had also pleaded 'not-guilty' – ended up paying out $10,000 in fines and costs after being found guilty of trespassing by a jury in Orange County. After a three-day trial, Zenger was fined $3,000 and given the choice of either a fortnight in jail or 180 hours of community service. He took the latter, bizarrely ending up patrolling the streets of LA with the National Guard during the riots.

When my attorney succeeded in getting the charges against me reduced to 'disturbing the peace', I pleaded 'no contest'. I also learnt an important introductory lesson about Californian lawyers.

The court fine was $50. My attorney's bill $2,500.

* * *

Disney is no stranger to litigation. But despite having hundreds of smart and expensive in-house corporate lawyers, Disney's bullying tactics have landed it with an embarrassing number of 'settlements' in recent years. In 1989, for example, Disney World employees – the company which created *Bambi* and *One Hundred and One Dalmations* – were accused of lying in wait at dusk for vultures strolling onto the theme park's Discovery Island, trapping them and clubbing the feathered creatures to death. Faced with sixteen counts of animal cruelty, Disney settled with a $95,000 donation to local animal groups. The following year 'squeaky clean' Disney was fined $500,000 by the Environmental Protection Agency for sewage violations and for failure to properly store toxic waste on their property.

Part of the reason, of course, for the opprobrium that has been heaped on Disney over the years stems from the corporation's enviably high level of success. Much of this is due to the energy and drive of Disney chairman Michael Eisner, whose success in restoring the magic to Disney's stock value in the eighties enabled him to cash in $197 million worth of personal share options shortly before President Clinton moved into the White House. Within four years of Eisner taking over, profits had quintupled to $444.7 million and Disney stock had rocketed from $2 billion to $10 billion. Bringing in Jeffrey Katzenberg to head Walt Disney studios, Disney's trademark stinginess (refusing to pay large sums to top stars – casting down-on-their-luck actors at a bargain price instead) and preference for making adult comedies over action pictures combined to produce a consistent string of box-office hits, ranging from *Down and Out in Beverly Hills* (which Eisner greenlighted on his first day at Disney in 1984) and *Pretty Woman* in the mid-eighties, to *Aladdin* (which grossed over $200 million).

Eisner used to boast that the nineties would be the Disney Decade. But despite buying Miramax for $60 million and clinching a studio deal with Merchant-Ivory ('like a billionaire buying an art-collection' one top studio executive sniffed to me) and bringing in Joe Roth, former head of Fox, to iron out Katzenberg's seemingly deficient personal skills at dealing with 'Talent' (as movie stars are reassuringly known in LA), Disney remains widely despised in Hollywood; a mountain of ill-will that Eisner seems resigned to accepting as the price of success. 'They hate us, I guess,' Eisner told *Vanity Fair* in 1991, 'and I don't know whether it's me, maybe Jeffrey, maybe the combination. It may be just a lot of history.'

One of the examples of their less than charming image was the well publicised case of how the studio prohibited a Florida nursery school from painting images of Mickey and Minnie Mouse, Donald Duck and Goofy on its walls without permission. After Jim Henson, the creator of the Muppets, died whilst putting together a deal with Disney, Henson's family were so outraged by the way that they were treated by Disney that they not only walked away from the deal, taking the Muppets with them, but sued the corporation, accusing them of 'sheer corporate arrogance' and 'corporate greed'. Disney, again, settled out of court.

But whilst an accusation of 'corporate greed' could almost be viewed as a backhanded compliment in the eighties, it is unlikely to win Disney many friends in the nineties.

The news that the opening day of Euro-Disney – or 'Eurodismal' – only lured 50,000 visitors, when they had been expecting 500,000, was greeted with unrestrained glee around Tinseltown. Attendance is still way down. When it was announced that the $2.2 billion resort was expected to lose $330 million in 1993, you could practically hear the champagne corks popping on Melrose Avenue and in Culver City.

But Disney's main problem appears to me to lie not so much with the stinginess of Mickey's sexless soul but in the sheer banality of its product. Is it an accident that Disney films – despite the corporation hiring veteran Washington lobbyist Happy Goday for $35,000 to advise on how to woo Academy members – can never seem to win any serious Oscars? This is because they are invariably so prissy and dreary. Many of Hollywood's most talented actors, directors and – in particular – writers, simply won't work for Disney. And they won't work for Disney simply because it is no *fun*.

As Joe Eszterhas, the highest paid writer in Hollywood history and widely regarded as the most successful screenwriter in the business, told me frankly: 'I'd never want to work with Disney because they are so hands-on. They sent me a script recently which they wanted me to rewrite. Along with the script comes this letter – which is, like, seven pages – about how *exactly* they want the re-write done. So I wrote Jeff a note saying, write the fucking thing yourself. You don't need anybody to do it.'

* * *

Probably the most extreme example of Disney's corporate greed was over a doggy cartoon. When, in 1987, Disney released the classic 1955 animated musical, *Lady and the Tramp*, it quickly became the bestselling videocassette ever, grossing Disney over $150 million dollars and toppling *Top Gun* as the No. 1 home video tape of the year. Yet despite the famous jazz singer Peggy Lee having written half a dozen songs for the movie, co-composed the score and given her voice to four of the characters, Disney refused to credit Lee with her work by insisting that she was not entitled to any cut of the millions of dollars of profits from the videocassette sales.

But *Lady and the Tramp* turned out to be a $3 million video nasty for Disney. The septuagenarian Peggy Lee singlehandedly fought Disney in court for four years for a share of the profits, arguing that her contract – drawn up before home videos existed – did not give them the right to sell *Lady and the Tramp* videos without her permission. After being awarded $3.8 million by Los Angeles Superior Court in 1988, with Disney found guilty of breach of contract, in addition to using the singer's name and photograph in advertisements without permission, the studio appealed. In 1992, the Californian Court of Appeals upheld the 1988 ruling against Disney in a precedent-setting case watched closely by studio executives, who now face a flurry of lawsuits from embittered actors and singers whose pre-1980s contracts did not specify the right to sell videos.

I was in the Californian Court of Appeals courtroom, in downtown LA, for the Miss Peggy Lee *v.* The Disney Co. hearing in September 1992. Seventy-one-year-old Lee – Frank Sinatra called her 'The Queen' – who recorded 631 songs, made 59 solo albums and composed more than 2,000 lyrics, sat hidden under a large-rimmed black hat in her wheelchair in the air-conditioned courtroom. In frail health after nine major heart operations, suffering from diabetes, and having recently been held up at gun-point, the scene could have come from Walt Disney's cartoons – the helpless underdog taking on the merciless and greedy corporate beast.

Facing her wheelchair, on the other side of the crowded and dimly lit courtroom, was Disney's team of lawyers, each dressed identically in white shirts, grey suits and hair clipped above the collar. Despite the fact that it was clearly stipulated in Miss Lee's 1952 contract (paragraph 12b) that the agreement between Disney and Lee specifically excluded the grant of rights for 'phonograph records and/or transcriptions for sale to the public', Disney's lawyers attempted to prove that – contrary to Judge William Huss's 1988 ruling – 'transcriptions for sale to the public' did *not* include videocassettes. The appellate judge was not impressed. Looking pained, the Disnoid lawyers hurriedly left in a convoy of black cars.

* * *

On a warm April evening six months after the end of her lawsuit, I was invited up to Peggy Lee's imposing château, high up in the winding hills of Bel-Air, overlooking LA and the Pacific ocean. After writing her bestselling autobiography, the seventy-two year old singer was now writing a book on Disney. Having heard – through a mutual friend in London – about my jailing by Disneyland, we agreed to trade interviews.

An immaculately uniformed young Spanish maid ushered me through the front door, into an entrance hall with a large grand piano and a chandelier that would not have looked out of place in Versailles. I was led into a huge drawing room, with French windows that opened on to a neglected swimming pool, that overlooked the city. The high-ceilinged room, with a freshly hoovered peach carpet, looked clinically clean. I was pretty sure not much ever happened in there. The dining room might as well have been a museum. One book prominently exhibited on the coffee-table surprised me. Lying on the glass like a chunk of white marble was a huge hard-back volume entitled *The Art of Walt Disney*.

I was ushered into Miss Peggy Lee's ground-floor

bedroom. Like the drawing room, it was decorated exclusively in glowing peach. Not just peach carpet and wallpaper but peach shutters, several dozen peach Peggy Lee roses (the American Rose Society named a rose after her), peach gilt chairs and framed paintings of peach cats and more peach roses on the walls. Miss Lee, with a white towel wrapped around her head like a turban, sat plumped up like a Technicolored Miss Havisham in a luxury king-size bed, swathed in peach satin sheets and pillows. Across the room was a huge TV set. Beside her was a pair of opera-glasses and what looked like a large scuba diver's tank, from which through a rubber tube drifted thick clouds of freeze-dried oxygen that swirled above the bed like stage-smoke. Despite the fact that I was sitting right next to her bed, the clouds were so thick at certain points that I could only catch glimpses of the famous singer. Beside Miss Lee, draped in a silk peach nightgown, was a wicker pet-transport basket. Tchaikovsky played in the background.

'This is Baby,' said Peggy Lee.

She pointed inside the pet-basket. Curled inside was a sleeping silver chinchilla cat.

'I think it's asleep,' I said. 'Better not disturb it.'

'I've had her for five years. She's an adorable and sweet little friend. I love her. All she eats is a special science-diet and water. She likes ice cubes in it. She likes to play with the cubes with her paws.'

'Really?'

'She knows I'm not feeling too well these days, so she stays on the bed like a little nurse. She's a little serious today.'

I asked how she was getting on with her research for the book. Her bed was heaped with files on Disney meticulously put together by her full-time personal archivist. In the office along the corridor, which is manned by a research staff of three, are three trunks containing over 150 files relating to Disney.

'One thing that is very important to me,' she began, 'is that people know that what happened to me was not to do with

Walt Disney himself. He would have been livid, I think. He would have been embarrassed. What happened to me is the result of a company becoming a big corporate giant. People are afraid to try to defend themselves.'

'Why?'

'They don't have the money. Fighting Disney costs a lot of money. They drag the case on and on. Their technique is to try and break you. To break your confidence. To try to bankrupt you. I had no idea the case would cost me so much money. I won. But it was very hard on my health. You know what one of Disney's lawyers told my lawyer once?'

'What?'

'He said that they knew about my fragile health. And that they were going to drag the case on and on, because if they dragged the case long enough, I might not make it.'

'That wasn't very nice of them.'

'I just couldn't believe what was happening in terms of justice,' she added. 'I had always heard that saying, you can have as much justice as you can afford. But I never believed it until I saw those Disney lawyers in action. They were very good lawyers. They were so good I even started to admire them.'

'What was their attitude towards you?'

'It was as if I totally didn't even exist. "Who are you little girl? – go away!" And I thought it was terribly wrong because Disney would have nothing if it wasn't for writers and artists. It was the principle of it. I suffered four years of terrible stress. The stress nearly did kill me.'

As soon as she started her action against Disney, Miss Lee found herself up against the Disney machine. She didn't receive as much support from the Hollywood community as she might have liked. Lawyers, to begin with, were reluctant to take on the case. Her publicist dropped out. 'People are afraid of crossing Disney. It's like a giant spider web – it goes everywhere.'

'A bit sinister, you mean?'

'Sinister. That's the right word. In the fifties, Disney was full of some wonderful people. There was an air of fun about the place. It was really fun.'

She began to stroke Baby again. Baby purred.

Looking more closely, I noticed that, beside the cat what I had taken for a pair of opera-glasses were, in fact, a pair of high powered 8 × 30 zoom racing binoculars.

'What are they for?' I asked, pointing to the lenses.

'Oh,' said Lee, picking them up and looking at me down the sights, 'I use these binoculars to watch TV. Here, look . . .'

She pressed the remote control. The evening news flashed onto the screen – thirty yards across the room.

I focused on the newscaster.

She flicked the channels.

'See anything?' she said.

'It's quite good vision,' I said, zooming up on the newscaster.

It was time to leave.

8

The Power and the Glitz

'WATCHING IT ON TELEVISION,' SAID Glenda Jackson of the 1979 Oscar ceremony. 'I felt disgusted, as though I was watching a public hanging. No one should have a chance to see so much desire, so much need for a prize and so much pain when not given it.'

The Oscars are the best example of how the world media now takes Hollywood absurdly, and excessively, seriously. They clearly illustrate why the popular idea that the movies represent the newest, most avant-garde and democratic of art forms, is a risible and disingenuous myth.

There are now over fifty annual ways of landing an award in entertainment, according to the *Hollywood Reporter Blu-Book* directory. That estimate is, in fact, very conservative – and does not include, for example, the legion of industry guild awards and the glut of annual 'Achievement' awards (invariably, in reality, for under-achievement). The real number is over one hundred. To talk of Hollywood's Oscar 'Season' is now a misnomer, since the season is now endless – with the award shows coagulating into each other like the Day-Glo globules in those sixties larva lamps.

The pain of losing has become especially acute in recent years when studio executives think of the millions of dollars they have spent on their Academy campaigns. Despite having filed for bankruptcy, Orion spent $325,000 promoting *The Silence of the Lambs* in 1992.

William Goldman is often cranked up and quoted for his

Hollywood maxim that 'Nobody Knows Anything'. With regard to the Oscars, at least, this is probably the most disingenuous bilge to come out of Tinseltown since John Wayne, in his overblown and manic 1960 campaign to win Best Picture for *The Alamo* (which he had directed and used $3 million of his own money to complete) hung up a banner across Hollywood Boulevard quoting his pal John Ford: 'This Is The Most Important Motion Picture Ever Made. It is Timeless. It Will Run Forever.'

Far from knowing nothing, the bulk of winners on Oscar night hold few surprises for the majority of Hollywood's well-placed industry insiders. This is not because the awards are rigged, or because of any Oscargate security violations, but simply because by the time the 5,000 voting Academy members send in their final ballot papers a reliable consensus of opinion has built up in town about who will win. This consensus is based on an established and respected Oscar campaign form-guide whose unwritten rules – built up over sixty-five years – are rarely radically swerved away from. The Academy of Motion Picture Arts and Sciences is, essentially, a trade union, with the Oscars, as is often dryly observed, being Tinseltown's annual general meeting. In Hollywood, where insecurity is a way of life, the herd instinct is strong.

Nobody, of course, just wins an Academy Award. You have to 'position' (in American PR-speak) for one. With expenditure on Academy Award toadying estimated at around $8 million in 1993 and specific campaigns that have cost around $500,000 or lasted for over a year (*Howards End* for example), speculation has been raised over the question of whether you can buy an Oscar. And if so, how much?

The answer, however, is no. What you may be able to do, however, is lunch your way towards one. Despite the popular idea of the Oscars as Hollywood's Derby Day, reality is that they are far from being any short-distance sweepstake; the Oscars are more like the Grand National.

Months before the Golden Globe awards, the first important hurdle on the Oscar campaign trail – especially for independent films – is to get your film picked up by an influential critic on the film festival circuit. This is exactly what happened to *Chariots of Fire* in 1981 after receiving a thumbs up from Chicago film critic Roger Ebert at Cannes. *The Crying Game* – originally, like *Chariots*, turned down by all the major studios – got its first Oscar campaign boost with a rave review from *Variety* during the Telluride (Colorado) Film Festival in September 1992. Unable to afford any expensive ads at the time, producer Steve Woolley (*Mona Lisa, Scandal*) stood up at the end of festival (the film also showed in Venice, Toronto and New York) screenings and asked people not to give away the ending.

Similarly, former BBC producer Jonathan Darby's short film, *Contact*, based on a true story about an Iraqi and an American soldier meeting in the Gulf War, was Academy nominated in 1993 after being acclaimed at the trendy Sundance Film Festival in January. It was made in six days. Getting a salutary review from a critic like Vincent Canby of the *New York Times* can often be more tactically important than being awarded a major prize. Winning the Palm D'Or at Cannes – such as *The Mission* did in 1986 – is invariably the kiss of death for Oscar gold. Too 'arty' for most Academy members. The crucial importance of being well received by the film critics was shown in 1993 when the Oscar playbill was clearly cast by the critics awards.

From about January onwards, the mail-boxes of Academy members are deluged with videocassettes, CDs, books and screening invitations for films, in conjunction with a glut of 'For your consideration' $7,500 double-page glossy colour ads in the trades that have little to do with winning an Oscar and everything to do with studio self-aggrandisement and tickling stars for future projects. As the closing date for ballot-papers approaches, *Variety* and the *Hollywood Reporter* swell up to the size of mail-order catalogues by the day, with telephone numbers for Academy members to call 'if you have not received your Academy screening cassette'. This is because no studio or PR firm in Hollywood has a complete directory of Academy members.

Since the official Academy list is strictly confidential (and is rumoured to sell on the black-market for around $5,000) the studios have absolutely no way of checking up on who the real members are. Most of the 'lists' circulating around town contain hundreds of bogus names. When I responded, for example, to a full-page Disney ad in *Variety* stating: 'Her Majesty, the Red Queen, cordially requests all Royal Academy Members to consider Adventures in Wonderland' an answerphone told me to leave my address and a tape would be mailed 'promptly'.

Sending out around 5,000 videos costs a studio around $50,000 (i.e. nothing). *The Crying Game*'s Academy campaign got off to a blundering start in 1993 when it was discovered that the video they had sent out to members had been made from a dud mastertape. For *Howards End*, Sony Pictures Classics sent out a boxed video cassette specially designed for Academy members. With most of their houses now resembling a Blockbuster video store, a move is underway to ban video campaigning on the grounds that it reduces the Oscars to the level of trial by telly.

If nominated, campaigns are taken over and beefed up – via large and expensive print and TV ads – by the studio marketing executives. If an actor or actress does not already have a personal press agent, one will be provided as a guide through the Oscar jungle.

Oscar campaigning traditionally ends with the trendy Independent Spirit Awards held on the Saturday before the Oscars. It's meant to be a relaxed afternoon as the twenty-two sealed Oscar winner's envelopes are already secured in a downtown LA bank-vault. Although the awards are for low-budget independent productions – i.e. often boring and pretentious 'arthouse' films – most of the major studios, many of the industry's top film-makers, like Oliver Stone, and agencies like William Morris, ICM or Mike Ovitz's CAA, show up because in nineties LA it is good form to be seen associating with fresh and upcoming 'Talent', and, more importantly, films that don't cost $45 million.

The Oscar trail is really about Hollywood's need to be loved. You receive no money, of course, for winning one of the thirteen-and-a-half-inch Oscar statuettes. Despite the sums lavished on the campaigns, and the extra millions that can be gained from expanded distribution after an Oscar nomination or win, Oscar toadying really has more to do with self-love than financial gain. Studios, producers, directors, writers, agents, make-up artists, costumers, and above all, the 'Talent' get to see their names blown up in self-promotional large type (Oscar vanity ads are often written into a star's film contract) around town. As Gerry Rich, senior vice-president of marketing at Miramax told me: 'The ads are simply to remind people. They are a prestige thing – an excuse to showcase your product and stroke the right egos.'

Insecurity, of course, is endemic in Hollywood. Nowhere can this be seen more clearly than on the giant billboards (usually 14 by 48 feet) that are splashed up along Sunset Boulevard in the run up to the Oscars. Often wishing 'to congratulate' films that were hurriedly taken off general release months before, a prime spot on the Sunset Strip – such as opposite Tower Records – can cost a studio up to $25,000 a month, whilst in another part of LA it would only cost $5,000. As the Golden Globe winners and Oscar nominations are announced the hoardings are plastered in go-faster 'snipes' (outdoor-advertising speak) trumpeting their tally of awards.

* * *

In 1993, the Golden Globe Awards celebrated their fiftieth anniversary. As the Tinseltown equivalent of the Two Thousand Guineas, the winners usually become short-odds favourites to become Oscar nominated. The Globes are handed out by the Hollywood Foreign Press Association, a gaggle of – mostly – star-gawping and aging pen-pushers who were once neatly summed up to me by a studio boss as 'one hundred stringers living off hors-d'oeuvres'.

It is no secret that the Hollywood Foreign Press Association has long been viewed by the film industry as something of an antiquated joke, a lazy throng of spongers and sycophants with incomprehensible Nordic or Far-Eastern names who write for publications that nobody in LA has ever heard of or cares about. If it wasn't for the fact that winning, or at least being nominated for, a Golden Globe has – bewilderingly – become a vital pillar to any would-be successful Oscar campaign, somebody would have had this extraordinary organisation closed down years ago.

The association has just eighty-seven members – 'unlike with the Academy, membership is strictly scrutinised,' one member told me. 'To remain a member you have to produce at least four clippings a year.' The HFPA has become something of an enigma in Tinseltown with its glamorous image on Golden Globe night, when the show is beamed live to over two million US homes, a marked contrast to its day-to-day reality. Its headquarters are the fourth floor of what resembles a Belgrade social welfare office on the fringes of Beverly Hills. Lino floors. Worn carpets. Soviet-style lifts.

'There used to be a joke that the HFPA only held press conferences on a Saturday morning, because the rest of the week the members were working in shoeshops, or whatever, around town,' said Douglas Thompson, a veteran member of the HFPA who has been writing on Hollywood for the *Daily Express* for years (he lives in the Esher-like suburb of Tarzana) in addition to writing celebrity biographies on the likes of Madonna, Clint Eastwood and Michelle Pfieffer. 'But that has changed,' he added hastily. 'It's got a lot more professional, more efficient. There are some highly respected journalists who are members these days.'

Some highly respected journalists. As for the remainder, Thompson admits there is a 'percentage' who, if not waiters or wine stewards, as is wearily joked each January, certainly supplement their income through a seemingly odd array of part-time jobs. Others do seem to be rather old. Several of the mug-shots of the HFPA's executive officers at the front of the 1992 Golden Globe programme, for example, look as if they were taken with a Brownie box-camera. 'Perhaps voting rights should be curtailed for those over sixty-five,' he added, only half joking. 'Around twelve to fifteen members probably can't make much sense of their computer these days.'

Twelve to fifteen members? That's nearly 20 per cent of the entire Hollywood Foreign Press Association.

With just eighty-seven members, there has been widespread speculation in recent years that, as *Variety* suggested a week before the 1993 awards, 'the Golden Globes are not so much earned as negotiated'. This accusation has hung like an albatross around the neck of the HFPA ever since the infamous 1982 Pia Zadora 'incident'. The singer was curiously voted the 'New Star of the Year in a Motion Picture', after a delegation of HFPA was flown over to a luxury hotel in Las Vegas and expensively 'entertained' by her multi-millionaire husband.

Despite the efforts of various recent HFPA presidents, such as Judy Solomon, who writes for publications in Israel, and Mirjana Van Blaricom, a Yugoslavian journalist for over twenty years, to clean up the HFPA's jokey image, they still seem to have a long way to go. Just when the embarrassing scars of the Pia Zadora scandal appeared to have healed, the association's credibility was seriously tarnished by an excoriating cover article in *International Variety*, followed a week later by a satirical flaying in the *New York Times* by the widely respected Bernie Weinraub – 'All is Glittery And a Bit Odd at Golden Globes'.

A bit odd is, in fact, something of an understatement. One of the HFPA's more peculiar rulings is that full-time foreign correspondents, West Coast bureau chiefs and major international TV and radio networks who are not affiliated to the HFPA are strictly prohibited from covering the Golden Globe awards. 'It's a strict policy,' I was informed by an apologetic Marianne Ruuth, the HFPA's press officer, 'only our own members and domestic press can attend. It sounds a little crazy, I know. But we have to say no even to the BBC. Sorry, it's just a rule.'

Few in Tinseltown have any real idea of quite what a motley collection the eighty-seven members really are. Significantly, their 1992–93 official directory lists only the countries that members write for (some don't write much at all, of which more later), not the names of any actual publications. 'Many members write for so many publications,' said president Mirjana Van Blaricom. 'It is often better that way. If I have a good story I can always get it published. I choose my editors. If you have a job working for a newspaper you can't do that.'

What is so bizarre about the HFPA is that despite it proudly decorating an entire page of its annual Golden Globe souvenir programme with forty-one flags from around the world, making it resemble a Boy Scout's almanac, few of the major international newspapers, magazines, or TV and radio networks with retained correspondents in LA are accredited with the HFPA. Take Britain as an example. According to the *Blu-Book*, under the heading 'Foreign Press Representatives', there are no less than *twenty-one* journalists who claim to work for British publications. Yet, absurdly, not *one* actual LA correspondent – with the exception of the *Daily Express*'s Douglas Thompson, who only writes on showbusiness – for a British national daily or Sunday newspaper is associated in any way, or would probably want to be, with the HFPA. Neither *The Times, The Sunday Times, Daily Telegraph, The Independent, Guardian* or *Daily Mail* are officially connected in any way. 'After two and a half years in Hollywood, I've never met anybody who is a member,' admits John Micklethwait of *The Economist*. 'I don't know who any of them are. Frankly, my understanding is they are a bunch of jokers. They are semi-ludicrous.'

Despite the jokes, however, and some evidence the organisation has improved its reputation, the annual Golden Globe awards at the Beverly Hilton in late January remain perhaps the most enjoyable, if most ridiculous, of Hollywood's award ceremonies to attend. The cream of Hollywood usually turn out in force.

Since *The Times* was not permitted to cover the 1992 Golden Globe awards in any official capacity – another condition of becoming a member of the HFPA is that you have to have lived in LA for two years, absurd when most foreign correspondents' postings are for around three years, I was, if I wanted to report on the Globes, left with no option other than to try and slip into the gala ceremony at the Beverly Hilton unnoticed.

With security organised by the HFPA it was – not unsurprisingly perhaps – absurdly easy to get in. I simply yanked open a side-door which led into some sort of back-stage dressing room and closed the door behind me. I was surrounded by rails of silk ball-gowns and sequin cocktail dresses hanging up in their dry-cleaners' wrapping, along with a medley of odd blouses, corsets, bras and suspenders. Not quite knowing what to do, I pulled the red curtain closed. Glancing around me again, I realised that I had, in fact, walked into somebody's – no, not just somebody, some female star's – private dressing room.

Standing next to me was an ironing board with an upright iron from which steam was hissing. Looking down at my crumpled dress shirt – my office had no iron – I realised that my black tie looked a disgrace. Seizing my opportunity, I stripped off down to the waist and swiftly ironed the front of my shirt – faster than any Chinese laundryman showing off on the *Generation Game*. Pulling the curtain open, I stepped confidently out and briskly made my way past a presenter practising on the tele-prompter, and some glaringly hot lights, through a stage door, and into the Beverly Hilton's noisy and capacity-filled International Ballroom.

It was like any other lavish gala dinner, with each round table's floral arrangement resembling something you might buy at Kew Gardens gift shop. The difference, however, was that wherever you walked it was almost impossible to avoid encountering some familiar celebrity actor, with people thrusting out their hand, or slapping each other on the back – 'Hey! Tom, remember me, met at the *Thunder* wrap party, my brother Mike, he was assistant grip' – with every yard they shuffled forward, as if they were doing a lap of honour after an 800-metres Olympic relay race.

All Hollywood was on parade in the Beverly Hilton that night. At the party afterwards it was even more ridiculous. It was like walking into the pages of a pop-up *People* magazine. Crammed into a room no larger than a large hotel suite were Jeremy Irons, Kevin Costner, Tom Cruise, Jodie Foster, Robin Williams, Michael Caine, Geena Davis, Bette Midler, Jamie Lee Curtis, Anthony Hopkins, Nick Nolte and so on. Since I had no press badge I was able to wander around freely, chatting to whomever I liked.

In 1993 I was there again. Necks swivelled when Sharon Stone, nominated for Best Actress for *Basic Instinct*, showed up at the party – clutching the hand of her twenty-three-year-old toy-boy Christopher Peters, the music executive son of hairdresser turned mogul Jon Peters. He had a greasy pony-tail and his dark eyes squirmed with the wounded concern of somebody who already knew his days of favour were numbered. Two months later Sharon Stone was engaged to *Sliver* producer Bill MacDonald.

My own effort to catch the attention of Sharon Stone was a miserable failure. Walking up the crowded steps out of the Beverly Hilton's International Ballroom after the ceremony, I saw that Sharon Stone was right in front of me. Glancing at her neck, I noticed that her triple pearl choker looked as if it was just hanging on by a thread. It was just about to fall off, with the pearls cascading all over the floor.

I tapped her on the shoulder.

'Excuse me,' I said, 'but I think your necklace is about to fall off.'

Swinging round sharply, she looked at me for a brief moment. We had met – briefly – once before. She didn't seem to recognise me. Luckily. Her eyes were icy green. Her entourage glared at me.

'No, it isn't,' she replied tartly, 'it's meant to look like that.'

And hurried up the stairs.

The questions that HFPA members ask are usually not – it has to be said – of the Mike Wallace or Brian Walden school of interviewing. One reason, of course, for the somewhat resentful and superior-than-thou tone of the domestic press articles mocking the HFPA is that, bizarrely, the HFPA – representing such countries as Pakistan and Malaysia – often get considerably better access to movie stars and directors than the most prominent national American newspapers and magazines.

During November and December – i.e. in the run-up to nominations for the Golden Globes – HFPA members find themselves deluged with up to three invitations *a day* from major 'A' list stars, desperate to get nominated, who suddenly want to talk – often not talk to, but also allow this elderly bunch of hacks to roam around their private houses all morning. ('I can't tell you which stars invite us into their homes,' one member told me, 'I would get into trouble.')

The scale of this joke becomes embarrasingly apparent if you obtain a transcript of an HFPA 'conference'.

An example. To maximise *Unforgiven*'s chances of winning a Golden Globe, Clint Eastwood and Gene Hackman spent an hour or so with the HFPA.

A question.

'Mr Eastwood, you are an environmentalist, and, in fact, always try to live close to nature. How do you see the future now of the United States and the world with the war and Mr Clinton heading the country? Do you think there is going to be more hope?'

'I'd hope so,' replied Mr Eastwood.

Unsurprisingly, perhaps, none of the heads of international publicity at the major studios I called up would talk to me on the record about the HFPA. The reply of Juliana Olinka at Warner Bros was typical: 'I have absolutely no comment to make about the Hollywood Foreign Press Association.'

It is a quaint tradition after HFPA conferences for members to queue up in an orderly line – as if at a celebrity book signing

– and take it in turns to shake hands and be photographed (two or three poses) with their 'favourite stars'. The slides or snaps are then mailed to the HFPA members, along with the Q and A transcript. Some members simply file the snaps away, others frame them and stand them proudly on their chimneypieces, hang them in their lavatories, send them to their editors, their mothers, and the more cunning, sell them – for excellent money – around the world.

The stars are invariably happy to oblige the HFPA members with these unusual fringe perks. Not to do so, indeed, could have regrettable consequences in their frenzied and often desperate quest for Globe gold. As one senior HFPA member confided to *Variety*, nominations and final awards often go to stars who are 'cooperative'. 'When they don't show up at the press conferences, we don't give them the goodies, you know?'

That the Oscars, watched by a billion people around the world, should be influenced to such a serious extent by this group of Dad's Army star-gawpers is incomprehensible. It makes a mockery of the Oscars. The Best Picture Oscar has been augured by the winner of the Best Picture Golden Globe in eleven of the last thirteen years – giving a clear idea of why the studios and stars are happy to go along with the HFPA's fun and games.

In 1993 there was some quiet sniggering around Hollywood following the Globes, however, after it was revealed that a delegation of HFPA members had been specially flown over by Universal to New York for a *Scent of a Woman* junket and interview session with Al Pacino and put up at a de luxe hotel, with dinner thrown in. Much to the surprise of the industry, *Scent of a Woman* won the Golden Globe award for Best Picture.

'We flew by airplane,' Algirdas Gustaitis, a widely respected Lithuanian writer who has been an HFPA member for over twenty-five years, told me. 'Then we took bus to hotel. At hotel we have nice rooms, like usually we have any place we go – because Hollywood Foreign Press doesn't go to cheap hotels, or cheap places.'

Mr Gustaitis is, in many ways, a not untypical HFPA member. I spent a morning with him at his pleasant West Hollywood house, just off Beverly Boulevard and Fairfax. He is a tall, charming old man, an old fashioned gentleman of the press. His eyes are quick and kind-looking. With his neatly combed grey hair and David Frost glasses, he looked more like an Eastern European classics professor than your conventional Tinseltown hack. Looking around his house, indeed, there were few immediate signs of Hollywood.

The walls, for example, were covered with rare and finely framed medieval and eighteenth-century maps of Lithuania. His study, far from resembling a video store, as with many Academy members, had a donnish feel to it – with the walls bulging with hard-spined rows of encyclopaedias and a sprawling library of books on Lithuanian history – along with the 1958 International Motion Picture Directory.

Many, it turned out, had been written by Mr Gustaitis himself. His books – he has written so many that he can't actually remember the exact number – include a definitive work on the cartography of Dniepras River, a classic reference work for Lithuanian cartologists called *The Real Lithuania*, dozens of other books on medieval maps and several childrens' books about a dachschund and a little boy on a farm.

'I keep all this a bit quiet,' he told me sheepishly, 'I don't know what the other Hollywood Foreign Press members might think.' He has his hundreds of HFPA photos – posing rather awkwardly beside the likes of Tom Cruise – hidden well out of sight in a dusty filing cabinet.

Although he frankly admits he is more of a qualified expert on medieval cartography than nineties Hollywood, he jumps to the defence of the Hollywood Foreign Press Association by arguing that the eclectic make-up of the HFPA is representative of world opinion, and is hence a useful divining rod for the Oscars. 'There are many special interests at stake when the Academy votes,' he told me. 'We are more like the public.'

He dismisses any notion that the *Scent of a Woman* trip had any influence on the votes of HFPA members as 'pure nonsense'. HFPA members simply liked the film.

He openly admits that he only goes on trips if they are free. He turned down the HFPA annual invitation to the Cannes Film Festival partly because he thought it would be prohibitively expensive.

'They ask everybody if they would like to go,' he said. 'But I'm not going to Cannes. I have no intention of going because in part we have to pay ourselves. It would be nice to go to France but I don't like to go there because first, I don't speak French, and second we must buy food ourselves. I don't know how much this will cost.'

'Couldn't you claim on expenses?' I asked.

'No,' he said with a sigh. 'Not with my publications.'

'That doesn't sound very fair.'

'Also we have to sleep two persons in one bed,' he added. 'You know, maybe somebody will snore.'

'You have to sleep in the same bed as a stranger?' I asked.

'Two persons in one room. We used to get a single room. No longer. Economy, they say. So you get somebody who snores – or maybe somebody trying to get some lovely girls into the room. And I don't like that. I like to relax. Maybe I like to write a little bit, or make my notes. So I'm not going. I don't like to waste my time. That would be wasting my time. Besides, I have things to do at home.'

HPFA president Marjana Van Blaricom insisted to me that studios regularly fly both domestic and foreign journalists to junkets, and put them up in de luxe hotels, as a matter of course. This may be true, but in two years of working in Hollywood I have certainly never received any such invitation. All studio-organised junkets I have been on involved sitting around a table with around a dozen other journalists for twenty minutes with an actor or actress – like, for example, Bridget Fonda, to publicise her film *Point of No Return*.

In the Fonda case there was simply no point in even playing back the twenty-minute tape-recording. The questions were fatuous. The film was unspeakably awful and

Miss Fonda seemed to have absolutely nothing to say.

It wasn't her fault – she seemed a very nice, polite, switched on young actress. But the patronising and aren't-you-lucky-to-be-here way with which the 'interview' – if that is the right word – was set up at The Four Seasons hotel, with a stop-watch ticking away for our twenty minutes of alloted time, turned the session into a ludicrous joke. Each person was rationed to a maximum of two 'friendly' questions. How any studio can seriously expect a quality newspaper or magazine to run a story on such a basis is quite baffling.

Several HFPA members declined to speak about the goings-on of the Hollywood Foreign Press Association. 'I would rather not talk about it,' said Howard Lucraft, who writes for 'UK and US publications'. 'We are under strict instructions to pass you on to our association publicist.'

My oddest conversation, however, was probably with HFPA member Lisa 'Liselotte' Trumpler.

I picked out her name at random from the *Blu-Book* directory.

After about six rings the phone was answered. All I could hear was a muffled gargling noise.

'Hello,' I said.

More muffled noises.

'Is that Lisa Trumpler?'

'Yes,' croaked a faint voice.

I introduced myself.

'There's been some speculation in the trades as to whether all HFPA members are professional full-time journalists. What's your view?' I asked.

'I'm . . . er . . . sorry,' the voice said softly. 'I can't give you an intelligent answer.'

'Why not?'

'I'm sleeping.'

'But it's 3p.m. in the afternoon.'

'I've been an active member for thirty-two years. What else do you want to know?'

'I'm sorry if I woke you up,' I said hurriedly. 'Shall I call back later?'

'No,' she said. 'I'd rather you didn't.'

Lisa Trumpler, I later discovered, is in her late seventies.

When I put a similar question to Mirjana Van Blaricom she became truculent: 'All the allegations are bullshit, okay.'

'I'm just talking about what I've read in the *New York Times* and *Variety*,' I replied.

'They are both unreliable.'

'In what way?'

'I can give you the example that everything they wrote is not factual and it's not true. They are malicious. They are not true. I don't understand the attitude of the domestic press. They have a problem – and they should take care of it.'

'What would your advice be to Bernie Weinraub?'

'He is a bad journalist. Everything he wrote are not facts. He must get paid on the side to write – or he must have a friend in one of the studios. It's simply envy.'

'Envy?'

'I don't want to talk about it. They are not worth it. They have nothing better to write about. There is a lot of nice stuff in this town which we write about.'

'Are you saying that HFPA journalists are more professional than those on the *New York Times*?'

'My journalists are professional – including me,' she said, her voice rising.

'I am the producer. I had a film in Cannes. I come from a good film school. I write for over twenty years. I'm more qualified than Weinraub or any of those people – so is any other member.'

'Of course,' I said.

* * *

The Academy Award ceremony usually takes place two months after the Golden Globes, on the last Monday in March at the Dorothy Chandler Pavilion in Downtown LA.

In 1992, I took up my position by the red-carpet alongside hundreds of TV cameras. Miles of thick cable hung down from the overhead trees like giant reels of soft liquorice. As the likes of Barbra Streisand, Warren Beatty and Jodie Foster sprang from their limousines, they were mobbed not only by the usual frenzied swarm of shutter-crazy paparazzi, squeezing down on the triggers of their motordrives like teenagers on a 7-11 store video game, but also by a legion of British celebrity-hunting tourists. Many, I discovered, had specially flown out to LA just to camp out royal wedding-style for two days so as to get a glimpse of the stars.

Standing beneath one of the thirty-foot-high gold-painted Oscar statues lowered into place the previous afternoon was thirty-three-year-old Tony Murphy, who worked in a wages office for the regional council in Glasgow. He was dressed in full Scottish football away strip and was well supplied with beer and crisps.

'You could say I am obsessed by films,' he said, swigging on a can of Carlsberg Export. 'After the Oscars, I'll be straight off to see the stars at the Spago party. It's a great atmosphere – better than most football matches.'

Further along the pavement was what I took to be a ragged collection of tramps. At least I assumed they were tramps, judging by the fact they were huddled up in dirty sleeping bags. Then I noticed a man in a natty blue anorak, sitting up reading the latest Tom Clancy novel. He was called Andrew Connolly and worked at a National Westminster Bank in Nottingham. He told me that he planned on impressing people with his Oscar night story for the next year.

'Nottingham isn't exactly the heart of the film-making world,' he said. 'I once saw Alan Rickman from a distance of ten yards, using our cash-point machine. I felt a sort of tingling feeling all over and my heart started pounding.'

The Achievement Award for the most inane TV interviewer of Oscar arrivals was easily won by KABC-TV Channel 7's Chuck Henry. In 1993, in fact, the perky, ever-grinning Chuck excelled himself.

His finest moment was when he stuck his microphone in front of Catherine Deneuve, Best Actress nominated for *Indochine*.

'I'd like to know the secret of your ageless beauty,' gushed Chuck.

The French actress raised her dark eyebrows in seeming bewilderment.

'I breathe,' she said.

And shuffled on.

At around 5.45p.m., the media were herded into various spartan press rooms above – and closed off from – the vast auditorium in which the Oscar ceremony takes place. A hundred-odd print journalists sit in a room that closely resembles a lecture room. I was ushered towards a wooden desk marked with the number 78. Paper, sharpened pencils and a bespectacled staff of Oscar researchers were provided. Cans of complimentary Coca-Cola and 7-Up floated in a large styrofoam ice-bucket.

It was not a memorable or especially enjoyable three hours. American journalists take their jobs – especially on Oscar night – manically seriously. Apart from the noisy clacking of computer keyboard buttons, the room had the desperate feel of an 11-plus examination.

* * *

The key to understanding the Oscar mentality is to understand that tempting as it may be to believe the cliché of Tinseltown as a town ruled by money, Oscar lobbying has more to do with vanity than greed. Most of its top players already have huge fortunes. The criterion for being Best Picture nominated is not box-office success (*My Left Foot* only grossed $2.65 million before it was nominated in 1990), but seriousness of purpose.

Some idea of the importance Hollywood attaches to the

medium of film can be judged by the Academy's new $6 million Center for Motion Picture Study on La Cienega in Beverly Hills. The building which houses the library was originally designed as an exact copy of a Spanish Revivalist church, with its steeple modelled after the Giralda Tower in Seville. Inside the centre has the hushed feel of a monastic library.

When the young Tom Stoppard was asked by London's theatre critics what *Rosencrantz and Guildenstern Are Dead* was 'about', after its successful opening night, he replied: 'I hope it's about to make me a lot of money.' Such candour is rare in Hollywood, where a simple desire to make money is viewed as a lowly form of ambition. As Raymond Chandler once wrote: 'Money will buy you pathetically little in Hollywood.'

The real ambitions of Hollywood are invariably more grandiose: a zealous and desperate quest for recognition, respect and legitimacy from peers. And, above all, to think they are making films that *matter* – films which help them to be taken seriously as people. Thus at the Director's Guild dinner, a fortnight before the Oscars, the normally reticent Eastwood said that his western was 'relevant' for the 1990s. 'The moral is the concern with gunplay,' said Clint, a little uneasily, 'it demythologises people who indulge in violent behaviour.' Well, um . . . maybe. The plot revolves around a bounty killer who murders a sheriff and half a dozen deputies after a slash-attack on a prostitute.

Uncharitable as it may sound, the real reason that so many 'quality' independent films have been up for Oscars in recent years is that it is simply the Academy's way of lending some much needed prestige to what otherwise – if looked at honestly – would be an embarrassingly thin list. It massages the ego of the Academy, as well as seeming to enhance its reputation, when a major studio film like *Unforgiven* is seen to beat off such arthouse opposition as *Howards End*.

The important difference between the Oscar campaigns for independent films and the big studio pictures is that whilst the independents are concerned with improving the profile of a particular film, the studios use the Academy Awards as a vehicle for corporate PR. 'The Oscars are taken far too seriously,' Oliver Stone told me, 'especially by the media. Most of the press don't know a damn thing about film-making.'

Self-congratulation has, of course, always been Hollywood's way of inuring itself from the banality of so much of its product. The self-love doesn't end, of course, with the final winner's envelope. You have to be invited to the right *après*-Oscar party; or rather, parties. Whilst Oscar nominees, Academy members and a rag-bag of LA socialites and dignatories are invited to the starchy Governor's Ball, for a number of Hollywood's elite the ball is simply a convenient place to wait for twenty minutes whilst their limos emerge from the car-park. Then it's probably on to Irving 'Swifty' Lazar's triple 'A' list party at Spago.

According to the *Hollywood Reporter*'s 1993 Academy Awards special issue, the day that your invitation comes to Swifty Lazar's Oscar party, you know you have arrived in Hollywood. That can't really be quite true, since I managed to get on Swifty's post-Oscar show list.

The moment I was nodded in through the glass doors on Oscar night 1992, past a wild cage of paparazzi, TV cameras and a crowd of several hundred shrieking fans lining the street, I entered into showbiz gossip columnist fantasy land: Madonna, Audrey Hepburn, Gene Kelly, Jane Seymour, Jacqueline Bisset, Michael Douglas, Rupert Murdoch, Lord White, Marvin Davis and so on. As Robert Osborne put it in his *Hollywood Reporter* column: 'You could say there was enough power-house weight in the room to single-handedly keep the movie business going for at least a decade.'

It was, indeed, just one large room – decorated with specially printed balloons, and filled with waiters weighed down with magnums of champagne. Other waiters carried around silver plates piled with delicacies, including slices of Wolfgang Puck's fresh Spago pizzas. The atmosphere was boisterous, friendly and raucous.

'You wanna know why it's like this,' said Mitchell Fink (*People* magazine's answer to Nigel Dempster) to me at the bar. 'The reason all these celebrities are having such a good time?'

'Why?' I said.

'Because they're not encouraged to bring their personal publicists with them,' he said. 'They don't have their flaks hovering around them, ruining their fun – that's why.'

Spotting Sharon Stone by the stairs, I went over and said hello. Short, slinky black dress, neo-Bardot ice-cream blonde hair – no sign of Dwight Yokam, her seriously bald six-foot-three country singer 'escort' (he was dumped shortly after this party – 'a dirt sandwich is better than Dwight Yokam' she sniffed after their split).

We chatted briefly about Cannes. She was shortly off to promote *Basic Instinct* at the Festival. We seemed to get on reasonably well.

'I went to Cannes last May,' I volunteered casually. 'I think I'm probably too busy this year.'

'That's a pity,' she said. 'What do you do in town?'

She sounded quite interested.

'Err . . . I'm a journalist,' I said hastily.

'Ah!'

She looked at me, put down her drink – and started talking to somebody else. As I stood recovering from this blow to the solar plexus of my ego, I saw Joan Collins, sitting down at a nearby table, along with Lord White and Roger Moore. She was glancing at me, eyeing me – as if she knew me from somewhere. As I smiled vaguely back, her fingers snapped sharply.

'Waiter,' she drawled at me. 'Get me a light please.'

9

Bad Boys

A FEW DAYS BEFORE GOING to interview Jay McInerney over a spring weekend in Nashville, Tennessee, I read in the May 1992 issue of *Vanity Fair* that his house '. . . feels regal inside, all soft white sofas and pastel-sponged walls. In one bedroom stands an imposing mahogany-posted family bed; beside it is a wooden easel displaying family portraits.'

'Regal' is overdoing it. Jay McInerney does not live in a sultan's palace. His 1920s Nashville town house is set back from a sleepy tree-lined road in a quietly prosperous bourgeois suburb favoured by lawyers, doctors and a handful of country-and-western music industry executives. After knocking a few times on the oak front door, I stepped inside an entrance hall dominated by a low-hung elk antler chandelier. This led into a high-ceilinged rococo drawing room with soft-peach walls, a large fireplace and some ancestral oil paintings. They weren't anything to do with McInerney. That much was obvious. They were heirlooms of his new wife, forty-three-year-old Helen Bransford, whose family is one of the oldest and grandest in Tennessee.

It was 7.30p.m. on Friday night. There was nobody about. I shouted 'Hello' a few times. Nobody appeared. On a gilt table was a large human skull. On another was a shiny cardboard jacket poster for *Brightness Falls* – a gold-and-black Cibachrome print based on a 1929 Hugh Ferris drawing of the *Daily News* building in New York – shortly to be published, beside which was a copy of *Bright Lights, Big City*, snugly fitted inside the hardcovers of an Everyman's edition of Emerson's *Essays*. The bookcase contained a set of nineteenth-century blue crystal glasses and bulged with dusty, leather-bound volumes – essays by Bacon and Rousseau, an obsolescent edition of a *Life of Napoleon*. No modern stuff. In a corner, was a fluffy pile of pigeon feathers.

A few minutes later McInerney wandered in. Freshly pressed blue jeans. Black suede lace-up shoes. Thick, wavy, black hair.

'Drink?' he said.

I followed him into an adjoining room – an austere ground-floor guest bedroom to be more exact – which housed a well-stocked cocktail cabinet and bar. Judging by the size of the stately mahogany bed, and the wooden easel, it was clearly the room mentioned by *Vanity Fair*. The last rays of evening sunlight flooded through the large windows, casting stripy shadows on the starched linen bedspread.

'That's a pretty amazing bed,' I said as McInerney plopped some ice cubes into my vodka and tonic. 'It looks as if it belongs in a museum.'

'It comes from my wife's family house, Belle Meade, in Nashville,' he said. 'You should get to see it while you're here. It's open to the public. Her great-grandfather was secretary of state for war under President Taft. He was born in that bed. My wife's mother was also born in that bed. She's very fond of it.'

Back in the drawing room, his wife, Helen, had emerged, also in jeans, and was sunk into a cream sofa. A ginger-blonde jewellery designer with a deep Southern drawl and sparky blue-grey eyes, she effused Old Money Southern charm. Her jewellery studio is just off the drawing room. She was wearing her best-selling piece, a silver bangle depicting the human vices. For $350 you get to choose five vices. Drink, sex, drugs . . . and so on.

I asked McInerney what his vices were these days.

'I'm not gonna tell you that,' he said ruefully. 'Let's just say I still do some of the things I'm not supposed to do.'

After another drink McInerney and I set off for dinner in Nashville in his blue Porsche 911 convertible. McInerney's vices and fast-living reputation have always, you sense, troubled the American media more than the author himself. His wild-craze image problem has hung around him ever since the success of *Bright Lights* sprung him to pop-star fame. Cast as New York superbrat and a literary John Travolta, his nightly dervishing with cocaine-sozzled supermodels had New York gossip columnists salivating faster than on the evening Norman Mailer head-butted Gore Vidal. But despite his new wife, and new life in the South, the idea that McInerney has suddenly transformed himself into a literary Mr Goody Two Shoes is naïve. The real change is that he has no interest in promoting his *enfant terrible* image any more. As we roar along the empty road, McInerney gives an example of how, back in the eighties, he felt obliged to live up to his party boy image. In 1984, after writing *Bright Lights*, he was so broke that he was reduced to working in a discount liquor store in Syracuse. One evening, whilst two drunks by the door were noisily fighting over a bottle of whisky, he got a call from a Paramount producer.

'How the hell he tracked me down to that liquor store, I don't know,' McInerney said as we hurtled along the empty road. 'But anyway, he told me I was about to become rich and famous because *Bright Lights* was being turned into a movie. By now the drunks were really shouting at each other. Before he hung up he said, "Hey, what's that goddamn noise going on? Where are you? – at *another* crazy party?"

'Er . . . yeah, I am actually,' replied the twenty-eight-year-old McInerney, too embarrassed to admit that America's soon-to-be most acclaimed new author in years was being paid the minimum wage for standing behind the till of a liquor store. 'It's a good party – everyone's just having a great time, actually.'

As he tells this story, McInerney has to shout above the turbo-whine of his Porsche as it roars along the dark Tennessee country road. With its hood down, the warm evening air rushes into his hair, standing it up like a preppy version of Dennis the Menace.

'You know, as a writer,' he added. 'I've always preferred the interesting lie to the boring fact.'

'Thank God the eighties are behind us,' he says, braking sharply before a narrow bend. The *Zeitgeist* at the moment is very fuzzy and ill defined,' he went on. 'New York is in a social and economic slump. I think an era has ended in New York, and I chronicled what interested me about it. The new Beast hasn't slouched into town yet. The *Zeitgeist* is taking a nap.'

Whilst he breaks off his monologue to light a cigarette, I asked how he responded to the criticism that Tom Wolfe might have already said everything possible about 1980s New York.

'That's absolute bullshit,' he sniffed. 'There is a hell of a lot that Tom Wolfe didn't even begin to say about New York in the eighties.

'I guess I am interested in creating a much more complex model of human behaviour than Tom Wolfe. I think he is a reductive writer – that's not to say at the end of the day he may not be a greater novelist than I am – but that he's no Balzac. Balzac had a far more profound conception of human nature than Tom Wolfe ever thought of having.'

He swings the Porsche in front of Nashville's fashionable Sunset Grill restaurant. For a surly moment, his cupreous eyes are fixed on a new black Mercedes 500 sports parked across the street.

'Shit,' he said, 'somebody's in my place.'

McInerney's life has clearly begun a grand new chapter in Nashville with his whirlwind marriage to Helen Bransford. Before his marriage, the only time he had been to Nashville was a sordid night in 1976, passing through on a six-month road trip with Gary Fisketjon – now his editor at Alfred Knopf – in a clapped out Volkswagen beetle. They ended up robbed of $150 and sleeping in a flea-bag brothel motel after being conned by a black drug dealer. The next day they were arrested for trying to break in to William Faulkner's house, nearby.

In Nashville, he candidly admits, he no longer has to shin up drain-pipes to get into people's houses. 'Society is pre-provided for me – which makes a change. I like it down in the South. It's like moving back to America after ten years. New York is another country, it has nothing to do with America. It's a country to itself.'

In New York, his posse of Bright Yuppie Things – editors Gary Fisketjon and Morgan Entrekin, former model and lover Marla Hanson and company – were caricatured as the *Vile Bodies* of New York, their lifestyle sometimes not so very different from the dark-ringed world of the critically drubbed *Story of My Life*: 'If Didi made a list of her favourite things I guess cocaine would be at the top and sunlight wouldn't even make the cut.'

These days the invitations are for turkey or quail shooting, and judging by the seriousness McInerney gives to the task of choosing the wine, any list of his favourite things today would have to include Grand Cru Bordeaux near the top.

'This place has a great wine list' he mutters, 'except that 75 per cent of the red wines are not mature. It pisses me off.'

'You choose the wine,' I said.

'I know the South has a reputation for hard drinking,' he continues. 'But since coming here, I've actually drunk a lot less than I used to. I used to drink every night. Now I'll go several nights a week without drinking. And I drink better now. I drink a lot of good wines. It's an endless hobby.'

'You like oysters?' he said. 'They're very good here.'

'Fine,' I said.

McInerney ordered two dozen oysters and an expensive looking bottle of Chablis. We both ordered the lamb.

The conversation drifted into literary gossip. He was shortly off to London to promote *Brightness Falls* – staying with his chum Julian Barnes for a few days – with whom he exchanges quirky faxes almost daily.

The Barnes and McInerney correspondence – scraps of which are stuck above the cooker in the McInerney kitchen – offered an unusual insight into the concerns of transatlantic literati. Barnes, for example, has recently been advising McInerney on his media career.

'Julian suggested that I shouldn't do any more interviews – but I know this is simply because he's trying to repress my sales,' he said laughing. 'I think he's terribly worried that I'm selling more books than him. It's not that he's worried about my privacy – he's just desperate to keep down my book sales.'

McInerney has only contempt for his own generation of critics who seem hostile to the idea of youth and the intellectual claims of popular culture.

'I like good clean popular culture rather than the sort of shit that the *New Yorker* publishes and pretends should interest us all.'

The *New Yorker*, of course, has long been something of a sore point with McInerney. After getting his Hemingway ex-pat thing out of his system in Japan, he got a job at the *New Yorker* in the Fact Checking Department. He was sacked for bad fact checking in 1981 – the first person, he said, in the history of the magazine to be fired from the department.

'I was humiliated. It was a big set-back in my life. But I was wholly unsuited to the job,' he said. 'I just wasn't interested in checking facts. If I was at a party I would always say I was from the *New Yorker*; I never mentioned I was a fact checker. I'd be very vague about my specific duties. I just gave the gentle hint that I was running the magazine.'

'It was a funny place,' he went on. 'Everything went through the Fact Checking department. There was a very paranoid, sepulchral feeling to the place. It was kind of like a church. You weren't meant to meet, talk to or greet people in the corridors. I used to try writing for them but I always got rejected.'

He paused and frowned at me.

'As a matter of fact I still do,' he added. 'They still reject my stories. *Can you believe that?* They've still never published anything of mine.'

I thought I had better change the subject. I steered the conversation back to *Brightness Falls*.

'I wanted this book to be ambitious,' he said as he slipped another oyster into his mouth. 'In my earlier books the culture at large had always been implied rather than filled in. This time I actually wanted to pull the camera back and get a bigger picture.'

What irked him considerably more than his literary bad boy image was the way that his success had started to become reviewed more than his prose. 'There was a terrible critical backlash against my success. There was this perception I had too much fun. In the kingdom of letters, you are not meant to smile.'

He was paid just $7,500 by Random House for *Bright Lights*. He refused to even so much as hint as to the size of his advances today.

'For a writer I guess I'm rich,' he said. 'I always wanted to live in the world that I have ended up living in. I wasn't born to it. The only figure I'll tell you, by the way, is that I pay my ex-wife $5,000 a month alimony.'

'Why are you telling me that?'

'Because I feel so sorry for myself about it.'

By this time we were well into the lamb and the second bottle of wine – a Grand Cru Bordeaux.

'My life really has changed dramatically in the last few months,' he volunteered. 'I've been waiting for it for a long time. I felt it would happen, and it has all to do with Helen. I found myself trapped in New York. I'm as happy as I've been since *Bright Lights* was published – my life has changed. My life got fucked up for years – I feel as if I lived in this bubble for seven years – and suddenly I feel I'm myself again.'

'And this was because you got too much attention?'

'Yeah, basically. In America anything that is new or exciting tends to get over-hyped. I was so tired of reading about myself, and knowing that people like James Wolcott would be negative, that I hardly read any of the American reviews. I only read the British reviews.'

One of the occupational hazards of having dinner with a local celebrity is that as the evening progresses various unordered glasses of brandy and port suddenly appear at your table. The brandy was from the Mâitre D' – a big fan of McInerney – the port . . . well, I don't know who the port was from. Neither, I think, did McInerney. But it seemed, as he put it, rude to refuse. More used to the drinking habits of LA, where the word 'alcohol' had practically dropped out of the dictionary, my head was starting to spin. Maybe it was the oysters. I don't know. Of one thing, however, I was certain. The mixture was not altogether healthy.

About half an hour later, I got the bill. We got back into the Porsche and roared off into Nashville in search of a country singer he knew about. Having switched my tape recorder off, my memory at this point becomes vacant. I have no recollection whatsoever of whether we did visit a country-and-western bar – although McInerney subsequently assured me that we did.

At around 1a.m. after a wild Toad-like ride in the Porsche through the darkly wooded lanes, we made it back to McInerney's house.

'William,' he said. 'You know, I really don't think you are in any fit condition to drive back to your hotel.'

'I'm fine, really.'

'No you're not, you'll crash and kill yourself,' he said. 'Look, stay here the night. Anyhow, you've got to come back in the morning to finish the interview.'

Without further ado, McInerney led me into the austere ground-floor bedroom with the mahogany Bransford bed.

'Sleep in here,' said McInerney. 'It's made up. It's a very comfortable bed. You'll feel much better tomorrow.'

McInerney pulled down the blinds, turned off the lights and within seconds I passed out, swathed in the starched linen Bransford sheets.

The very best nightmare guest stories are passed down, over the years like an endless game of Chinese whispers. Mistaking your host's cat for a cushion and squashing it to death. Running over your host's dog on arrival. I have a friend who, during a late-night game of sardines in a large house in Scotland, opened the door of an unfamiliar room and walked – she was wearing steel-pointed stilettos – *over* a priceless set of family oil paintings that had been laid on the floor for restoration. That, I admit, was *bad*.

For those who enjoy the misfortune of others, what follows are the unexpurgated details of my own little nightmare. Normally the sunlight wakes me. On this occasion it was the smell. A noxious, amino smell, like rotten onion stew blocking a sink, There was an acidic, taste in my mouth. I felt disturbingly unwell. I sat up and opened my eyes. My eyeballs stung as if they had been squirted with vinegar. Then I saw it – or, rather, I saw the first of it: a lumpy pool of claret-based vomit beside me on the bed. I jumped up. I was, in fact, covered in the stuff. As if I had just rolled around in a vat of strawberry custard. I was *smothered* in undigested bits of red and yellow coloured sick.

Worse, it wasn't simply the bed and sheets. On the floor by the bed was a large pat of more solid looking sick. It resembled a discarded giant cheese-and-tomato pizza. Pulling myself out of the bed, it got worse. The wall and curtains behind the mahogany head-piece was sprayed with sick in a style that bore a close resemblance to a De Kooning painting.

The cause was irrelevant. I had been a guest in Jay McInerney's house and I had redecorated the walls, curtains and bed of his principal guest bedroom in a colour scheme best described as Hint of Tomato.

It was nearly 7a.m. I had to get to work. And I had to act *quickly*. Helen McInerney had said she was going riding in the morning. After ten minutes or so of desperately rummaging around in the kitchen, and in various storage rooms, I finally found a plastic bucket and an old-fashioned mop with a wooden handle. I decided to use the bathroom next to the bedroom as my mopping-up headquarters.

I had no idea what sort of disinfectant you used to mop up sick. I squeezed about a third of a bottle of washing-up liquid into the bucket and added scalding hot water. I added a couple of squirts of lavatory cleaner. I swirled it round with the mop and then set to work on the wooden parquet floor. Apart from leaving a large brown wet patch, that seemed to work well enough. That was fine. That would dry.

I flushed the first bucket down the lavatory and returned with another bucket of my concoction of soapy water. I got down on my knees and, using a scrubbing brush from the bathroom, set to work on the mahogany bed. Bits of lamb and spinach were stuck to the frame and the carved legs. It was easy to get off. I was beginning to quite enjoy myself.

The wallpaper and curtains presented more serious difficulties. I opened the windows to let in some much-needed air. I was beginning to smell like a hospital. To tackle the sick on the wall I began by using a hot flannel. Most of it came off easily enough, like freshly sprouted mould. But there was a large patch behind the bed that I simply couldn't reach with the flannel. I was becoming increasingly worried about the time.

There was only one thing for it. After filling up my bucket with fresh water, I ingeniously began to use the wooden mop as a kind of paint brush. Dipping the mop in the bucket as if it were a paint pot, I started to dab the wallpaper with the mop. My method was sound. So effective was this technique, indeed, that I abandoned the flannel – whose blue dye was starting to run anyway – and began to mop down the curtains with bold, flourishing strokes, as if it were a feather duster. The dabbing technique was surprisingly effective. Any stubborn lumps were dealt with by pushing the mop firmly into the wall and twisting it like a bayonet. Finally, to finish the job off, I rubbed a bar of Pear's soap evenly over the curtain's affected patches, letting it soak in for a while, before applying hot water.

The sheets presented the most awkward problem. I had, I was quite aware, to be very careful of the linen sheets. They were probably, for all I knew, the same sheets that President Taft's secretary of state for war had been born in. That Jay McInerney's mother-in-law had been born in. I stripped the bed and ran a hot bath. The sheets – blotched in pinky-red stains – went in the bath. They needed to soak. After much ineffective scrubbing, I added a few kettles of boiling water. Next about half a pound of salt. To this I added the rest of the washing-up liquid, a few capfuls of paint thinner and a mugful of washing powder. But still the red blotches remained. At about 7.30a.m., fearful of either Mildred, the housekeeper, or Mrs McInerney, I opted to return to the Nashville Sheraton where I could get the sheets properly laundered. I would try, I thought, to slip the sheets back on when I returned to complete the interview later in the morning.

I made up the bed minus the sheets. There was a gentle morning breeze which was helping to air the room. The floor was dry, the curtains looked fine – although they smelt a bit – and I congratulated myself on a job well done. I replaced the mop and bucket and poured half a bottle of after-shave around the bath and basin to confuse the nostrils of anyone happening to stray into the downstairs bathroom.

I picked up the bundle of screwed-up sheets – one under each arm. I made for the back-door. *Tempus abire tibi est*: It is time for you to leave the scene.

Tiptoeing as quietly as possible out of the back-door, with the sheets under my arms, I darted across the back-yard and jumped into my Hertz hire car – a two-door silver Thunderbird coupé. I gunned the engine, shifted the gear into reverse, and began to turn the vehicle around.

To my horror, as I was about to speed off down the drive, Helen McInerney came running towards me in her dressing gown. That was it, I thought. It was all over. She knocked on the window.

I had no excuse. I was feeling too unwell to think how I would explain myself. I had been caught. Fair and square. It was my turn to be humiliated. The electronic window whirred down.

Her family's wet sheets were sitting in a screwed-up heap on the passenger seat.

'Morning,' I said.

'William,' she said, 'You left your briefcase behind.'

'Thanks,' I said, grabbing hold of it through the window.

I placed it on top of the sheets.

'Don't you want some breakfast?'

'Er . . . no,' I said. 'I've got to go back to the hotel. I need to make some calls.'

'So we'll see you later.'

'I'm not feeling very well,' I said. 'I might have had a bad oyster.'

Without so much as a wave, I accelerated down the drive and made my escape back to the hotel. After handing over the sheets to housekeeping, I collapsed on my king-size bed and went back to sleep. I did not feel well.

Around noon, I sheepishly returned to the McInerney house. *The Times*'s photographer, Graham Wood, who had flown over from London, was already setting up his tripods. I was hardly in a spirited mood for interviewing Jay McInerney. I had recently altered the colour scheme of his spare bedroom and stolen his best linen sheets. I decided to come clean. To his wife.

'Helen,' I said. 'I'm terribly sorry. But there was rather an unfortunate accident during the night.'

She gave me a puzzled look.

'I was unwell,' I said hurriedly. 'Unwell in your bedroom.'

'Unwell?'

'Sick,' I said. 'I was sick last night. I was sick in your bed. The family bed. I don't know how it happened – or why. I think it must have been the oysters. Oysters never agree with me. I don't know why I had them. I'm sorry.'

I was surprised that the McInerney's seemed so unfazed by my disgraceful behaviour. Helen McInerney took it very much in her Southern stride. In fact, she seemed to think it was quite funny. Down South, they were used to such things.

'Are you all right?' she said.

I nodded.

'I've got your sheets, back at the hotel,' I gulped. 'I'll make sure I get them back to you when they come back from the laundry.'

'Don't worry about it,' she said. 'Things happen like that

every weekend. Our friends wake up in the yard, around the swimming pool. . .'

'I'm really very sorry,' I said again.

'Don't think about it. William. I tell you it's dangerous coming here. I had an old boyfriend come to stay recently – Isaac Tigret . . .'

I knew who he was. He started the Hard Rock Café in London.

'Well, Isaac has a Range Rover. It was late at night. It had been quite an evening. He got in his car and the next thing we heard was this crash. Somehow he had jumped the drive, driven over the lawn and crashed into the neighbour's car. Completely crushed it. It belonged to a Japanese lady.'

Suddenly I was feeling a lot better.

'What did you do?'

'Jay and I had only just moved into the house. We had hardly met the woman. I was so embarrassed. We pinned a cheque to her front door the next morning.'

* * *

I was not a fan of Hunter S. Thompson, you understand. I had read *Hell's Angels* and *Fear and Loathing in Las Vegas* some years ago and did not rank them exactly as literary masterpieces of the twentieth century. The latter was probably of a certain medical interest.

But I was curious to meet Hunter S. Thompson. Not, as I said, as a fan but simply as a literary tourist. What drew me to him was probably his extremism. America has a problem with excess. It can't help loving it – swerving past critical or moral judgement.

I sent a fax to his farm in Woody Creek, Aspen, requesting an interview. No reply. I sent another fax. No reply.

I tried getting him on the phone.

An answerphone picked up. There was a strange and incoherent message recorded in a middle-aged woman's voice followed by a tone.

I left a message. No reply.

About two days later I tried calling again. Half way through the message, the phone picked up.

There was a loud noise like a glass smashing on the floor.

'Yeah,' said a husky voice. 'Who is it?'

I asked if he had got my fax.

'I remember something about it.'

Could I see him?

'Yeah, I don't see why not.'

I wasn't going to Aspen simply to visit Hunter S. Thompson. I wasn't that foolish. Despite his assurances, I was aware that the likelihood of actually meeting the Doc was not particularly high. His methods and working hours were very much his own. But if nothing else, his invitation was – at the very least – an excellent excuse for a skiing holiday over the President's Weekend.

'Where are you going for your holidays?' is one question you are hardly ever asked in LA. There are several reasons for this. First, many of Los Angeles's more affluent citizens are addicted to their designer West Coast lifestyles far too much to want to leave California. They have their beaches. They have their suntans. They have their mountains and swimming pools, gyms, Jacuzzis, steam-showers and saunas. After spending millions of dollars building their dream Bel-Air or Malibu mansions – each with more luxury fittings, *en suite* marble bathrooms and fitness facilities than the Regent Beverly Wilshire – they enjoy, as they say, spending 'quality time' at home.

The other reason that Angelenos do not really much enjoy leaving their Californian Connoisseur Class existences is that the LA mentality is acutely paranoid. Most actors, executives, agents, managers, directors and producers rarely take long holidays because they are afraid they will miss a would-be Oscar winning job, or find somebody else in their desk on their return (the average life-expectancy of a studio executive is just eighteen months). Besides, they already spend a large part of their professional lives jetting off to exotic locations for meetings and film shoots, i.e. spending non-quality time hanging around sets.

What Hollywood really likes to do is to take reassuringly expensive, short-distance, long-weekend breaks – with opportunities for pampering and shopping. This is why Aspen has long been so popular with LA society – to the chagrin of long-term local residents like Hunter Thompson. In 1970, the Doc had, indeed, run for Mayor in Aspen – partly as a joke, partly out of anger at the way the old mining town was being developed and turned into an international luxury playground for the super-rich 'greedheads'. Calling his grassroots movement 'Freak Power', the Doc set up headquarters in the bar of the Jerome Hotel, launched his own newspaper, *Aspen Wallposter* – which publicly pilloried dishonest drug dealers – and declared he would rechristen the town Fat City. Standing as the Freak Power Party candidate he lost out on becoming Mayor by a few votes.

Since then, the belligerent Doc voiced his opposition to the gliztification of Aspen with direct and covert action – usually of a violent and explosive nature. His skirmishes with the law nearly put him in jail in 1991, however, after ex-porn film producer, and actress, Gail Palmer-Slater accused him of trying to sexually assault and shoot her during a visit to his house late on a winter night. After arresting Thompson, Aspen deputies uncovered a hoard of drugs at his Woody Creek ranch – along with dynamite and gunpowder. The charges were later dropped, partly due to the chaos inside his house. 'We beat them like stupid rats. We beat 'em like dogs. They had a bad case,' he told *Sunday Times* journalist Sam Kiley after leaving the courthouse – *en route* to a 'humdinger of an orgy' victory celebration at his local, The Woody Creek Tavern.

For my trip to Aspen over the President's Weekend in February, the LA glitz quotient was back in force – for a series of weekend parties, pro-celebrity ski races and a charity gala dinner (in aid of The Race to Erase Multiple Sclerosis) for 750 in the ballroom of the brand new Ritz-Carlton. Before the gala dinner, hosted by LA charity queen Nancy Davis, there was a Silent Auction, which involved putting written bids in for a bizarre selection of donated gifts, jewels, holidays and memorabilia laid out like a village jumble sale.

It was a strange sight – LA and Denver millionaires and celebrities, from tycoon Lee Iacocca to singer Michael Bolton, scrawling their names under such items as:

> *Hollywood, Here I Come! – Do you dream of appearing on the Big Screen? Of capturing the bright lights of stardom? Welcome to Hollywood with this incredible opportunity to be in the upcoming Ivan Reitman* (Ghostbusters, Kindergarten Cop) *feature film with a walk-on part.*
>
> *Value: Priceless*
>
> *Minimum bid: $500.*

The most extraordinary items were too small puppies – a little black labrador in a cardboard box and a fluffy little white thing, no larger than a mop. The tiny animal was in a wicker pet-carrying basket. A card above it, framed by love hearts, said 'I need lots of love and affection. So please promise to spend a lot of time playing with me.' A charity volunteer was patting the animal on the head.

'Had much interest in the dog?' I asked.

'This is a pretty exciting evening for a little pup,' she said.

I noted on their auction form that both dogs had offers of $300 – the minimum bid.

'Three hundred dollars – not bad for a puppy,' I said. 'That's about what it costs in LA to see a vet.'

'She needs a nice home,' the woman went on. 'But she's getting nervous – I can feel her little heart pounding.'

About half an hour later, just before the bids were closed, I checked up on the two dogs. By now there was quite a commotion beside the fluffy white thing's wicker basket. A quick glance at its auction form revealed why. The first bid for the dog was $300. The second bid, scrawled by tycoon

Lee Iacocca, was for $25,000.

The charity worker was relishing the attention.

'It's wonderful,' she squealed. 'Everybody wants to pat the $25,000 dog.'

I gave the dog a quick pat and went into the gala dinner.

The Ritz-Carlton in Aspen has to rank as one of the most extraordinary hotels I have ever stayed at. With 259 rooms – priced from £325–$2,000 a night in high season – the hotel had developed a simple policy designed to lure people away from the comfort of their Bel-Air or Hollywood Hills mansions. Namely, to out-de luxe all previous pretensions towards five-star luxury. 'The Ritz-Carlton mission is to enliven the senses,' I read in a brochure in my room, 'instill a sense of well-being and fulfill even the unexpressed wishes and needs of all guests.'

The quality of service did, strangely, seem to border on the telepathic. On checking in, I was given a special elevator key to reach my room. Without it, the fourth-floor was inaccessible. On stepping out of the lift, I entered an elegant drawing room. Three beautiful young women, in russet red uniforms, smiled brightly. One of them, a blonde with apple-green eyes, showed me the complimentary cocktail and champagne bar. You simply helped yourself. All day long.

Which was all very well. For a day or two. For a day or two of leaving messages on the Doc's Woody Creek answer-machine and getting no reply. Nothing. A muscular barman at the Ritz told me that he had heard Hunter had gone away somewhere to write his novel. A blond-haired luggage boy told me he had tried to get Hunter to autograph a copy of *Fear and Loathing in Las Vegas* before Christmas – and had been shot at as his pick-up approached the Doc's bat and vulture iron statues.

After three days in Aspen – I could ski until lunch without concern that the Doc would call (he usually goes to bed around 8.30a.m.) – I got bored with abusing the champagne bar. Taking out a sheet of headed hotel writing paper, I faxed Hunter S. Thompson an ultimatum:

Dear Dr Thompson,

You kindly said that you would see me for an interview. I have flown to Aspen from LA in the hope that this will be possible. I am writing to ask whether we can meet for a drink at the Woody Creek Tavern at 7p.m. on Thursday – i.e. tonight.

I sent you a fax about my coming to Aspen a few days ago. I have tried leaving several messages on your answer-machine – but without success. Frankly I don't know what to do. I will simply turn up at the Woody Creek Tavern at 7p.m. in the hope that you might be there or come in; failing that, I will try again tomorrow. I realise this is a somewhat unusual method of setting up a meeting but I have, as I have said, flown from LA, so please forgive my somewhat desperate-sounding tone.

Yours sincerely

William Cash

Woody Creek is about ten miles from Aspen. By 6.15p.m. it was getting dark and snowing heavily. It was cold. The town's row of chic boutiques (a pair of designer cowboy boots will cost you $450) were empty. The odd 4 × 4 Cherokee Jeep or Range Rover drove slowly past, headlights on full, four-wheel drive engaged, thick snow-tyres churning. I ordered a cab. About ten minutes later what resembled a gleaming black hearse arrived. It was about fifteen feet long, with tinted windows and thickly rutted snow-tyres that could have come off a JCB.

'Your car, Mr Cash,' said the luggage boy, flashing his dental work. He was dressed in a Napoleonic officer's great-coat.

This wasn't any ordinary cab. It was a mountain stretch limo. Inside it was like a plush 1930s Chicago pool hall. Black leather and crushed-velvet seats. A fully stocked cocktail cabinet, with cut-glass whisky tumblers. Standard limo-sized colour TV, video, electric windows, magazine rack, telephone and enough wall-to-wall carpeted leg room to massage a hippopotamus. The car was, in fact, two four-wheel-drive pick-up trucks welded together. My ride to the Woody Creek Tavern – turning right down a twisting mountain road to nowhere – cost $30.

'When do ya wanna be picked up?' the driver asked after dropping me off at a rickety old barn with a selection of rusting Ford and Chevrolet pick-ups outside.

'I don't know,' I said.

I negotiated some icy concrete steps. Snow was piled in lumpen mounds by the door, like burst sacks of granulated sugar. Above the door was the head of what looked like a giant wild-boar. Creaking the door open, I walked inside and pulled up a stool at the bar. A few bearded locals, dressed identically in lumberjack shirts, jeans and cowboy boots, rolled their eyes.

The barman was in his mid forties, with greasy black hair, and wire-frame glasses. A sign above the bar informed me that the house speciality was a locally brewed beer called 'The Doggy Position'.

'A Doggy Position,' I said.

The beer was a dark substance that resembled linseed oil.

I sipped it and attempted to look as if I was interested in the NBA basketball game playing on the TV. I wasn't. Stuck on a huge fridge with a metal pull-handle was a bumper sticker: 'This Planet's Finished – Let's Party.' Near it was the evening menu: 'Dinner Special: $9.95, Roast Turkey, mashed potato, gravy, veggie salad.'

The woody Creek Tavern was an odd place. Cheap plastic fairy lights – shaped as pink elephants, underpants, trains – were strung across the tavern like a washing line. The walls were adorned with more heads and fish than a taxidermist's boot sale. Slapped up on a wall was a Tavern bill on which was scrawled 'Dr Hunter Thompson promises not to throw smoke bombs in the Woody Creek Tavern' signed by the Doc. In one corner was a wooden table over which hung a large stuffed buffalo head. That, I recognised from a photo in

E.J. Carroll's biography, was Hunter Thompson's private table. It was empty.

I tried to look as if I was waiting for somebody. After a second beer it became more difficult to look convincing. When a dozen or so female members of the over-fifties branch of the Ski Association of America walked in, I welcomed the chance for small-talk at the bar. After they were seated at a long table, it was back to sitting uneasily at the bar waiting for . . . waiting for Gonzo.

By 8p.m. it looked fairly obvious that he wasn't going to be turning up. I decided to call a cab.

'Seen Dr Thompson around recently?' I casually inquired of the barman as I finished my last Doggy Position.

'Nope,' he said. 'Haven't seen him for a week.'

I asked to borrow his phone.

'Wanna cab?' he said.

'Yes I do.'

He dialled a number. It would be here in fifteen minutes.

The cab arrived.

'Err . . . by the way,' I said across the bar as I got up to leave. 'I had an appointment to meet Dr Thompson here this evening. If by any chance he shows up, can you say I was here. And to call me. My name is William Cash. Thanks.'

The barman and a local on a bar-stool smirked at each other.

'Told ya,' he said. 'Haven't seen him in days.'

Then the phone rang.

Grudgingly, the barman handed me the receiver.

'It's for you,' he grunted.

'Hello,' I said.

'Mr Cash, yes, hello, this is Deborah, Hunter's secretary, I'm sorry but I've been away. I've just read your fax. He says he will see you – but not tonight.'

'Tomorrow?'

'Tomorrow night, late. How do you feel about scheduling for around two o'clock in the morning?'

'Two in the *morning*?'

'That would be the best time.'

I asked her to call me at my hotel in the morning to confirm the exact time and place. But when I got back from skiing the next morning there was no message. I left a final, not very hopeful, message saying where I was having dinner.

At about 11p.m. having resigned myself to the fact that I would not be meeting the Doc, a waiter came up to the table.

'Telephone call for you, Mr Cash,' he said.

'William, hello,' said a younger and frisky female voice. I'm Hunter's editorial assistant. He says he will see you at midnight at the Woody Creek Tavern.'

'In an hour, you mean?'

'Right.'

'Fine. I'll be there.'

'One thing,' she said matter-of-factly. 'The Woody Creek Tavern may be closed. Don't worry. Just knock hard and somebody will unlock the door.'

I took a regular cab this time. By the time it picked me up, it was 11.40p.m. Despite the blizzard, I ordered the driver to drive like a madman. Swerving and sliding around the narrow mountain roads, we passed only one car on the hazardous ten-mile journey. That was just as well. Because of a heavy snow-storm, visibility was practically zero. The view through the windscreen was like pressing one's nose up against the glass door of a washing machine.

As I was dropped off at the edge of the empty road, just after midnight, the Tavern looked ominously silent. The pick-up trucks were gone. As the blizzard swirled around me, and the freshly fallen snow creaked under my boots, the scene became increasingly Dickensian. I could see no light. There was no country music. I knocked loudly on the door. Three times.

Not a sound.

It was perfectly quiet. Above me the moon glowed dimly under the heavily falling snow. To each side of me the road simply disappeared into a tunnel of darkness. As I stood by the door, I could feel the snow melting on my head and streaming down my face.

'Who's there?' a deep voice finally muttered.

I said who I was.

The oak door slowly opened and was quickly locked behind me. The tavern was empty except for the barman and Hunter S. Thompson, sitting at the bar like a huge grizzly bear in a hat and red trucker's shirt. He was cutting up a large carrot and some red and green chilli peppers with a hunting knife. Beside him was his assistant, a foxy twenty-something blonde with a thin nose and sharp eyes. She had the smile of a first-class air stewardess.

I ordered another 'Doggy Position' and shook hands. Big, beefy hands. Dr Thompson was, in fact, a good deal larger – larger in every way – than I had expected. He also looked a lot fitter. He had his customary dark glasses on; so I couldn't see his eyes. But his chubby face was the texture of a gristly sausage, streaked with the odd rogue vein. His whole body bulged as if it had been inflated with a foot-pump. He exuded brute strength.

Chop. Chop. Chop.

He was chopping up the red chilli and popping it in his mouth.

'Here, try some of this,' he said, holding out his DIY smorgasbord.

'You look fitter than in some of your photographs,' I said.

In *Songs of the Doomed*, Thompson had written: 'My soul and body chemistry are like that of a chameleon, a lizard with no pulse. They call me "Lizard Man" and I laugh smugly.'

The barman leant over towards me.

'The man before you has the constitution of a mule,' he declared. 'He's an amazing human being. I've known him for a long time. He's an amazing human being.'

I looked at the Doc. That was a difficult one to follow.

'It's that fucking comic strip,' he said, referring to the Doonesbury cartoon. 'It makes me look small. Makes me look an ass-hole.'

I asked why so many Americans were seemingly obsessed with the Hunter Thompson phenomenon.

'I'm afraid of most of my fans,' he said. 'I don't care who

they are. I don't want to see or meet them.'

'You don't like them?'

'EXCUSE ME?'

I asked for some examples of manic fandom.

'There were two occasions I had to turn letters over to the secret police.'

'Why?'

'They sounded dangerous. But not because they were threatening me – I'm always getting death threats and dirty letters. They say things like, "You dirty son of a bitch, you ruined me, you ruined my children".'

'Who are these people?'

'I dunno. Usually people who beat their kids so long they went off and did drugs. I get threatened by all types of people. I seem to get on the wrong side of the people I write about – Bill Clinton, I'm writing about Bill Clinton now . . .'

He was referring to his new book. Hoping to repeat the success of Thompson's classic account of Richard Nixon's victory over George McGovern for the Democratic nomination twenty years before – *Fear and Loathing: On the Campaign Trail '72* – which had sold over 1.5 million copies for Random House, his publishers were hoping to recoup some of the $1.2 million advance they paid for Thompson's as yet unwritten first novel (supposedly called 'Polo is My Life') by getting the Doc to churn out a book on the Clinton campaign, provisionally called *Fear and Loathing: On the Campaign Trail '92*. There was, however, an awkward technical difficulty. Apart from on election night, when he was down at the Clinton HQ, Hunter was not actually *on* the 1992 election trail. He watched the campaign on TV at home in Woody Creek. The book is largely made up of faxes sent to friends around the country as he sat watching the telly.

'Bill Clinton has threatened you?'

'No.'

'You know the President?'

'Yeah.'

He wouldn't elaborate any more on that point.

I asked how he first met him.

'Down in Texas. When he was Attorney General of Arkansas, he was comparable to normal.'

The trouble was I was starting to have serious difficulty understanding what the Doc was saying. I don't know whether the years of drugs have simply burnt out some of his mental circuitry, but he slurs and mumbles his words so badly that understanding him is almost impossible. It soon became clear there was no point in asking him to repeat himself. I had to content myself with simply listening and nodding – picking up the odd phrase here, the odd name I recognised. It wasn't uninteresting. It was just, from an interview point of view, frustrating. I might as well have been fishing on a beautiful autumn day for a monster pike – seeing him there, in front of me, circling my bait – with just a piece of string on a bamboo shoot.

As he spoke, he discreetly stroked his editorial assistant on the leg. The exact role of his young female supplicants has always been a bit fuzzy. According to one close Hunter source one of their chief purposes is to act as honey-mouthed *femmes flatteurs*. They will stand over his typewriter and offer wild adulation as each paragraph is squeezed out. 'An editorial assistant will read it out loud,' I was told, 'and will then give praise. "Oh I love that!", "that's brilliant Hunter", "Oh go on – I can't wait to hear the next sentence".'

When his assistants aren't around, he is understood to type phrases like 'now you're golden' on the page.

His conversation was strangely staccato. Unfathomable sentences interspersed with short bursts of clarity.

We spoke of Jack Nicholson.

'Jack's very comfortable with his celebrity. He knows how to handle it – for which I envy him.'

'You mean you don't feel comfortable?'

'We went down to the LA Forum once – for a basketball game. I was on the end seat and people were reaching over me for his autograph. None of them wanted *my* autograph.'

'Do you care for LA?'

'The way I write is an interior monologue. It's not for the

movies. I've fooled around Hollywood. It was a great disappointment.'

At about 1a.m. – with the stroking of his assistant's leg getting progressively less subtle – the barman said he was closing up.

'Let's . . . er . . . continue talking tomorrow,' Hunter said, catching the eye of his assistant for a moment. 'You're in town for a few days. We've got plenty of time.'

'Fine,' I said.

We agreed to talk in the morning.

I sunk the remains of my Doggy Position – the Doc had been drinking Wild Turkey – whilst the barman called a cab.

But there was no message. During a late Valentine's Day dinner the next evening at the Caribou Club – my last in Aspen – I received another phone call.

'Mr Cash, it's Deborah here,' she said. 'Hunter will see you again at midnight, up at the house . . .'

There was a bellowing sound in the background and the sound of something crashing. The line suddenly went dead.

'Hello,' I said, shaking the receiver.

Ten seconds later, Deborah came back on the line, gasping for breath.

'Mr Cash – can you call back in half an hour? We have an emergency.'

That time the Doc answered.

'It's William calling,' I said. 'I was told to call back in half an hour – is the emergency over?'

'No,' said the Doc. 'It fuckin' isn't. A mad beast of a woman has driven her car damn well nearly into my house. The mad drunk! Had to take her to hospital. Second time she's crashed like that in a month, I don't think we can talk tonight. Tomorrow maybe?'

I explained I was going back to LA.

'The goddamn mad whore!' he said again.

'Goodbye Dr Thompson,' I said.

'THE BEAST!'

I hung up.

10

Deathwatch

'WE'VE BEEN SO BUSY THIS morning' said the smiling blonde Avis girl at San Francisco international airport as she handed over my car rental keys. 'All I have left is a Chrysler convertible. Red okay?'

'Fine.'

'Here's your map. Have a nice day.'

San Quentin state prison, where thirty-nine-year-old Robert Alton Harris, convicted of killing two teenage boys in 1978, was scheduled to be buckled into a metal chair and executed by lethal gas that night at 12.01a.m. was not officially marked on my free map of Northern California. To assist the international media circus descending on the postcard seaside village of San Quentin, thirty miles north of San Francisco, the girl at the Avis desk had highlighted the quickest route from the airport to the prison with a flourescent yellow felt-tip pen.

With Robert Alton Harris set to become the first man to be executed in California for twenty-five years, the American media's obsession with Harris's fate had built up to a frenzy over the 1992 Easter Holiday weekend. Executions, of course, were traditionally always held on public holidays. Whilst in Rome in 1845, Dickens got up at dawn and queued for seven hours for a prime spot to watch a robber publicly guillotined: 'Priests and monks elbowed a passage for themselves among the people, and stood on tiptoe for a sight of the knife . . . suddenly, there was a noise of trumpets . . .

the cigar and pastry merchants resigned all thought of business, for the moment, and abandoning themselves wholly to pleasure, got good situations in the crowd.'

Moving executions inside the prison walls coincided with the rise of the mass media in the nineteenth and twentieth centuries. This ensured that they remain a public spectacle. The American media likened the frenzy of interest in Harris's execution to the circus attending Gary Gilmore in 1977. In *The Executioner's Song*, Norman Mailer's exhaustive account of Gilmore's execution there is a macabre moment which catches the scale of the American media's appetite for executions. When journalist Larry Schiller, who had struck a cheque-book deal with Gilmore for his exclusive story, gets inside the Utah prison at dawn for his last interview, he realises that in the panic of the last-minute legal wrangling, he has forgotten his reporter's notebook. Desperate, Schiller pulls out his cheque-book and scrawls down Gilmore's last words on the back of cheques.

America's relative moral indifference – albeit massive media interest – to the execution of Robert Alton Harris raised speculation as to whether the country has lost its capacity to be morally shocked. Harris ended up being executed by fax. Most of the seventeen American media witnesses of the final execution said they had no personal feelings in watching the farce. This surreal sense of moral obfuscation was not reported on. The execution of Robert Harris seemed indicative of how death has become such a banality in America today. The sense of passiveness surrounding Harris's death made it appear – to a European perspective at least – that America is now in danger of becoming inured to its own reality.

Although it is probably true to say that not since Gary Gilmore's death by firing squad had America been so gripped by an execution, for the media to compare Harris with Gilmore was naïve. With the exception of their last-minute legal and constitutional wrangling, their cases could hardly have been more different. Whilst Harris could hardly write,

Gilmore had an IQ of 140, was a gifted painter and could quote Shelley. Whilst Harris's lawyers succeeded in stretching his appeals for years, Gilmore expressly asked to be executed – the eleventh hour wrangling came from state lawyers who wanted to stop the execution. 'You sentenced me to die,' Gilmore told them as they tried to get a last-minute stay, 'unless it's a joke or something.'

* * *

Driving over the ramp of the airport rental car-park, I put on my sunglasses and pushed a button that electronically whirred open the black canvas hood. 20 April 1992 was a glaringly hot spring day. Californian barbecue weather. I was soon heading over an empty Golden Gate Bridge with the balmy sea breeze blowing in my face like a blow-dryer. I did not feel especially comfortable driving a lipstick red Chrysler sports car on Easter Monday to report on the first execution in California for twenty-five years.

'The Sunset Slayer' – a neighbour of Harris's – was also in line for the gas chamber. But I wasn't going to be dropping in on him – for a rubber of bridge, game of dominoes or anything else. His letters to me had abruptly ceased shortly after I arrived in LA as a consequence of *The Times* publishing an 'Inside the Mind of a Serial Killer' piece I wrote about his letters to me rather than his unsolicited 900-word article.

The question of whether Robert Alton Harris actually had a mind of his own had enabled his lawyers to stretch out his appeals for over thirteen years. Harris had been regularly beaten and abused and molested as a child and had spent almost all his adult life in prisons. At the short time he spent at school he averaged grade E. Born two months prematurely after his father, a US army soldier, had kicked his mother in the stomach during a jealous rage, Harris suffered severe psychological impairment from foetal alcohol syndrome throughout his life.

As I drove on towards San Quentin, with Alcatraz island

looming across the San Francisco Bay to my right, local radio stations kept up their frantic coverage of the execution. At midnight the night before the 9th Division Court of Appeals overturned a ten-day stay of execution granted by federal judge Marilyn Hall Patel to consider whether lethal gas constituted 'cruel and unusual punishment', after a last-minute civil rights lawsuit filed by Harris's lawyers and the American Civil Liberties Union, on behalf of California's other 330 condemned inmates, that claimed execution by gas was 'barbarous and torturous'. The lawsuit stated that the same gas scheduled to be used on Harris – Zyklon B – was used by the Nazis to exterminate over a million concentration camp inmates at Auschwitz. Radio stations replaced their normally cheery morning-drive shows with live phone-ins devoted to discussing various methods of execution. It was practically impossible to find any good music.

Whilst thirty-six states in America still carried out the death penalty, only three – California, Arizona and Maryland – still used lethal gas. Whilst the inventor and designer of San Quentin's gas chamber – the only one in the state – had proudly boasted that his submarine-style chamber would 'snuff out life' in fifteen seconds, it took a grown pig three minutes to die in the first test execution. Many humans took well over ten minutes to be pronounced dead, with eyewitnesses being nauseated as the victims twisted and gurgled, strapped into the chair.

Just a few weeks before, in Arizona, media witnesses to the execution of murderer Don Eugene Harding reported how they had stared aghast as it took ten minutes and thirty-one seconds for his body to stop thrashing after a prison guard released a lever dropping sodium cyanide pellets into a vat containing a lethal cocktail of distilled water and sulphuric acid. Charles Kelly of the *Arizona Republic* wrote: 'His head falls and rises, and a violent trembling is visible in his upper arms and back – an involuntary flicker of nerves and muscles, as if bugs are racing underneath the skin.'

The history of capital punishment in California had been a

1 The author buys a bottle of White Diamonds perfume in order to have tea with Liz Taylor at Robinson's department store. The meeting lasts fifteen seconds. Note the use of left elbow to obstruct path of oncoming journalist. (Photo Lee Salem)

2 Desperately seeking an interview with Madonna. At the 1992 Jean Paul Gaultier Fashion Gala at the LA Shrine.

3 David Hockney in his studio in the Hollywood Hills. (Photo Graham Wood, *The Times*, London)

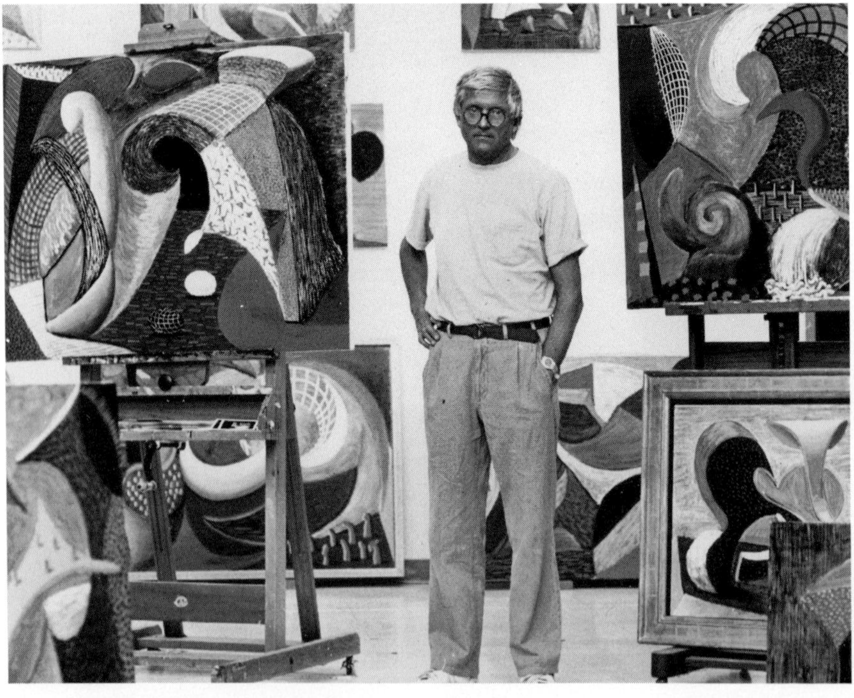

4 Posing at Elton John's 1993 Oscar night party to benefit the Elton John Aids Foundation. Note the jaunty angle of tie.

5 With Bob Lazich of KNBR radio station, who witnessed the last execution in California twenty-five years ago, a few hours before the death of Robert Alton Harris at the seaside resort of San Quentin.

6 Marooned at the Playboy Mansion with Corinna Harney, 1992 Playmate of the Year, in the middle of the LA riots. The romantically named 'Love Grotto' glistens enticingly behind. Left hand comes in useful once again.

7 In the back garden of the Playboy Mansion. Hef wore one of his 175 pairs of silk pajamas. I wore my suit.

8 Eleven good men and me: cricket on a Saturday afternoon under the Hollywood sign. Mick Jagger, Julian Sands and TV cameras on pitch are a regular feature. Team footwear is yet to be approved by the MCC. (Photo Clement von Franckenstein)

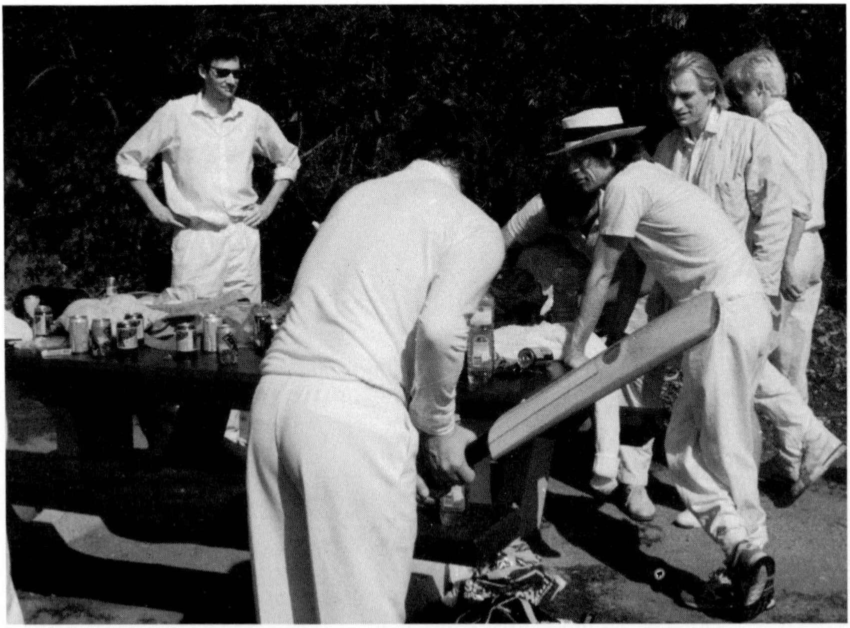

9 With 'room mate' Simon Kelton in Times Mirror Square, Downtown LA, at the start of our twenty-six mile walk down Sunset Boulevard. Simon, a student on UCLA's Master of Fine Arts in Screenwriting course, came along primarily for the free meals.

10 The author in his office waiting for that call – anorak and mobile phone at the ready. (Photo Michael Stinson)

messy saga. No condemned inmate had been executed in California since 1967, largely because of legal yo-yoing in both state and federal courts. In 1977, however, the Californian State Legislature finally re-instated the death penalty. Harris was sentenced to death on 9 March 1979.

On Wednesday 5 July 1978, twenty-five-year-old Harris woke up and simply 'decided to rob a bank'. After persuading his younger brother, Daniel, to help him out, and then deciding on which local bank to raid – the San Diego Trust and Savings Bank – the pair went off to a supermarket car-park in a suburb of San Diego to steal a getaway car. Seeing two sixteen-year-old boys, Michael Baker and John Mayeski, happily eating hamburgers in their car, Harris walked over, pointed a 9mm Luger pistol at them and told Mayeski to drive east towards an isolated canyon area. When they arrived at the deserted spot, Harris – for reasons that even he has never been sure of – shot the two boys, and then went off in their car to rob the bank. Wearing ski-masks, they stuffed $3,000 into two pillowcases and then drove home – followed by a witness. Harris put the stolen vehicle in the garage. When the police arrived, his clothes were smouldering in the fireplace. One of the police officers who arrested Harris turned out to be the father of Michael Baker.

What had always really irked Californians about Harris's case, the *really* unforgivable thing he did that lodged in the minds of the public, was that after shooting the boys he casually sat down and ate their hamburgers. 'It seemed funny at the time,' he told a police psychiatrist after he was arrested. 'I wish I could explain it better because it would make me feel better. There was no thought at all in my head, just like I was a robot, just like I was empty inside, just like there was nothing there.'

As the day of Harris's execution approached the *Los Angeles Times* introduced a quirky 'Execution Journal' which described in detail how the media were preparing for the big day. Local San Francisco newspapers featured hour-glasses on special 'Execution Countdown' pages. In June the previous year, a federal judge ruled against the KQED-TV San Francisco broadcasting station that came close to being allowed to film the execution. The grounds for the court's decision were that broadcasting the execution would provoke a panic among inmates with access to TV sets. A judge did, in fact, rule at the last minute that a video camera would film the execution but not for prime-time television; rather, for experts to determine whether death by lethal gas could be deemed 'cruel and unusual punishment'.

It was shortly after noon when, following a signpost, I turned left up a wooded hill and finally arrived at the seaside resort of San Quentin, over which the prison looms like a giant concrete sand castle. With its palm-tree lined beach, and row of painted wooden houses looking out across the San Francisco bay, it was hardly the most likely place to find California's only lethal gas execution chamber located. Boasting a pair of six-foot-high gleaming gates, San Quentin prison itself looked – from a short distance – like one of those self-contained luxury time-share resorts in Southern Spain or the Caribbean, with tight perimeter security to keep the locals out. There were, in fact, very few locals about. Most had been paid off with thousands of dollars by TV producers wanting to park their satellite vans in their drive-ways and turn their houses into round-the-clock 'death-watch' headquarters. A white stretch limousine with smoked windows drove past me, throwing up a cloud of dust as it turned into the neighbouring drive-way. A TV crew jumped out. Standing in bermuda shorts and a T-shirt on the balcony of a pretty beach house set back from San Quentin's main street on a pair of huge stilts was an ABC news producer, called Max, who was speaking to New York on his cellular phone.

'The focus of the story is gonna be what, then?' he barked. 'Just what the hell is going on outside? If we're gonna be the only package, you'll want both inside and outside. Right?'

I asked Max how he had negotiated the house, which belonged to a Californian civil servant. It had been turned into a CNN-style newsroom headquarters.

'It's a lovely house. We got it about three weeks ago,' he said, folding away his cellular phone. 'We were lucky to get the best house on the block. I'm not particularly competitive about these things but from our point of view, in terms of having lots of microwave possibilities for signals out, and camera positions, this is by far the best location.'

The small high-street had a carnival atmosphere. Its dusty road thronged with police cars, satellite trucks, a gaggle of anti-death penalty protestors holding up amateurish placards and a handful of pro-death penalty supporters who had come up to San Quentin for the afternoon to celebrate. Local resident Todd Morris, for example, was dressed in black leathers and was accompanied by a Rottweiler on a silver chain. 'I'd like to see Harris fry,' he told me matter-of-factly. 'I think the gas chamber is too good for him. I think he should die a slow death. I don't think it's inhumane at all. What's inhumane is his shooting two kids. This will be justice.'

A pro-death penalty supporter held up a placard which read: 'Plop, Plop, Fizz, Fizz – Oh, What a Relief it is.' Sunbathing on a yellow deck chair in an open polyester shirt and sandals, his nose thickly dabbed in sunscreen, was sixty-five-year-old Reverend Bill Fling. He was eating a home-made corned beef sandwich for lunch. Rev. Fling preached the gospel at the Church of Christ in Orangevale. 'What we have before us is the murder of two teenage boys. What is the punishment of God for a murderer?'

'Hell,' I volunteered.

'Not just Hell. But that he should surely be put to death.'

Journalists accredited to report on the execution from inside the prison had to pass through a special security post set up at the West Gate of the prison by 2p.m. Each of us was frisked for a weapon, had our bags and briefcases searched and were made to sign a release form.

'What does that mean?' I asked after signing.

'It means that in the event of a prison riot you agree that the prison does not have to go to any special efforts to save your life.'

We clambered into an old mini-van and were driven along a winding drive, through a rock-landscaped garden rather like the entrance to a Scottish estate. By the Warden's House was a Victorian folly. The prison grounds, originally laid out in the nineteenth century, were overlooked by a 40-foot-high Colditz watch-tower. The grounds bloomed with spring flowers – hundreds of wild red roses, thyme, poppies, purple heather and a small jungle of giant cacti with thorns up to ten inches long. 'It's all part of our landscaping,' our stocky female driver told me. 'San Quentin tries not to be a local eyesore. We try to make the best of this very beautiful spot.'

We were dropped off in what used to be – appropriately for the drama of the night ahead – the old prison theatre. 'Please clean the soles of your shoes prior to entering the hall,' a sign outside the door stated. It was a high-ceilinged room, just like a school theatre, with its walls covered with old sepia photographs, prison memorabilia and what looked like sixth-form geography or history projects. Peering a little closer, I noted that the wall displays were limited to just one subject. We were, in fact, locked up in a local museum – complete with audio-visual learning aids – devoted to the science and history of executions in California. In a corner was a TV set which continually played a video about the gas chamber. Many of the exhibits and photos had hand-written explanatory labels. Under a black-and-white photo of the gas chamber was written:

> Lethal gas, as a replacement for hanging, was provided by the state legislature on August 27th, 1937. A total of 194 persons have been executed in the gas chamber, including four women. There have been 22 multiple executions. The last execution took place on April 12th, 1967. Aaron Mitchell was put to death for the first degree murder of a police officer.

'I saw the last execution here,' said a man in a checked red tartan cap standing next to me, and also staring into the glass exhibition case. 'I watched Aaron Mitchell die.'

Wearing a checked jacket and a button-down shirt, with a large pair of binoculars slung around his neck, he introduced himself as Bob Lazich. He worked for KNBR radio station in San Francisco. In 1967, he was thirty-six and had had no difficulty getting to be one of the media witnesses to the execution. Ronald Reagan had been Governor at the time.

'What was it like?' I asked.

'I'll never forget it. It was one of the most dramatic moments of my life – watching him. There were twenty-four of us in the witness room. Tonight it's about fifty. I was pressed up against the window of the gas chamber. I wanted to get a good view. I had a front row seat. Mitchell was a big and tough looking guy, and he had to be virtually dragged into the gas chamber. He was barefoot and dressed in prison blues. They had to pretty well force him in there and strap him down. He did not want to go in there. I can tell you that Aaron Mitchell was frightened to death – excuse the pun – when he got to the chamber door.'

'I can understand that.'

'I wasn't surprised,' Lazich went on. 'After they strapped him in and closed the door, I tried craning my neck to see the cyanide pellets being lowered into the acid vats under the chair. But I couldn't see them. There was a lot of pushing to get the best view. What I remember most vividly is his head started to bob up and down. Somebody said they heard him say he was Jesus Christ – I didn't hear that. After about sixteen minutes the warden came out and declared he was dead.'

'What about the others?'

'Some of the reporters stayed back from the windows. They didn't want to look. But nobody was actually sick. A lot of my colleagues didn't want the assignment. It was a kind of feather in my cap at the time. I wanted to do it because I'd never seen something like that before. I'd like to be in there tonight – but I lost out on the lottery.'

Like Lazich, I was a bit disappointed not to be one of the official media witnesses to Harris's actual execution. Why? A morbid sort of curiosity, I suppose. The condemned prisoner story has fascinated the public imagination ever since Crito wrote up his last conversations with Socrates. Death has always been a crowd-puller. The reason Roman spectators watched gladiators mauling each other to death, or Lazich again wanted to press his face up against the glass of the gas-chamber, is to be able to walk away into the warm evening air with the comforting feeling of being a survivor.

Executions, however, are meant to invest death with moral point. America's obsession with capital punishment when the practice has been abandoned by most of the industrialised Western world cannot simply be explained as fear of an ever-growing crime rate. Part of the modern appeal of executions in America is that they provide a communal focus for evil in a society where confidence in traditional sources of comfort against life's uncertainties, such as religion and the law, is at a record low. Executions offer some illusion of order in a world that may seem to be spiralling out of control. They also provide an element of social catharsis by reassuring the public that the system is working. The execution of Robert Alton Harris coincided with the final days of the Simi Valley trial of the four LAPD officers charged with beating Rodney King.

There must have been around eighty journalists confined inside the old prison theatre. You could tell, without asking, who most of the eighteen official media witnesses were. They were either rather nervous looking – unwell looking, I should say – or else they swaggered around together in little huddles trying not to look smug. Those who weren't on the witness list sat around like football team reserves who knew they hadn't a chance of getting a game.

In an attempt to get *The Times* a place in the witness chamber as a 'foreign press representative' I had been told by the Warden of San Quentin to write to Douglas Willis, president of the Capital Correspondents Association, based in

Sacramento, whose organisation was responsible for allocating the media witnesses. Despite pointing out that *The Times* had reported on historical executions for over two centuries, my letter got me nowhere. No foreign press would be included in the media witness pool, although they agreed to let me inside the walls with the other American media.

Later that afternoon, we received our first – of many – briefings from Vernon Crittendon, San Quentin prison's media spokesman. A softly spoken black man in his mid-thirties, Crittendon stood up on the old prison theatre stage and made a short announcement.

'The mood on Death Row is rather solemn right now. There's very little conversation between staff and inmates. It's relatively quiet – they're all on "lock-down", that is they are restricted to their housing units and are not involved in their daily programme.'

'Has Mr Harris said his last goodbyes?' asked a reporter.

'Yes. As he passed other Death Row inmates earlier this morning, he began to give what staff thought were his final goodbyes.'

As the afternoon dragged on, I started to feel restless. Outside on the tarmac, we were restricted to a taped-in area that stretched for about fifty yards and was grid-locked with TV satellite trucks. Looking out across the San Francisco Bay, as the late afternoon light began to turn a streaky mauve, it occurred to me that San Quentin looked quite an easy place to escape from – if you could swim. I asked a freckled young uniformed guard whether anyone had tried recently.

'People are always escaping,' he slurred.

'Swimming?'

'Somone tried that once. We pulled him out. Usually they just walk away – we had one recently. People don't like it here. They are on one of the work crews, and they just walk off.'

'So it's not a very secure prison.'

'No prison is secure – not even Alcatraz.'

I walked over to the official snack-bar. They had a special execution menu set out on green photocopy paper. In addition to a choice of gastronomic sandwiches there was a sizzling barbecue serving hot-dogs and polish sausages for $3.50.

'We were told no alcohol,' the chef told me. 'And no burgers. They thought it would be distasteful.'

Every time I went back inside the old prison theatre, stepping over thick reels of TV cable, boom poles and camera equipment, there was usually at least one TV reporter – often three at the same time – talking to camera with their back to the prison.

We were handed a 'San Quentin News Update' press release which detailed Harris's last meal request. The food order had, in fact, been placed two weeks before.

21 piece Kentucky Fried Chicken (extra crispy)
2 large pizzas, no anchovies
6-pack Pepsi
1 bag jelly beans
1 pack Camel cigarettes

By a grim coincidence, the lead story on KCBS Channel 2 – Robert Alton Harris's execution – was followed by a commercial which featured a condemned man being asked what toppings he wanted on his Tombstone pizza. This of course was wholly inappropriate. Harris had expressly ordered two Dominos pizzas. They arrived cold but were re-heated.

Shortly afterwards, Steve Futterman, NBC radio's veteran LA reporter bounced up to me like an excited hare.

'Heard the news?'

'What news? An execution stay?'

'No, no, no. Benny Hill has just died. Just heard it on the network news. BIG story.'

I had never much liked Benny Bill.

'Did you know that Harris is a big Benny Hill fan? In fact, he got real depressed when he heard the news.'

Futterman broke off into a loud cackle.

It was strange. It wasn't an especially funny joke. But the little crowd of reporters huddled around Futterman chuckled loudly. Like Orwell, who found himself unable to stop laughing after witnessing the execution of a puny Hindu in 1931, I couldn't help laughing as well.

Shortly after 6.30p.m. came the first execution stay of the night. Issued by a lone judge at the Federal Appeal court, the appeal contended that Harris had been denied adequate legal assistance at his 1979 trial because the defence had not thoroughly investigated his psychiatric history. It also contested that new evidence could prove that Harris's eighteen-year-old brother, Daniel, may have shot one of the two teenagers.

Harris learnt about the execution stay whilst watching the news on his TV set. Having spoken with Harris after bringing him his last meal at 8.15p.m. – whilst Attorney General Dan Lungren frantically attempted to get the stay overruled by the US Supreme Court – Vernon Crittendon said: 'He seems to be very well composed. He is still able to 'kid around', although he seems somewhat withdrawn.'

' "Kid Around"?' asked a serious-looking reporter with thick glasses. 'What exactly do you mean?'

Crittendon paused for a moment to collect himself.

'He seemed quite light hearted – but I also felt that he sensed the seriousness of the situation he is in. When I brought the food in, he was joking around about which he wanted first – food or mail? He ate the pizza first.'

'You say he was eating the pizza,' shouted a reporter. '*How* was he eating it?'

'Big bites. Big bites.'

The second appeal came at approximately 10.15p.m. Signed by ten Circuit Court judges it asked for a vote to consider arguments as to whether death by lethal gas constituted 'cruel and unusual punishment'. The following legal wrangling between San Quentin, the US Supreme Court and the 9th US Circuit Court of Appeals made a mockery of the US legal system. At 11.20p.m. the US

Supreme Court lifted the first stay of execution. Shortly after midnight, the scheduled time for Harris's execution, a third stay was issued by the Circuit Court – contesting the use of gas in the chamber as a possible environmental health hazard.

For the next two hours, we simply sat – or slept – and waited. The old prison theatre now resembled a refugee camp, with reporters asleep on desks, under tables, and lying across rows of chairs. Bodies were curled up in the old stage curtains. People read novels, played cards, or clacked away on their lap-tops. There was the occasional whirring of an electric razor, before some reporters filed early reports for their network's breakfast news.

At 3.06a.m. the US Supreme Court finally lifted the two remaining stays and it was announced the execution procedure would start. Wasting no time, the media witnesses were quickly rounded up and told to get inside the clapped-out prison mini-buses that would take them to the gas-chamber. They were instructed to leave their wallets, credit-cards, pens, paper and notepads behind. *En route* to the chamber, one of the buses crashed into a gate-post.

'Keep going! Keep going!' ordered the senior prison officer. The important thing was to get to the witness chamber before another stay might be issued.

According to witness Dan Morain of the *Los Angeles Times*, they were then ushered into an employee lounge where they were each searched (including the inside of their shoes), and handed a legal pad of white paper and a pencil. The gas-chamber itself was bathed in an eerie luminous green light. On the other side of the room were the witnesses of the family of the teenagers that Harris shot. These included the sister and mother of John Mayeski and San Diego police officer Stephen Baker, who had arrested Harris two hours after his son had been shot. Detective Baker stood in front of the chamber where Bob Lazich had pressed his face against the glass in 1967. At 3.49a.m. Harris, dressed in a blue workshirt and jeans, was brought in to the chamber by two prison guards. He was quickly strapped – twice around his chest, each arm and each leg – into one of the two chairs, during which time he nodded and gave a thumbs-up sign to his brother. He appeared to be smiling.

At 3.57 a.m., witnesses heard the gurgling sound of the water gushing into the vat under his perforated seat. Just as the lever releasing the cyanide pellets was about to be pulled, the chamber echoed with the ring of a telephone.

'Oh my God!' a witness cried out.

When it was established that another stay of execution had been issued, just seconds before Harris was about to smell the cyanide fumes, Crittendon ordered the witnesses to move out of the chamber. Harris was quickly unbuckled from his chair by four guards and led back to the 'death-watch' cell fifteen yards from the chamber.

I had been standing on the old theatre steps talking to Kip Kendle, spokesperson for the California Department of Corrections, moments before the execution was interrupted. We assumed that Harris was probably now dead.

Kendle's cellular phone bleeped.

'Okay,' he said, his face unemotional.

'Right. I was going to ask the obvious question.'

'Okay, okay, is there any other detail? . . . Okay, I'm not surprised at that. I'll go make an announcement.'

Kendle hurried up onto the old theatre stage.

'I have a brief announcement to make,' he said quickly. 'We have information that there has been another stay by a federal judge.'

There was a loud groan of despair from the media.

'Was Harris in the chair?' asked a reporter.

'Err . . . I understand that Harris was in the chair.'

Once the witnesses were shuttled back to the old prison theatre, several described the surreal spectacle they had witnessed as being, indeed, like a scene from a horror film.

Exchanging stories on the steps outside the theatre were two female witnesses who appeared to be shaking with after-shock. 'It was outrageous,' shrieked a female local reporter. 'It was, like, unbelievable . . . it was outrageous.

You couldn't write a better script. You couldn't make this shit up. We had to sign these things. I was so nervous I didn't know what I was signing. I mean I never recognised my handwriting. I didn't know whose it was. Then this councillor guy – he thought I was so pathetic he stayed with me the whole time. I held onto him.'

Futterman, his eyes alight with excitement, bounced up to me again.

'Unbelievable,' he exclaimed. 'Of course this is how California has to execute someone. In true Hollywood style.'

After the initial drama had quietened down, people went back to sleep, back to their books or wrote their stories. Most were resigned to the expectation that Harris would not be executed that night. There were, indeed, bets being made. At 5.45a.m., however, a sudden announcement was made that the US Supreme Court had lifted the fourth stay and in an unprecedented move had stipulated that the 9th Circuit Court could not issue any more stays without its permission. 'There is no reason for this abusive delay,' the order said, 'which has been compounded by last-minute attempts to manipulate the judicial process.'

The witnesses were rounded up so fast that two very nearly got left behind. Once back inside the employees' lounge, they hardly had time to pick up a pad of paper let alone be searched before they were marshalled into the witness chamber. Harris was led in for a second time. This time he looked frightened. His head was bowed. His eyes flicked nervously and painfully across the assembled audience. There was a sudden rush of water gurgling under Harris's seat, and the signal was given to commence the execution. As he sat, motionless, strapped down, his head suddenly keeled back to look at Detective Baker and mouthed 'I'm sorry'. The police officer, standing right over him, nodded.

He sat still as the lethal gas clouded around him, breathing in quick gasps. His eyes rolled for a moment and he convulsed for about thirty seconds before his head flopped forward. According to witness Jerry Wilcox his face then turned red and a vein stood out on his forehead. His cheeks puffed up as if he was struggling for breath. After several minutes his head dropped forward, only to suddenly rise again slowly. He then seemed to lose consciousness. The red light of the video camera ordered to film the execution glowed against the thick glass of the gas-chamber. At 6.21a.m. Harris was declared dead.

It was now after dawn, with the early morning sun above the San Francisco Bay, bathing the prison in a misty light. Back inside the old prison theatre, the witnesses – many of whom looked sick and had trouble collecting their thoughts – answered more questions. I was surprised by the level of detachment – American Journalism School – claimed by a number of the witnesses. When asked what it was like to watch the planned death of another human being, UPI's Chris Crystal said: 'I couldn't allow myself to feel anything. I felt it wasn't the time to make any kind of judgement or for floods of emotion . . . So I didn't feel anything other than trying to get the time straight'; 'It wasn't as bad as I thought it might be' said another; 'I was there to be a witness and just describe what happened. I really don't know how I felt.'

Finally, the Warden of San Quentin Prison, Daniel Vasquez, emerged from the back-stage of the old theatre and made a brief formal announcement of Harris's death. He ended by revealing the words – from the film *Bill and Ted's Bogus Journey* – by which Harris asked to be remembered: 'You can be a king or a street-sweeper – but everybody dances with the grim reaper.'

11

Postcard from South-Central

UNTIL THE EARLY EVENING OF Wednesday 29 April 1992, my knowledge of South-Central Los Angeles had been limited to lounging for an hour and a half in a crushed velvet French cinema seat watching John Singleton's *Boyz N' the Hood* on a rainy afternoon at the 1991 Cannes Film Festival. I had it noted as a place to avoid.

I was in my office at Fox TV when the Simi Valley – a lily-white middle-class suburb forty miles north of LA – jury returned from deliberating on the four white LAPD officers charged with beating twenty-five-year-old black motorist Rodney King on 3 March 1991. One of the mail-room boys poked his head through my door.

'The Rodney King verdict is just coming up,' he said. 'It's on live in the newsroom.'

I hurried down the corridor. Editors, reporters, cameramen and technicians had stopped working and were staring at the flickering images of Judge Stanley Weisberg and the emotionless and down-cast faces of officers Stacey C. Koon, Theodore J. Briseno, Timothy E. Wind and Laurence M. Powell on several wall-mounted TV sets. There was a strained silence.

The minutes dragged on. For nearly fifteen minutes, the only sound in the tense courtroom was Judge Weisberg turning the pages of his papers.

Over the three months of the televised trial, I had seen so

many repeated clips from the eighty-one-second world-famous Rodney King beating video that I had become semi-anaesthetised to the sight of his writhing body being clubbed like a wounded animal on the tarmac.

Shortly after 3.15p.m., ten 'Not Guilty' verdicts were read out by the court clerk to Judge Weisberg. Each successive 'Not Guilty' ruling drew gasps. On one remaining assault charge against twenty-eight-year-old officer Laurence Powell, the jury was dead-locked. A charge of nervous tension rushed through the newsroom.

After the verdict was announced in Simi Valley's Courtroom Number 3, the four elated police officers – who had not always been on good terms with each other during the trial – threw up their arms and hugged each other and their lawyers.

Their joy, however, was short-lived. As the defendants and attorneys attempted to leave the court-house, they were ambushed by a chaotic stampede of panicking reporters, TV crews, trial junkies and locals. Abuse was shouted from hundreds of angry black protestors. Some hurled stones and gravel at Powell.

The Fox newsroom quickly resembled a war-zone command-centre. Helicopters were ordered on the phone with a casualness normally reserved for take-away pizzas. All reporters were called in. All leave cancelled. Researchers dispatched to the Fox vaults for footage of the Watts riots of August 1965. Until that night, the Watts riots in South Los Angeles had been the worst city violence in modern American history.

In one of the studio dressing rooms along my corridor, I noticed a veteran news reporter trying on a bullet-proof jacket. A pile of multi-sized navy blue 'Point-Blank' body-armour suits were heaped on the floor like life-jackets on the jetty of a South of France water-skiing school. 'Help yourself,' he said. 'If you're going out tonight, you'll probably need one.'

'Thanks,' I said.

Designed to withstand the impact of a Magnum bullet at close range, the jackets were alarmingly heavy. I tried one on for size. Glancing at myself in the stage-mirror, framed by a dozen 100-watt bulbs, I decided I looked like a deflated Michelin Man. I passed on the offer.

By 6p.m., hundreds of enraged blacks had begun venting their anger over the verdict with a rowdy demonstration outside Parker Center, the downtown LA headquarters of the LAPD. As the light began to fade, the crowd became increasingly belligerent. They demanded LAPD police chief Daryl Gates's resignation.

Despite having lived in LA for seven months by now, I was still renting my car from Hertz. I usually swopped them about every fortnight at Burbank airport. On that warm and blancmange-pink early evening on 29 April, I had a gleaming navy-blue two-seater Ford Cougar with an electronically adjustable driver seat, that whirred up and down like a de luxe dentist's chair. With its sharply pointed aerodynamic nose and flashing high-tech computerised LED dashboard controls, it felt like the cockpit of a small fighter jet.

I pulled my Hertz map of downtown Los Angeles from the glove-box and closely examined it in the Fox car-park. According to Pete Demetriou of KFWB News 98, who was live at the scene, the 'incident' had now moved to the intersection of Florence and Normandie avenues. Several hundred blacks, many armed with bottles, had now assembled at this junction. I had no idea where either Florence or 71st Street were other than they were somewhere in the heart of LA's South-Central gangland. My Hertz tourist map of LA ended worrisomely at 23rd Street – 48 blocks short of the trouble-spot.

As I sped south along the Hollywood 101 Freeway, the road was unusually empty. Across the steel dividing barrier, the other side of the freeway – heading north – surged with the roar of speeding, swerving traffic.

I exited and swung right onto Normandie; the neighbourhood took on the desolate feel of the outskirts of

Manilla in the early hours of Sunday morning. Pressing down on my central-locking switch with a reassuring clunk, I clattered over an old railway track and began driving past hastily boarded up stores. Even the palm trees seemed scraggy, casting long shadows on the side-walks which were swelling with gangling black youths by the minute. Some were burning American flags or holding up bed-sheets on which were crayoned 'No Black Justice'. A muscular man in cut-off jeans was thrashing a liquor-shop door padlock with an iron scaffolding pole.

Nobody looked in the mood for an interview.

Driving under the 10 Santa Monica Freeway, shaggy gourds of jungle-like vine hung off the graffiti-scrawled over-pass. Continuing down Normandie, I passed Adams Boulevard. I was now south of 23rd Street – off the page of my Hertz tourist map. The light was fading fast. As I headed on along the empty road I resorted to navigating by the flashing green and red tail-lights of two low-flying media helicopters that were swooping in the sky up ahead like angry piranhas. Their blades sounded like the roar of a powerful chain-saw.

On my radio, I could hear Pete Demetriou's voice drowned out by the sound of menacing shouting in the background of his broadcasts.

I pressed on, thinking it could only be a few blocks before I came across the usual circus of police-cars with their blue siren lights flashing, road-blocks and TV satellite trucks. But there was no sign of any media on the ground. Only an army of blacks that seemed to emerge from nowhere, overspilling onto the road. For about a mile I hugged up behind the bumper of an LAPD police car until it suddenly – at about 60th Street – swerved into a car-park, screeched around, and sped back in the opposite direction. All police in the vicinity, I later discovered, had been pulled out to a bus terminal at 54th Street and Arlington – 30 blocks away.

With each block – I was now on 68th Street – the sea of black youths swelled larger. There were almost no other cars about. Switching on my headlights, I twiddled nervously with my car-radio. The radio crackled and then I heard a noise like a microphone being dropped to the ground, followed by some hasty running along a pavement.

Still gasping for breath, Demetriou said: 'I can see a man lying ahead of me on the road. He has been dragged from his truck and beaten. He is just moving. I can see him moving. His face is covered in blood. He's trying to get up. Nobody is helping him.'

The TV helicopters above me were now broadcasting the scene live. At 6.30p.m. KTTV cameras zoomed in on the half-dead body of thirty-six-year-old truck driver Reginald Denny, sprawled on the road. After he had pulled up at an intersection, several blacks surrounded his eighteen-wheel lorry, pulled open the driver door and dragged him out onto the road. He was knocked to the ground, kicked repeatedly in the face and had a fire extinguisher smashed over his skull. As he lay on the asphalt, he was pick-pocketed by one of the black youths – who then did a victory dance.

The radio spluttered: 'The situation is getting out of control. Rocks are being thrown at us. I'm getting outta here . . .'

KFWB cut to commercials.

After helping a Korean woman, whose nose had been split open by a rock hurled in her face, to safety, Pete Demetriou ran back to his KFWB pick-up truck, threw his gear in the back and started the engine.

Then he heard a smash on his door and the squeal of grinding metal. Two burly black men were pulling on his door – one attempting to lever it off with a tyre-wrench.

Pete Demetriou – a seasoned LA reporter and former war correspondent – was well prepared. Pulling out a .37 Magnum, he pointed it at the forehead of the man with the tyre-wrench.

'Come a step closer,' Demetriou informed him. 'And I'll blow your fucking brains out.'

It was now difficult to drive on because of the numbers of angry blacks swarming onto the road. By the overgrown lawn of a crumbling episcopal church, I had to slow right down. Ahead of me a car was on fire and a crowd were heaving on the metal security grid of a liquor store.

A fat teenager with small, blood-shot eyes and a gold necklace dangling around his trunk-like neck sat on my bonnet. He grinned goofishly at me – bouncing up and down as if trying out the springs on a showroom bed. By now I was nearly surrounded by blacks.

'What y'a doing here?' he scowled. 'Hey, man, see this . . .'

In his fat hands was a rock the size of a basketball.

'This is from Rodney King.'

The rock bounced off my bonnet with a heavy clatter. To my left, a surly teenager in a nylon tracksuit, his eyes seething with hate, hurled another rock at my windscreen. It smashed, showering me in splinters of glass, with the concrete missile flying past my head.

Instinctively, I screeched the car around 180 degrees in a rather poor imitation of *Starsky and Hutch*. I could hardly see anything. A volley of rocks and stones followed, clattering on the car as if someone was attempting to play the drums on a set of dustbin lids with a baseball bat. Pressing my foot right down I drove down the wrong side of the street for five blocks at about 60mph – weaving and swerving my way through the thick crowd on the road, pursued by some unsavoury-looking characters in the South-Central equivalent of a customised Ford Capri, an old Pontiac Firebird.

As my pursuers honked their horns and yelled at the mob in the streets for support, I concentrated on speeding north, through what now seemed a wasteland, a no man's land that seemed to divide a city by race. I picked up a rock that had smashed through my passenger window and knocked a hole through the windscreen to see where I was going. I switched my head-lights onto beam and flicked on my hazard-warning lights.

The black Pontiac had trouble keeping up with my Cougar. One of the passengers, dressed in wrap-around sunglasses and what looked like a Crips gang head-scarf, leant out of his tinted window and fired several shots at me.

Crack. Crack. Crack. Crack.

He was a lousy shot.

Crack. Crack.

He missed again.

Nobody was paying any attention to red lights – or to any other laws. There were no police anywhere. Nor any whites. Had I knocked somebody over – killed someone – as I sped away, I wouldn't have stopped. Wouldn't have cared. I would have driven on. Faster. LA does that to you.

After about twenty blocks, with the Pontiac skidding to a halt outside a burning petrol-station, I swung under a disused railway bridge and – phew! – onto the Santa Monica Freeway.

As I drove back into downtown LA, the protest outside Parker Center had turned into a street fight, with police cars turned over and kiosks set alight. An army of helmeted riot police finally moved in and broke up the violent crowd. The thick line of riot-police that remained guarding the building seemed more suited to South Africa than Southern California. The mob surged west, down 1st Street – banging on my new car roof as I attempted to pass them. It was like a Dadaist safari park trip – grinning faces squashing their noses up against my windscreen and windows, pulling on my door handles and shouting abuse.

This crowd seemed to be in more of a party mood. They weren't anything like as dangerous-looking as the South-Central LA gang-members I had encountered earlier. Many were Latinos and didn't look as if they had spent too much time worrying about Rodney King recently.

These were mostly opportunist rioters, or rather trophy hunters. Most scuttled away down back-alleys with their arms loaded not with brand new videos or CD players – they already had those – but with new Reebok sneakers, Levi jeans or as many six-packs of Mexican beer as they could carry. It was a shopping expedition. At a café on Vermont, I saw a black man sitting down to eat a huge steak while several youths emptied the till and slunk off with some mini-sized liquor bottles in their pockets.

By about 10.30p.m. it was no longer necessary to listen to the radio for reports of violence or looting – wherever I drove in the maze of Downtown streets, I came across shops with their windows smashed in and looters helping themselves to goods. When I poked my head inside a looted hi-fi and electronics shop on Pico, for example, I saw a thirty-something man dithering behind the counter.

'What are you looking for?' I asked.

He looked startled. 'You a cop?'

'No.'

'I'm . . . er,' he stuttered. 'I can't decide between these two games. D'ya know anything about Nintendo?'

'I don't,' I said. 'Take both.'

'Na,' he replied. 'I just want a souvenir.'

I didn't need any more souvenirs (I use the chunk of South-Central pavement that smashed through my windscreen as a paperweight). But one final image was branded into my memory as I headed back to my Sunset Boulevard office. Driving north along the eerily empty 101 Hollywood Freeway, I hardly needed to switch on my headlights. In an act that seemed to symbolise that evening, a number of palm trees along the freeway had been set alight and were blazing like forty-foot medieval cresset-torches.

I finally got back to my desk at around 11p.m. Walking through the near-empty Fox car-park, the moon glowed pastily through the dense fog of smoke swirling above the burning city. There was a message on my answer machine from Dennis Taylor, a senior editor on *The Times* foreign desk in London, left at 4a.m. GMT.

'Just a word of warning, William,' the message said. 'We've seen the TV pictures from Los Angeles – seems to be a bit hairy in South-Central, so *please* take care, and don't go around in dangerous situations just for local colour. You can watch an awful lot of it on the box.'

* * *

I didn't get much sleep that night. Not even to sleep for thirty minutes on the sofa in my office. It wasn't simply the LAPD who were caught embarrassingly unprepared for the worst urban unrest in America this century, it was also the world media. Lacking any sort of TV news staff presence in LA, let alone a camera crew or a West Coast bureau, the BBC in London resorted to some desperate emergency measures for their coverage of the riots.

'We know you're busy, Mr Cash,' said a friendly, if deeply anxious sounding, BBC producer down the phone. 'But if you could just say a few words on camera about what is happening in LA – for *Breakfast News* – we would be most grateful . . . we haven't got anybody on the ground you see . . .'

'But I'm not a TV reporter . . .' I said.

'Doesn't matter,' he interjected hurriedly. 'We just need someone to describe what the hell is going on in LA.'

'Okay then.'

'Do you know CBS Television City?'

He was referring to the megalithic West Coast headquarters of CBS Broadcasting – the oldest national TV network in America. Located in the heart of West Hollywood the stadium-sized TV City was almost impossible to miss. It was like asking a Londoner if he'd ever heard of the Post Office Tower.

'Yes.'

'Get over there as fast as you can,' I was instructed. 'We'll try to get a live satellite feed for the next news. I'll let them know you're coming.'

'You the guy from the BBC?' a burly looking producer in a flak jacket and baseball cap asked. He was from New York.

'Yes,' I replied. 'I think so.'

'You'll be on in five minutes – take a seat.'

'Hungry?' he said pointing to several giant pizza boxes by his desk.

'No, I'm not,' I said. 'But I would like somebody to tell me what I'm supposed to do?'

'What do you mean?' he exclaimed. 'You're the BBC aren't you?'

'Not exactly,' I said. 'I'm sort of temporary BBC.'

'Just sit in the chair and talk,' he said. 'Want any make-up?'

I looked at myself in a mirror. It was not a pleasant sight. I was unshaven, my hair was uncombed and my chin, nicked by a splinter of flying windscreen glass, was spotted with dried blood.

'You've got three minutes.'

'Just pad out this,' I said, pointing to my chin.

I was told to sit in a high-standing director's chair. The idea was to get the 'CBS Los Angeles' newsroom logo in the background.

Suddenly I felt a cold hand running up my back.

'Undo your shirt,' a technician told me. 'Pull this cable through.'

That was my microphone.

Another technician squashed a plastic jack into my ear and handed me a volume-control.

I twiddled the knob.

'Los Angeles, this is London, can you hear us?'

'Yes,' I said 'Just.'

'One minute,' the producer said.

'Is that William Cash?' a voice said.

'Yes.'

'Nicholas Witchell here, we'll be going live in about a minute. Can you hear me all right?'

'Just about.'

'You've done this before haven't you?'

It wasn't the time to mention that my TV studio experience was limited to appearing on *Love Connection* at KTLA on Sunset. That had been a week ago.

'No, I haven't,' I said.

'It looks nasty out there. I'll just ask you to fill us in on the latest position.'

'Is it live?'

'Yes.'

I was beginning to quiver from nervousness. I was beginning to regret agreeing to go on. It was all a terrible mistake. I gulped down some water.

Apart from losing the sound at one point, my live 'link' went smoothly enough. Half an hour later I went on again.

I was just about to leave the CBS studio when the phone rang. It was for me.

'Hi,' said a confident English voice, 'I'm the ITN News foreign editor in London. I've just seen you on the telly.'

'Hello, there,' I said.

'We were hoping you might do a live link for the lunchtime news.'

I explained that I had quite a bit of writing to do.

'It would be a great help to us,' he said. 'We need this story covered. We've got absolutely nobody out there.'

I agreed to do a pre-recorded link.

Whilst I was being wired up again, the ITN foreign editor continued chatting amiably away. I had no idea who he was or what he looked like.

The phone rang again. The CBS news producer handed me the receiver.

'You deal with it,' he said. 'It's New Zealand television. They want somebody to do a satellite link out of LA. Our guys are way too busy. Give them sixty seconds if you want. And that's it.'

'Mr Cash,' chirped the phone. 'New Zealand here. Could you please do us a quick two-way?'

I explained that I was just about to do a link for ITN in London.

'What about straight after?'

He sounded desperate.

'I'd like to,' I said. 'But I've got a lot to do.'

'Mr Cash, please listen,' he went on, his tone rising. 'Los Angeles looks as if it's going up in smoke. A lot of New Zealanders have friends and family in LA. They want to know how bad it is. I mean it looks *bad*. How many people are dead? We don't know. We've heard it could be thousands.'

'About ten,' I said. 'So far.'

'I guess that's some good news.'

I had to get this man off the phone.

'I'll do a brief two-way,' I told him, 'in ten minutes.'

There was a technical problem with the ITN link-up. I heard in my ear-jack what sounded like the *Magic Roundabout* music played too fast. New Zealand TV had, in fact, bumped ITN off the satellite feed. I had no choice but to do the New Zealand link live. I kept my answers monosyllabic.

After apologising to ITN, I finally did the feed to London.

'It happens the whole time,' the unflappable ITN foreign editor told me afterwards, 'it's like a crazy game of Space Invaders.'

'I never realised.'

'Nice girl, isn't she?' he added breezily. He was referring to the news presenter (whose name I have forgotten) who had interviewed me. I had no idea what she looked like either.

'Yes. Very nice.'

'You should take her out when you're next in London,' he went on. 'Go out for a drink. Dinner maybe.'

'Take her out?' I choked.

ITN was beginning to sound like a highly unusual blind dating service.

'Yeah, she's a great girl,' he went on. 'Give me a call. I'll fix it up.'

'Right,' I said 'I will.'

On my way out, I wrapped a large slice of pizza in a paper napkin and placed it in my briefcase. That would be my supper. Just as the studio door closed behind me, I heard my name being yelled out.

'Mr Cash,' the producer shouted across the room. 'Line two. Pakistan television want a two-way link.'

'I've got to go,' I said. 'Tell them to try somebody else.'

International TV news was, I thought, a peculiar business. I managed to shave but not sleep before my final TV riots broadcast – for the BBC *Six O'Clock News.* After somebody called from London to say I looked like a street tramp, I changed into a suit.

'I thought the BBC always wore a tie,' was the rather gruff opening remark I received from the NBC executive producer.

'I don't work for the BBC.'

'Still, you ought to wear a tie – I'll see what I can find.'

He came back five minutes later with a navy blue Giorgio Armani tie patterned with white diamond triangles.

'Put this on,' he said. 'And come this way.'

To my bewilderment, this time I was given my own mini studio. It bore a close resemblance to a BBC *Panorama* studio. This time the ear-plug appeared to be a luxury model – the whole experience felt as if I had just been upgraded on an international airplane from economy to first class.

'This is the *Six O'Clock News,*' I heard in my hearing-aid. 'From the BBC.'

I was interviewed by Anna Ford and gave an up-date on the riots – there were now at least twenty-five people dead, a state of emergency had been declared and police had advised everyone to stay at home.

Afterwards, I received no offer of a blind date with her.

I did, however, have to make an important local phone-call.

It was now 10.30a.m. and I had a long-standing lunch engagement.

I dialled the number.

'Playboy Enterprises,' answered a bubbly female.

'Excuse me,' I asked. 'Is Mr Hefner's lunch party still on?'

'Oh, yes, yes, yes,' she replied. 'It's on. Limousine shuttle from the Beverly Hilton to the Playboy Mansion starts in an hour.'

* * *

A week after the memorable Playmate of the Year lunch I was to return to the mansion to interview Hefner. The day before, a glossy white package arrived on my doorstep. It was from Hef 's PR man, Bill. Inside was a one-and-a-half hour Playboy video entitled *Hugh Hefner: Once Upon a Time*. 'It's a new documentary about Hef 's life,' I was told down the phone. 'He wants you to get an idea of what he's really like.'

It began like a Playboy Channel soft-porn film. Shots of nude classical sculpture, a child on a swing, a twitching pet rabbit, a white peacock, fading to a leggy blonde Playmate – Mrs Hugh M. Hefner – slowly unhooking her orange and pink lace suspenders and panties as she smiles tantalisingly into the soft-focused camera. '*Reality or fantasy*?' drooled the deep-voiced narrator. '*For millions of Playboy readers, a fantasy*,' – fade to bare-breasted Playmate now sitting in an empty ballroom and staring aimlessly at a silver coffee set – '*but for* Playboy*'s publisher, she became his reality . . .*'

You need a loud voice to be allowed through the Playboy mansion's wrought-iron gates. A remote-controlled camera whirred out of a wall towards me. After hearing my name, a guard's voice instructed me to proceed up the drive and park behind the white Porsche. Leave the keys in the car.

In front of the sprawling ivy-clad house – an architectural cross between a 1920s Surrey golf clubhouse and a luxury Torquay hotel – is Hef 's Mercedes. He doesn't use it much. Doesn't go out much. Doesn't go *outside* much. But Kimberley is in the garden. She's gone for a bicycle ride. Not a long one – in fact, it's just around the front lawn. Weaving under the willowy trees, in and out of the classical statues. 'Hi,' she says as she wobbles past. She gets off and catches her breath. Huge aquamarine eyes, girlish cream dress.

I asked if she ever went bicycling outside the gates.

'No,' she says, 'only around the garden.'

Hef has just bought her a mega-dollar Malibu beach house retreat. 'Hef will never go there,' I was assured by a *Playboy* executive. 'It's a place for her – and the kids. To get some privacy. She never gets to do anything on her own with all those people (the mansion has a staff of around 50) milling about the whole time.'

The interview took place in Hef's by now familiar panelled study. Hef strides regally in, swathed in imperial-purple silk pyjamas and black-velvet smoking jacket. He makes straight for a mini-bar fridge and pulls out a gold can of Diet-Pepsi. For a man aged sixty-six whose lifestyle has always been the very model of self-indulgent excess, he looked remarkably fit and well.

I asked him about his wife.

'What particularly set Kimberley apart from the other girls is that she is a very classy lady and somebody I would want to have as the mother of my children,' said Hef briskly. 'I'm committed to this marriage. What I am seeking now is a safe harbour – I've ridden the waves and that time had its own excitement and pleasure.'

The former King of the Love Grotto – aged sixty, he estimated having slept with 'around 1,000 women' – says today that he is only too glad that his party is over. For all the claims of his 250,000-word *Playboy* Philosophy – bottom line: '*nice girls like sex, too*' – he now frankly admits that much of his former playboy life-style was superficial.

'Was it shallow? Sure, it was shallow,' he said. 'Most of life is shallow. It was an adventure. And I managed to re-invent myself at various times in my life. There's a wonderful line in *Lawrence of Arabia* when Omar Sharif says something like "It is written" and Lawrence says "It isn't written until I write it". I think I've done that with my life.'

Hef was sitting under the leaded window where he often plays backgammon. Behind him was a model of the 'Big Bunny', his famous DC 9 private jet with the elliptical bed – sold in 1974 for $4 million. As the mid-afternoon sun streamed through the glass, showering him in a soft focused haze, he soon settled into interview auto-cruise. Every few minutes he swigged on his Diet-Pepsi.

'Life has stages,' he continued. 'If I was still trying to keep alive my playboy life-style today that would be kind of sad and pathetic. If my life has meant anything it has not simply meant that one should pursue any number of romantic relationships – it means that one should have the right to pursue one's own individual dreams. I created an empire of dreams. The fact that my own dream had an obsessive side to it was because I was raised in a very puritan home . . .'

I put down my notebook and began nodding politely. After sitting through Hef's ninety-minute biographical video and reading up some old interviews, his script was familiar: 'In many ways I am the microcosm of the American experience related to the Victorian puritan part on one side and rebellion against that on the other . . .'

Hef went on like an old record. 'When I had my stroke in 1985, I called it a stroke of luck which gave me permission to lay down the luggage of my life. After the stroke I decided – hey, I've got another chance here. I think it was Scott Fitzgerald who said there are no second acts in American life [Hef 's favourite interview quote]. And I've managed to have a third act.'

Hef now spends much of his day 'in reflection' up in his attic study, surrounded by old trunks and mumbling into a tape-recorder. (He's been working on his autobiography for a decade. He's reached the chapter on Bonnie Arnstein, his former secretary and lover who committed suicide in 1974 after dragging *Playboy* into a cocaine-trafficking scandal.) Or else he will peddle away on his Tunturi exercycle in the master suite, screen an old *Flash Gordon* or Fred Astaire movie or play on the bouncy front lawn with his two young children. He likes to hop on a plastic yellow duck and ride his two-year-old-son Marston's personal merry-go-round.

'This is, without question, day by day, the absolute happiest time in my life,' he goes on. A dreamy smile lights his eyes. 'I am not driven as I was but I think I can look back on what I accomplished with great pride. I have managed to live a life that most people would kill for. I don't need to prove anything anymore. My place in history is rather clearly established.'

Part of Hef 's problem is that the *Playboy* myth is now a lot mightier than the magazine. A sticky fog of popular clichés lingers around Hugh M. Hefner. Yet for all the opprobrium that has been heaped on him over the years, his critics like to forget that in the sixties *Playboy* was one of the most original and best-written contemporary magazines around. *Newsweek* and *Time* both congratulated it on its editorial excellence. And for good reason.

With each chunky issue weighing in at an average of 300 glossy pages, contributors included: Saul Bellow, Woody Allen, P.G. Wodehouse, Kingsley Amis, Roald Dahl, Gore Vidal, Norman Mailer, John Updike, Robert Graves, John Paul Getty, Kenneth Tynan, Malcolm Muggeridge and Kurt Vonnegut JR. Prepublication serialisations included Ian Fleming's *You Only Live Twice* and Len Deighton's (*Playboy's* travel writer) *The Ipcress File*.

The literary standard began to slip when Hef, faced with growing competition from such lewd imitators as *Penthouse*, decided to go pubic in 1972. When you flick through the skinny and dated issues of today, it's easy to see why Hef should say he finds himself in this 'nostalgic state'.

But for all its wild-crazy success, he says he has always been a lousy businessman. 'I have nothing in common with people who make money. There are few business people who are my friends. I've never been interested in business. I'm a guy who doesn't give a shit about business. I'm an entrepreneurial genius who understands *people*.'

He describes himself as an 'incurable romantic' who has sought refuge from the real world in songs and movies (he is a fanatical Cole Porter and Dennis Potter fan) ever since he was a boy. His second favourite interview quote is from *Pennies From Heaven*, when the hero says: 'Somewhere there must be a world where the words of song are true.' That, says Hef, describes the sentiment of his life.

'There is a strong tendency in America that wants to bring their heroes down,' he sniffs. 'I have managed to survive and prevail. Standing for the things I have done, I have made enemies. That is the price you pay for writing your own life instead of having it written for you.'

Besides, he is used to criticism. When 1980 Playmate of the Year Dorothy Stratten was murdered in unsavoury circumstances by her first husband in 1981, a string of films and books (*Death of a Centrefold, Star 80* and Peter Bogdanovich's *The Killing of the Unicorn*) began casting sinister aspersions over *Playboy*'s 'empire of dreams' image. The malevolent picture that emerged was of the *Playboy* mansion as a Golden Cage – with the Bunnies kept under control like a gaggle of KGB-trained starlets.

But his fiercest critics have long been the army of radical feminists who have accused Hefner of reducing women to the level of sexual playtoys. It is a criticism that he is uncomfortable with. The difficulty is that Hef has always seen himself as being a champion of the oppressed, with *Playboy* being a forum for left-wing minority views and trendy political causes from anti-Vietnam to marijuana use.

In his biographical video, he attempts to counteract feminist odium by assembling favoured former Playmates to reflect on the 'happy days' they spent up at the mansion. 'It was a place where you could be exactly who you were – nobody would judge you,' remembered Monique St Pierre, Playmate of the Year 1979. 'There was this tremendous amount of freedom – and, oh boy, I just tried everything. I knew I would never get another chance in my life, and I was safe, so I said let's go – and I did.'

Quite. Hef is at his most acutely philosophical on the subject of natural beauty. 'These feminists are against beauty contests,' he goes on, 'And that's *bullshit*. We should be celebrating our sexuality. It's almost impossible to hear a kind word about pornography. But what is pornography? There's no violence in pornography. It's just people making love to one another. Is that what we are afraid of ?'

Hef took me on his Mansion Tour.

'I am a big fan of Tarzan. A lot of the good times for me now are revisiting the childhood stuff. I always loved the idea of living with animals and nature. And that's what I tried to do with *Playboy* – to say that beauty was everywhere – and that natural beauty is the nicest beauty of all.'

Hef has, indeed, created his own mini safari park. I refrained from inquiring into the health of his white llamas. One of the cherished herd, prized for its ability to step over frying nude sunbathers by the love-grotto swimming pool, had recently died – apparently after eating a monogrammed Bunny bathing robe.

After winding up his Jacobean-style oak staircase, and past a bronze sculpture of a female bottom (the 'Brass ass') which his staff use to display messages, we enter the master suite. It is scattered with toys, soft-porn videos, children's clothes, gym equipment, stuffed teddies and various sleeping cats.

His bed is the size of two billiard tables. By the head-board is a Concorde-style panel of dials and gadgets to control lights, curtains and temperature.

'Look, it's automatic,' he said with a grin, flicking a switch. With a whirring noise all the curtains close and the room is bathed in a cosy darkness.

Hef 's dressing room resembles a Mayfair tailor shop with a row of mahogany cabinets lined with dozens of identical pairs of silk pyjamas shipped over from Italy in a rainbow of colours: lime-green, black, turquoise, scarlet, orange, dark blue, chocolate brown, canary yellow.

'Do you always wear pyjamas?'

'It's absolutely true that I do spend almost my entire life in pyjamas,' he said. 'I wear them because they're so comfortable. And because I can get away with it.'

'How many pairs?' I asked.

'Gee – that's a tough one,' he said. 'At least a hundred. Probably twenty colours. It's the only decision I have to make at the start of each day.'

12

The Unloved Ones

It's a responsibility, I can tell you, and in various degrees every Englishman out here shares it. We can't all be at the top of the tree but we are all men of responsibility. You never find an Englishman among the under-dogs – except in England, of course. That's understood out here, thanks to the example we've set. There are jobs that an Englishman just doesn't take . . . We don't want any poor Englishmen hanging around Hollywood.

Evelyn Waugh: *The Loved One*

MATTHEW ANDERSON, AGED TWENTY-EIGHT, from Walthamstow, East London, who has lived in LA for the last five years, is one of many thousands of British living in LA in the nineties who would have little respect for such remarks. Each morning before breakfast he slips into his undertaker's outfit before setting off – or at least hoping to – on his 'Death-Styles of the Rich and Famous' tour of Hollywood in one of his two 1960s, eighteen-foot-long silver Cadillac hearses, modified with aircraft-style seating for eight. Requiem music pipes out of quadrophonic speakers.

His award-winning tour costs $30 and takes in the restaurant where James Dean ate his last hamburger, the hotel in which John Belushi overdosed on drugs and a faked copy of Alfred Hitchcock's death certificate. Despite having been acclaimed by CNN, the *Wall Street Journal* and dozens of British newspapers, business has become increasingly bleak. Following the riots, tourism in LA remains down by up to 50 per cent. His cars have started to break down, and worse, when it rains, the roof of the hearse leaks – so he has been sued by angered customers.

His only real competition in LA is, in fact, from another British entrepreneur, thirty-three-year-old Dennis Smith, from Ilford, Essex. Smith offers a chauffeur-driven Marilyn Monroe tour – touring such sites as the Brentwood apartment where her naked body was discovered – in a glinting 1959 Fleetwood Presidential limousine that once belonged to a Belgian diplomat who had it fitted with bullet-proof doors and a midnight-blue velvet interior. After buying the car for $7,500 and investing another $25,000 with a partner in rebuilding it, Smith was faced with the prospect of selling up when demand went down to an average of just one passenger a week. 'I'll be frank with you,' he told me. 'Business is bloody terrible.'

Like so many British lured to LA he has found the Californian Dream falling far short of his expectations.

There are around 400,000 British living in California. When the British Consul General told me this at a BAFTA cocktail party in his garden, shortly after arriving in LA from the Far East, he glanced somewhat uneasily around at the crowd of tanned and brightly decked out members of the British film industry gulping down Napa Valley chardonnay by his fun-sized swimming pool. Staring down into his glass of Scotch, he added sheepishly. 'Actually that figure is out of date. Most people don't register with us. We have really no idea how many British are living here – other than its an awful lot.'

Far from being put off by California's crippling recession, the number of British flocking to the West Coast with Dick Whittington hopes has rapidly increased in the early nineties. Their exodus has a close affinity to the expatriate rush to

Spain in the early 1970s. Southern California has, indeed, turned into the Costa del Sol of the nineties.

And it has brought along its inevitable share of undesirables. The example of Ian Spiro, a self-styled 'international commodities broker' who worked out of a bedroom in his family's expensive ranch in the San Diego hills is not untypical of the entrepreneurial expatriate type attracted to Southern California. He bought the *Daily Telegraph* at his local newsagent and gave the quiet impression that he was always about to strike a million-dollar deal on the phone. Exactly what he sold nobody was ever quite sure. No one knew that his French house had been re-mortgaged and his flat in Swiss Cottage repossessed, together with a boat moored in the Cote D'Azur. As a close friend commented: 'He was the kind of man who was financially up and down all the time.'

It was intriguing to observe the contrasting ways that his death, and the murder of his family, were covered by the US and British media. The Americans blandly and briefly reported the case as if it were a straightforward murder and suicide – which you didn't have to be Inspector Morse to work out – probably rooted in financial problems. The British press seemed glamour-struck by the fact that he lived in California. Despite the fact that Spiro had nothing whatsoever to do with Hollywood, the story was quickly invested with all the elements of a Tom Clancy novel – spy rings, poolside parties and a desperate search for celebrity neighbours. It was first thought that he had been kidnapped by an Arab hit-squad. Reality was doubtless less exotic. He couldn't afford to pay his $4,000 a month rent.

In trendy London media circles Hollywood is the nineties cultural capital of the world. A visit to Los Angeles is now viewed as cultural advancement. At a lunch party in the Hollywood Hills, Elizabeth Emmanuel – the dressmaker who designed the Princess of Wales's wedding dress – gave me an insight into British thinking about LA. 'Whenever I'm ill or just don't feel like going into work, I phone up the office and tell them to say I'm in LA. People are impressed.'

The numbers of British in LA began swelling in the 1960s when giant aerospace corporations like McDonnell Douglas employed thousands of British-trained engineers at their Long Beach factory, an hour's drive south of LA. Having been recruited through British newspapers, many ended up settling by the ocean in rent-controlled Santa Monica.

When the centre of the world's entertainment industry transplanted itself from New York to LA in the seventies, the British colony expanded with an influx of creative 'talent' – if that is the word – scurrying away from, in particular, the sinking ship of the British film industry. Yet few of the army of actors, producers or directors who have descended on LA are so naïve as to imagine that the streets of Hollywood really are paved with gold, knowing that the likelihood of becoming the next David Niven, David Puttnam or Ridley Scott is practically nil.

It is often assumed that most of the British in LA are involved – or want to be – in the film industry. But the turnover in small businessmen with get-rich-quick hopes is far greater than that of aspiring movie stars. Perhaps the worst hit by the recession has been the legion of now ruined British property developers who swarmed over to LA in the 1980s. Commercial property in California has slumped in value by up to 50 per cent in the last three years.

I was once invited along to the 'Colonial Club', a British collection of estate agents and property speculators who meet together once a month in the VIP section of a trendy pool hall on Sunset Boulevard. The night I went, the small gathering was relegated to the public bar – sitting huddled in a corner sipping glasses of mineral water. 'Shouldn't ask too many members what they are actually doing,' I was flatly warned beforehand by the member who invited me. 'Most are probably bankrupt or about to lose their jobs.'

To anyone brooding over their unpaid credit card bills in drizzly England, the superficial allure of LA is obvious. Petrol is around eighty pence a gallon, swanky restaurants and BMWs are roughly half the second-hand London price, taxes are comparatively low and the sun is always shining. Not forgetting the idea of a gaggle of Californian swim-suit calendar girls rubbing sun-oil into your back by a David Hockney-style swimming pool. Hordes of British flocked across the Atlantic to start new lives in LA when the exchange rate was nearly two dollars to the pound.

It only takes the most cursory of looks at the British colony in LA today to see that the days of any sort of pool-side paradise are long over. Santa Monica, with around 18 per cent of its 92,000 odd population being British, has the flaky and washed out feel of off-season Marbella. Its bay is polluted and in its huddle of half-empty and air-conditioned British bars you can keep up, via satellite, with the FA Cup soccer. A man was knifed to death, in broad daylight, not far from the door of The Kings Head, the best known British pub in the town.

* * *

After about five months of living in LA, still without having found any satisfactory home, and having slept on my office sofa for about as long as I could reasonably expect to get away with, I received a temporarily life-saving phone call from a *Times* executive editor in London. The paper was doing some sort of travel promotion offer to various cities around the world.

'Sorry to trouble you about this,' I was told. 'But would you mind spending a night at the Universal Sheraton. Check the place out. Write it up. All on expenses. Give readers some idea of what they can expect if they stay there.'

Would I *mind*? I didn't just spend one night at the Sheraton Universal. I was given a presidential luxury suite. Michael Jackson, in town to film a music video for his *Dangerous* album, was also in the hotel. The room, which looked out over LA, was larger than my entire Vine Street apartment. It had a vast bed and a large mahogany desk. Tourism was seriously down in LA at the time and the hotel was not completely full. I stayed in the suite for a month at a super-discounted rate of $45 a night.

But that couldn't last for ever. The next solution to my accommodation problem came when I overheard a middle-aged Englishman in a bar arguing in a loud voice about the plummeting quality of LA's famous nudist colony. He had a raffish air about him, with silvery hair, slightly flared trousers and, for some odd reason, was wearing a shiny pair of formal dress shoes with black satin bows on the front.

'I mean it's a disgrace,' he boomed in his Terry-Thomas voice. 'In the mid-seventies it was a civilised place to go for an afternoon's bathing. Now its full of punks and queers.'

The Englishman introduced himself and handed me his business card – Clement Von Franckenstein was engraved on it in thick black Gothic script.

I gave him a quizzical look, but said nothing.

'By the way,' he drawled before getting up to leave. 'Do you by any chance play cricket?'

'I do, actually,' I said.

'I think we may be a man or two short on Saturday. Fancy a game?'

Many people arriving in LA have scant idea of how long it can take to become successful. The career of forty-eight-year-old Von Franckenstein, an old Etonian whose father, Sir George Von Franckenstein, was Austrian ambassador to London from 1920–39 is not untypical. Having come out to LA in the seventies, after a disastrous start to his career as an officer in the Scots Greys, followed by failing to make it as an opera singer, it took him nearly *twenty* years of TV soaps, commercials and violent kick-boxing films, to get his recent break into major Hollywood films. Whilst the likelihood of Clem picking up a Best Actor Oscar in the immediate future remains small, the days of him being cast as the dead body in *Murder She Wrote* are probably over. His credits now include a hugely successful Jean Claude Van Damme action movie (which required Clem to work out for six hours a day for two months to get into shape) and such mega-budget movies as *Shining Through*, with Michael Douglas and

Melanie Griffith and *Death Becomes Her*, with Meryl Streep and Goldie Hawn.

I not only made my debut for the Hollywood and Beverly Hills Cricket Club through Clement Von Franckenstein but also ended up sleeping on a mattress on his dusty and bare wooden floor for a month before I – finally – moved into a house. (My mother arrived in LA and asked me where I lived. Nowhere, I said. Two days later she replied to an ad in the *Los Angeles Times* and I moved into a Hollywood Hills house with a view of the Hollywood sign.) Clem's bedroom was decorated with curled-up posters of old movies in which he had strayed into camera shot before his career took off, as well as a number of dusty Etonian house photographs and a picture of him in his Scots Grey's greatcoat. The *Daily Mail* has dubbed Clement the 'Baron of Beverly Hills'. 'I don't like using my title in Hollywood,' he said. 'It gives the wrong impression if you're a working actor.'

The Beverly Hills and Hollywood Cricket Club, for whom 'Clem' usually opens the batting and fields first slip, is a Hollywood institution. The sheer numbers of British arriving in LA in recent years had meant that, for some games, getting selected can be as tricky as getting into the I Zingari. It is run by the affable Lord Alexander Rufus Isaacs, a very successful thirty-six-year-old Los Angeles lawyer trained as a barrister in London who is also an active member of the Oxford Dangerous Sports Club. Mick Jagger (who, twice when I played, hit his first ball for six and was then promptly clean bowled), Julian Sands and TV cameras on the pitch are regular features of the games, which are played most Saturdays in the summer under the Hollywood Sign above Lake Hollywood. The cricketing standard, it has to be said, is abysmal.

The club-ground – in fact a dog-walking park – is mown once a week. Not with a sit-down machine, but with a manual rotary mower that needs to be pushed. Since my house in the Hollywood Hills is less than ten minutes' drive away, my garage has doubled up as a groundsman's hut. The house was owned by an entertainment lawyer – and manic vintner – called Martin Cohen, who lived next door. Not only did he have his own private vineyard and farm, with geese, ducks and turkeys that clucked away at all hours, but he also had one of the largest private wine cellars in California.

I furnished the house in an afternoon, buying out half the contents of an estate sale from a country house in Rio de Janeiro which was shipped over to LA. The only problem, of course, was that it soon began to take on the jaded look of a Welsh mountain youth hostel, doubling as an international post-office, thanks to the incessant stream of British visitors – 'I'm-just-passing-through-LA-can-I-have-a-bed?' I once had fourteen – or maybe it was thirteen, I lost count – people staying, which gave my drawing room the look of a Somalian refugee camp. Each morning, bodies were slumped on my cream sofa cushions and wrapped up in my Afghan rugs.

The trouble with so many Europeans descending on the city *en masse* is that LA, which has for so long liked to hype itself as the City of the Twenty-First Century, is turning into Losers' Capital of the World. The important difference between the British à la Mayle (his next book is rumoured to be about doing up a house in California), who have for so long been accused of invading and ruining places like Provence or Tuscany, and the British in LA, is that – hazarding a guess – about 90 per cent of those Brits who arrive on their Virgin flights at LAX to make their fortune are broke. And, often, not very talented.

And they often remain luckless – for years and years. I was fairly surprised to discover, for example, that the famous sixties British film actress Judy Geeson had recently been forced to work as a sales assistant behind the till of a health and body product shop in Santa Monica. She had to commute nearly forty miles a day from her house in the Hollywood Hills – which was faced with repossession – in a clapped-out old Subaru. Having once turned down a chance to earn up to $1 million a year with a Hollywood contract committing her to ten films, she was earning around £180 a week. After we had lunch one day our waitress had a problem operating the American Express machine. Seeing the girl was having difficulty, Judy jumped up and put the transaction through herself. 'It's all right,' she said, 'I do this every day.'

While the talented and lucky few – very few – do amass fortunes many more are miserable failures, spongers and escape artists who are, frankly, wretched national advertising material. The result is that a reverse discrimination against the British now seems to operate in California. A new strain of Anglophobia reverses the popular cliché of Americans loving English accents. The fact is that a good many British have been abusing American hospitality for years – and they're getting what they deserve. What does seem rather absurd is that while the Californian Dream is widely regarded as extinct in the US it seems to remain so alive and well in the leafy suburbs of Middle England.

* * *

My house in the Hollywood Hills was in the middle, I soon discovered, of a mini-British colony. I had not realised that David Hockney lived next door. After a few weeks, I sent him a note, saying that I was a young Englishman just moved in, and invited myself to tea. The next day I got a message on my machine.

'This is David Hockney speaking,' he drawled in his deep Yorkshire accent. 'Why not come for a drive tomorrow, down at beach?'

I swiftly accepted.

Noxious clouds of purple-black exhaust smoke swirled around a clutter of unstretched canvases and two-gallon paint tins stored at the back of David Hockney's Malibu cottage garage. Whilst the V8 engine of his leather swathed, Mercedes 500 SC sports convertible growled impatiently away, Britain's most famous living artist was hunched studiously over the LED programming controls of his ten-disc state-of-the-art Sony CD car stereo system. It pumps out 150 watts from *twelve* speakers.

After five minutes, Hockney raises his bleached head – his hair is the colour of fresh pop-corn – looks at me with a boyish grin and waves a hand-held remote-control device ahead of him. He swops his usual owl-rimmed spectacles for dark green sunglasses. The car's automatic drive gear is engaged with a noisy clunk. There is an electronic whir and the garage door is slowly raised like a mechanical theatre curtain. We roll out onto the dusty tarmac of the Pacific Coast Highway, into the baby-pink warmth of the Southern California early evening sunshine.

David Hockney's Wagnerian tour of the Santa Monica Mountains takes nearly two hours. Normally, it's quite difficult to stop Hockney from talking. He tends to be garrulous and argumentative. Like W.H. Auden, he likes either to work – alone – or to hold court at home, glass of red wine and cigarette in hand, firing off the odd expletive, flooding (some would say swamping) the evening table-talk with his eclectic knowledge, endless theories, opinions, well-polished anecdotes, quotes, self-mocking wit, mischievous gossip and crude jokes. But for the mountain tour he insists on silence.

With the Mercedes gliding along the winding coastal road, overlooked by towering cliffs, Hockney punches the CD play button with a vulgar smile. A ghastly, orchestral tune is piped out at ear-deafening volume: the American National Anthem. This prank is followed by a sub-popular classic rendition of the *Blue Danube*. Only when Hockney swings right up a narrow canyon, cutting through a rocky forest, does the Wagner begin – starting with the subtle grandeur of *Rheingold*, and then, as the mountain reaches its jagged peak, exactly as the blood-orange sun begins to sink into the ocean he blasts the *Entrance of the Gods into Valhalla* into the highest orbs of the Californian sky.

But a warning. Hugely enjoyable as this all was – magnificent acoustics, inspired cinematography – I was worried about the *driving*. As *Parsifal* accompanied our snake-like mountain descent, the dangers became obvious. The extent of Hockney's absorbtion in the music appeared to border on the mystic. As the light began to fade, the car weaved ever closer to the precipitous edge of the canyon. Whenever I glanced at Hockney, he seemed to have his eyes closed (in addition to keeping his dark glasses on). Sunk deeply back in his seat, both hands clutching the steering wheel, his buzzard-like face stared rigidly ahead. I noticed he had an unlit Marlboro cigarette hanging from the corner lip of his mouth for five minutes.

By now it's around 8p.m. We are sitting in the breakfast room of his Malibu cottage, only a few yards from the soft lapping of the Pacific on the silvery sand. The ocean shimmers through the glass like oils on a wet canvas. As he has been talking, the small room has slowly been plunged in Stygian darkness. No effort is made to switch on the lights. I can see almost nothing – just making out his dachsunds, Stanley and Boodgie, who sleep under the sheets in Hockney's bed each night, stretched out in front of the smouldering log fire. John, an unshaven, good-looking young Englishman who lives with Hockney – *officially* he is the gardener – is clattering around in the kitchen, mashing potato for the evening's cottage pie. Hockney is slouched deep into an armchair, engulfed in the hazy fumes of a 'vegetarian' cigarette.

'I'm not sure whether tragedy is a theme for painting,' he says with a melancholy sigh. 'Strauss always said "I thought artists were for providing beauty" and I must admit that I am very sympathetic to that attitude in my art in general.'

Matisse once said that he wanted his art to be as soothing as a comfortable armchair. When Hockney went to the Matisse exhibition in New York, a small picture caught his eye. It was a little vase of flowers with a bust on a table. And it was beautiful. Unbelievably beautiful, he thought. 'I looked at the date, and it was 1942. And, of course, Europe was ripping itself apart. But I thought, well, I'm *glad* he painted it. I'm glad that there was somebody just frankly ignoring that and making something beautiful from the world around him. I found it touching. And, sometimes, I think, well, maybe I have to do that now in some way.'

One of Hockney's reservations about England has always been that there are no shadows. He has always been drawn to the wide open spaces and rich colours of America. He has lived in Los Angeles since 1963, lured by the thought of visiting the seedy offices of *Physique Pictorial*. He once told me he's been buying his pornography in the same shop in LA for the last twenty-five years.

'How much do you think you've spent?'

'About twenty thousand. I have to keep buying more because people come round and steal them. The whole time. Friends drop round – and I have to make another trip again.'

His meeting with W.H. Auden was, in fact, somewhat awkward. This was due to Hockney – typically – dragging along various members of his entourage, including his boyfriend, Peter Schlesinger, and the artist R.B. Kitaj. 'Auden reminded me of a school headmaster,' Hockney recalls. 'He complained a lot about pornography, which I thought was amusing – I knew he was just being perverse. Anyway, when we left, I remember Kitaj's comment: "If his face is like that – I wonder what his balls look like?" '

But the way he lives now is very different. With at least thirty of his friends having died from Aids – 'I have watched them rotting away' he sighs painfully – a real shadow has been cast over Hockney's pool-side paradise. Coupled with the hearing loss that has made him increasingly anti-social, forcing him to only eat in half-empty, fourth-rate, restaurants so as to avoid crowds, and his recent suspected heart attack, which involved emergency surgery, after finding himself so tired and overworked that he began having to crawl up the steps to his studio, Hockney is now retreating back into his own time and space.

'I have always thought the world was a bit mad, frankly,' he says matter-of-factly. 'I see now that it probably always will be. I think you have to make your own version of it. I've made it here – I've made an environment for myself which I intend to stay in and do my work.'

It is, however, a private, somewhat dotty and comic world that seems increasingly removed from the popular clichés so often recycled in magazines. A long stop-off for *steak au poivre* lunch *chez* Hockney by the verandah of his Hollywood Hills house has now become a popular tourist attraction.

These days, the form is well established. Visitors get to see the studio (a converted concrete tennis court, painted blue, shrouded from the road by red pepper creepers and a pair of curtain-like palm trees); are shown his aquarium (cut-out plastic shapes of zebra-striped fish, dangling from bits of string) and – if they are lucky – hear him play the piano. Or rather, see his impish grin when, shortly into his recital, his two hands appear – and he reveals that it's just a trick tape-recording.

When he left Bradford Grammar aged sixteen, his headmaster wrote: 'He will be glad to be rid of the "figure of fun" and to establish himself as a sincere and serious personality.' But Hockney, of course, did no such thing. He has always loved playing truant, indulging in clever, attention-seeking games. Above his Canon Laser Copier 500 in his studio is a colour reproduction of a recent *Life* cover asking 'Who is God?' – upon which Hockney has mischievously transposed a raffish mug-shot of himself decked out in a thickly knotted seventies silk tie.

Unsurprisingly, perhaps, the steady shuffle of journalists, students, fans, assistants, lackeys, secretaries, camera crews, collectors, stragglers, gallery owners and boyfriends who always seem to be meandering through the house are happy accomplices to his colourful circus. I remember poking my head over the rickety wooden fence by his studio early one Sunday morning to find Hockney waving around two long paint-brushes, like giant sparklers, delivering an impromptu lecture about Isaiah Berlin's essay on Verdi to a sweaty trio of Beverly Hills racing cyclists, kitted out as if for the Tour de France – one of whom was his doctor – who happened to drop by on their way up the leafy hill.

Their attention soon wandered over the walls, which are decorated with a turquoise freize of colour laser collage prints of his closest friends. The vast studio is awhirl with creative energy. Blown-up photos of a grassy church-yard in Bridlington, Yorkshire, where his ninety-two-year-old mother lives, are slapped up next to child-like doodles of his beloved dogs ('They're dear, dear little creatures, you know'). The odd fax from the Royal Opera House, pleading penury, lays about, as do Polaroid snaps of grinning young men in pea-green trousers, pinching each others bottoms. Propped up above an old book called *The Costumes of Yorkshire in 1814* is a heavily crested Royal Academy certificate which he received on being accorded an honorary doctorate in 1992. 'You wouldn't believe it,' Hockney volunteers gingerly, his fingers twitching around the loops of his maroon polka-dot belt. 'They wouldn't even let me keep the bloody hat, as souvenir.'

Behind the piano in his kitchen are over thirty giant volumes of photographs, framing his life snap-by-snap. As a rule, he has only been drawn to subjects that have a meaning for him personally, i.e. close friends, lovers in swimming pools, his houses, or a road – such as the spaghetti highway of Mulholland Drive, which he uses almost every day. He is usually a slow-working perfectionist, and rarely does commissioned portraits.

Hockney's choice of living high up in the Hollywood Hills, flanked by multi-million dollar movie-star mansions, has nothing to do with any interest he has in the famous. He once went to Swifty Lazar's Oscar night Spago party but left as soon as he could. 'It was just so boring,' he told me. 'We just sat there and watched the thing on these TV sets – I'd have been better off sitting and watching it at home.'

He did have a party himself, some years ago, in his studio – but somebody stole an original painting he had done for a *Vogue* cover and he didn't even know the last lot of people to leave, which bothered him.

But he paints or draws every day and has a loyal nucleus of bohemian friends in LA. The most vivid example I can remember of the Hockney clan out in force was Christmas dinner at his Malibu beach house – me and a dozen or so evidently gay men. It was a Saturnalian evening. Somebody bought Hockney a Macmillan's *Visual Dictionary* in which everyone enjoyed looking up certain obvious and crude parts of the human anatomy. The book was passed around – amidst great whoops of laughter and excitement– like a decanter of port. After dinner Hockney sat transfixed for about half an hour, staring out at the ocean as the wood fire crackled in the late-evening breeze.

Despite the prodigious industry of Hockney profiles, documentaries and retrospectives, there has only been one biography, *David Hockney: A Portrait* (1988) by Peter Webb, which Hockney said he has never bothered to look at. 'I told him I'd never read it. He didn't believe me. But I haven't read it. Why should I? I found Webb a little bit humourless. When he used to phone me up – to check facts or something – I used to say, well, why don't you just make it up? I don't mind.'

Hockney also remains disenchanted with Jack Hazan's famous 1974 semi-documentary, semi-fiction film *A Bigger Splash*, which captured the frenzy of the early Hockney zeal, along with the chaos of his helpers and hangers-on. 'It's a portrait of me by somebody else. He got me to act a few things in it. I always thought it was a daft idea. When the film was finished, I thought it was rather humourless. He was filming at a time when my life was a bit topsy turvy [his break-up with Peter Schlesinger] and I regarded it as his work. If I had done a portrait of him, and he didn't like it – then, frankly, too bad. I wouldn't care.'

Hockney will occasionally curl up with his dachsunds on the sofa and watch a film like the *Thief of Baghdad*, with Douglas Fairbanks, or *Citizen Kane*, on his giant stereo television set.

I asked him why he so rarely went to the cinema.

'Welles used lots of perspective tricks with sets to get the effects he wanted. Nobody takes the trouble anymore – or even to think about it. The moving image isn't magical to us anymore. That is why I go on about the TV picture – and how bad it is. And why I rarely go to the movies. They just point the camera and pick up what's there.'

When he was a child, he says, the moving image was special. Now it's bland and ubiquitous, with the camcorder enabling people to make instant and incoherent movies. 'To me, films today are so *lacking* in space. The theatre and opera are thrilling because they are a spatial experience. The cinema just isn't. I do wonder whether it will ever be possible on the screen to present grandeur anymore. I am an incurable aesthete. Mass culture doesn't interest me much. I just assume that a lot of the things you do are for a small audience.'

Yet with the death of Francis Bacon, David Hockney's pre-eminent position in the contemporary art world seems indisputable. In January 1993, Hockney held a major new exhibition of new paintings at the André Emmerlich gallery in New York. The days of the Tate Gallery being able to pay just £2,000 for his exotically domestic masterpiece *Mr and Mrs Clark and Percy* (1971), are long over. His paintings have sold for over £1 million at auction.

He has a sardonic sense of humour. After he came back from the opening of his exhibition, I asked him if he knew who had bought the eight paintings he had offered for sale.

'Rich people,' he said with a grin. 'Very rich people.'

His development as an artist has much to do with his understanding of visual space – everything now is much deeper and, indeed, bigger. He spends much more time looking out at the Pacific than sunbathing by his swimming pool. In fact, in all the times I have been over at his Hollywood Hills house, I have never seen Hockney – or anyone else – showing any sign of using the pool, or frying out in the sun. The pool area has a distinctly neglected feel. Hockney's daily exercising takes place on one of his two professional automatic trotting machines – installed in his studio and the Malibu cottage respectively – upon whose rubber conveyor belts he runs for half an hour each day whilst watching breakfast television.

Since his hearing has deteriorated, he has developed an even more acute sense of space. 'I used to play a lot of music on the gramophone whilst I was doing other things,' he said. 'Now I don't like to. I either sit on my own and listen or it is not on at all. I actually *listen* to music, playing it quite loud. I hate background music. I probably always did.'

It is supper time.

'I must tell you,' he said as he finally turned on a light in his sitting room. 'I don't see myself as a celebrity – I'm not. Artists aren't. If I go out I always introduce myself by name. I assume people have never heard of me.'

13

The Graduate

As a seventeen-year-old, I cherished two ambitions about the United States. The first was to spend a warm summer evening at an American drive-in movie theatre, sitting beside a Californian blonde. The other was to spend time on campus as an American college student. I wanted at least one date with a cheerleader in my life.

To be honest, until September 1992, when my friend Simon Kelton moved in to share my house shortly before the start of his first term on the screenwriting graduate programme at UCLA's Film and Television School, I'd somewhat forgotten about all this. I'd met Simon in rather odd circumstances. We had been opposing team captains for the 1988 Oxford *v.* Cambridge Cresta Run Race in St Moritz.

One warm evening I visited the UCLA campus in Westwood for the first time – to see Ian McKellen in the National Theatre's tour of *Richard III.* Although the UCLA theatre acoustics were a disgrace (Simon and I could hardly hear a thing) what I saw around me – rows of tanned, tall, demure, ice-cream Californian blondes – certainly exceeded my most Paphian of teenage fantasies.

As we strolled through the floodlit and grassy campus, towards the car-park, my eye was caught by a small purple poster pinned to a tree opposite the Melnitz theatre. The flier advertised a new ten-week course, part of UCLA's Independent Film and Television Program, entitled 'Hollywood the Media'. Course 291 A was to be taken by mogul

Peter Guber (who green-lighted films like *Batman* and *Rain Man*), chairman of Sony Pictures Entertainment – which oversees both Tri-Star and Columbia studios – and Robert G. Friedman, president of worldwide publicity and advertising at Warner Bros.

'Hollywood and the Media' sounded like an interesting series of lectures. Guber and Friedman were exactly the sort of Hollywood brass who refused to return my phone-calls. Back home, I looked up course 291 A in Simon's bulging file of UCLA Film and Television School lectures. The directory came complete with an index of hundreds of 'Entertainment Industry' UCLA Extension courses for part-time students.

I was surprised, I have to admit, to find the 'Hollywood and the Media' course come under the heading 'The Role of Management in the Entertainment Industry'. *Management*? Ummm . . . an odd word to use. The syllabus, I read on, would focus on how the 'fixation of the media on Hollywood is equalled only by Hollywood's fixation on the media'. It would examine why, although the most successful films were seen by less than 10 per cent of the American public, 'the amount of time and space the print and electronic media devote to the theatrical release of motion pictures often surpasses the time and space given to Washington DC and the capitals of every other country on the planet'.

I had wondered about this too. I had written about it: the strange symbiosis between Hollywood and journalists. But what I had never been able to do was to get any sort of answer from the likes of Peter Guber or Rob Friedman. Probe too deeply, and . . . well, as I said, you don't get your calls returned. Simple. I had been warned about that. After just a few weeks of arriving in LA, I had lunch in the Carolco building on Sunset Boulevard with the president of one of the biggest international public relations firms in the entertainment business. At the end of lunch the PR firm president turned to me. 'William, there is something I must tell you about journalism in this town,' she said. 'People either last a year, *maybe* two – or else they stay for twenty. There is no in-between. No beating the system. The studios set the rules. You play their game – or you leave.'

The three-hour lectures would take place every Monday evening in the Knusden lecture hall on the Westwood campus. The reading list for the course required students to be 'thoroughly conversant' with *Daily Variety, New York Times, Wall Street Journal* and *Premiere* magazine – in addition to watching *Entertainment Tonight.* An attendance sheet would be circulated and 'missed classes for which there was no medical or other urgent excuse will result in the student's final grade being lowered by 5 per cent for each absence'. Classes began promptly at 7p.m.

This all sounded very intriguing. At Cambridge, on the infrequent occasions that I had gone to lectures, there were always a few unlikely looking people – middle-aged Open University students with library books bulging from Sainsbury's bags, the unemployed, pensioners, tramps, the odd drunk – sitting quietly at the back. Technically, perhaps, they shouldn't have been there – but nobody protested.

Likewise at UCLA, nobody seemed to mind me sitting at the back. Guber and Friedman's 'Hollywood and the Media' course was not only one of the most popular of the term but also attracted some of the most interesting guest speakers. These included Jack Valenti, president of the Motion Picture Association of America, John Singleton, director of *Boyz N' the Hood*, Susan Lyne, editor-in-chief of *Premiere* and the *New York Times*'s Bernie Weinraub. Sony chief Guber, who paced around the podium like the senior partner of an East Coast corporate lawyer's firm, wore either a slick Armani – at least it *looked* like Armani – suit, or freshly pressed designer jeans, shiny black moccasins, college-style blazer and jazzy tie. The greying and bearded Friedman sat across the podium in an expensive grey suit. It always looked like the same one.

In the first class we were strictly informed that *on no account* should we attempt to approach Peter Guber – let alone pitch him any story ideas – in any capacity *whatsoever* outside of the classroom. In total, the classes spanned over twenty-four hours. I certainly didn't go to all of them. And I certainly didn't bother any of the written homework that the class was set. What interested me, however, was the point that Guber repeated, time and again. The reason, he said, the media was so obsessed by Hollywood was that both attempted to interpret the American 'situation', both dealt in manipulating perceptions and images – and hence, along with politicians in Washington who also sought to define how Americans perceived the world, the media and Hollywood were natural *competitors*.

'Movies are like bananas,' Guber explained in another lecture. 'When they come out they are beautiful and everybody wants them, but if they're not sold within a day or two they go rotten and nobody wants them. So we have to sell them fast.'

The major studios, Guber insisted, remained concerned only with the bottom line. If they think a movie will be profitable they'll make it – if not they won't. Artistic considerations did not figure. 'Fuck fair,' he repeatedly exclaimed. 'This is pure business.'

'Hands up those who think that Hollywood manipulates the media,' Guber asked the packed audience on another evening.

There was an embarrassed hush. Whispers and shuffling of notebooks. Roughly a third limply stuck up their arms. Nobody seemed to have thought about this before.

'This is the point I want to stress,' Guber smugly declared, his dark and curly eyebrows glistening under the hot spotlights. 'We don't manipulate the media – we manage it.'

Ah.

* * *

'Hollywood and the Media' wasn't the only course I sat in on that fall term. A few days before the beginning of term I spent two hours in the office of Professor Richard Walter, faculty chairman of UCLA's Master of Fine Arts Screenwriting programme – talking to him about a piece I was doing on the rapidly increasing number of high-flying young graduates from Oxford or Yale who were now turning down well-paid (and scarce) jobs as bankers or lawyers to seek their professional fortunes in Hollywood.

In the Wolfean eighties, of course, the irresistable destination of all those who insisted on being *where things were happening* was New York. In the nineties, however, with Wall Street badly hit by the economic slump, and the entertainment industry (i.e. Hollywood) now America's second biggest export – contributing $5 billion a year to the US balance of payments – LA seems increasingly to be the gladiatorial arena for the financial and deal-making *action*.

Screenwriting remains the fast-track way to become seriously rich. Unquestionably the easiest route is to win a place on a graduate screenwriting programme at one of America's three leading film schools: at New York University, the University of Southern California (USC) or – preferably – at UCLA. The once avant-garde USC boasts such late sixties students as *Star Wars* creator George Lucas; but the *Zeitgeist* has now moved down the freeway to the UCLA campus.

This, I quickly discovered, was not unrelated to the fact that under the aegis of UCLA screenwriting chairman, Professor Richard Walter, the programme offers a red-carpet entrance into the suites and Roladexes of Hollywood's most inaccessible and powerful studio chiefs, agents and players. Walter, a loquacious and lizard-thin forty-something ex-hippie is usually dressed in tight-faded jeans, brand new sneakers and a baseball cap covering his practically bald head. Described by the *Wall Street Journal* as the 'prime broker for one of Hollywood's hottest new commodities: student writers', Walter has inadvertently found himself in the position of Hollywood's equivalent to an MI6 Oxbridge talent scout.

Several times a week – especially on a Monday morning – he is called by top Hollywood agents wanting to know if he has read any saleable scripts. They want to know, quite simply, who the best student writers *are* – and their telephone/fax numbers. Of his fifty or so screenwriting students, two-thirds normally have agents (many with William Morris). Shortly before the start of one term, he told me, he had *six* agents from Michael Ovitz's top CAA agency (who represent the likes of Madonna, Dustin Hoffman and Kevin Costner) sitting around his chaotic office, earnestly quizzing him about the new intake.

'In the early eighties, I couldn't give away student scripts,' he said. 'Then we began to have some huge successes.' Former student Gregory Widen wrote *Highlander* as a class project (for which he received $400,000) and *Backdraft* (students are required to write at least five screenplays in two years); UCLA graduate Shane Black received $1.75 million from Warner Bros in 1990 for his latest *Lethal Weapon* script; others wrote such films as *RoboCop* and *Repo Man*. TV fortunes have been amassed writing for *Miami Vice, Cheers, Twilight Zone, LA Law* and *Star Trek: The Next Generation*.

In a town which is forever craving validation and legitimacy, the stamp of UCLA works as hugely effective cultural snob value. Another benefit is the network of highly placed student internships with the big studios, and with producers like Oliver Stone, that often lead to real jobs. As a result of this, several hundred applicants – many of whom are British graduates eager to escape the depression in London – are now applying each year for just fifteen places. Competition is so intense for the $24,000 a year course that Walter now has to be given legal advice before trawling through the year's vast piles of application forms and writing samples. 'Not much in this town surprises me any more,' Walter said, slouching deeply in his motel-style office sofa. 'But when rejected candidates start to sue . . .'

My friend Simon was one of the fifteen successful candidates for the Class of '92. After degrees at Oxford and Stanford, he turned his back on a career in the City, rented out his Kensington flat and took out a £30,000 overdraft to support himself before he sold his first script. He was, in fact, just one of around half a dozen contemporaries of his from

Eton and Oxford – such as Beechwood Canyon roommates Benjy Fry and Andre Burgess, who ran the Oxford Film Foundation together before enrolling at the USC and the American Film Institute (AFI) respectively – who decided to make studying the business and craft of movie-making the culmination of their academic careers.

'No writer in a garret ever had a five-figure overdraft,' he used to grouse whenever his statements arrived, 'but then again they couldn't get $1 million for doing their homework.'

The only snag with the UCLA Film and Television School is that a considerable number of students drop out because they have been *too successful*. Their agents have advised them that they cannot *afford* to continue with class work when they have six-figure assignments being offered by the major studios. Twenty-seven-year-old Rob Long, educated at Andover and Yale, dropped out in order to earn a fortune as an executive producer and writer of *Cheers*. 'Go for it!' Walter exclaimed after he was offered the job, despite Long having several terms of his course left. A friend of Long's, who also quit was called up and asked if he would read the script of Adrian Lyne's new film *Indecent Proposal* which needed surgery after William Goldman had been paid $1 million to do a re-write. The ex-UCLA student said he would fix it – but wanted to be paid the same as Goldman. When Paramount refused, tempting him instead with a new $90,000 Porsche, he simply walked out of the project.

Walter also does extensive script-surgery. The huge amount he is paid is, he admits, rather embarrassing. 'A lot of people approach me – the work is very lucrative,' he said. 'To be honest, my university salary is becoming a nuisance.'

After turning up with Simon on the first official day of term – meeting the professors, posing for some freshmen group photographs and familiarising myself with the Film and Television faculty, I quickly settled into the campus. After sitting a little uneasily through Walter's opening lecture, attended by hundreds of serious-looking students with the same squeaky Reebok sneakers and regulation blue-nylon knapsacks, it was clear that nobody objected. I soon relaxed.

In the hot, hazy weeks of that fall term, I spent quite a lot of time hanging around campus dressed in tennis shorts. It was enjoyable to be a student again. I attended whatever lectures and classes I felt like. I joined the UCLA library. I started to go out with a six-foot first-year history student. She had gone to the trials to be a UCLA basketball cheerleader – but was told she was too tall. I joined a student cross-country cycling club. I auditioned for a part in a student production of *The Winters Tale*. As I said, nobody seemed to mind.

No LA education can be complete without some time spent at UCLA and I like to think of myself as having been something of a model student – except, of course, that I wasn't paying. After the fall term, I voluntarily dropped out of the UCLA Film and Television School – and enrolled as a part-time UCLA Extension (i.e. nightschool) student.

Just as in the eighties, when health clubs, Alcoholic Anonymous meetings and Aids galas became the hip places for out-of-office deal-making and Roladex-expanding, so in nineties LA one of the trendiest evening activities is to enrol as an adult student on one of UCLA's many hundreds of nightclass or weekend Extension courses. Since starting in 1917, UCLA Extension has become not only the largest single campus continuing higher education in America – and probably the world – but has become known as one of the most popular pick-up scenes in LA (for both teachers and students). I enrolled for a weekly three-hour class – Tuesdays at 7p.m. – called 'The Stardom Strategy: The Art of Career Management in the Entertainment Field'.

Every weekday, just before 7p.m. the concrete multi-levels of UCLA's labyrinthine car-parks take on a curious metamorphosis. As the university's regular students swing out of the various exits in their old Volkswagen Golf 's and noisy Mustang's, a long queue of gleaming new Cherokee Jeeps, Mercedes and BMWs lines up in front of the entrance barrier – with a small army of uniformed attendants taking $5 from each driver as they rumble over the ramps.

The appeal of UCLA Extension is clear. First, apart from going out to a restaurant, or to see a movie (which in LA doesn't really count as going out), there is really not very much to do in the evening. There is very little theatre. Unless you enjoy standing in a dark, sweaty room, pounded by deafening rap-music, there are few night-clubs. That you have to drive everywhere means there is little sense of a local community – and UCLA's landscaped Illyria allows you the luxury of walking somewhere for a change. The evening courses also offer people a chance of meeting new people, encourage a sense of 'belonging' and – most significantly – provide a ready-made topic to talk about over dinner afterwards (the course syllabus comes complete with a list of local restaurants).

From a networking or potential dating point of view, some courses were – clearly – more suitable than others. Only a truly desperate lonely heart, I guessed, was likely to sign up for the 'Living as a Single' series of classes. As you trawl through the 246-page UCLA Extension catalogue of courses, careful judgement is required to understand what is really on offer. The courses include: 'Extraterrestrial Intelligence: The Search Begins'; 'Emergency Treatment for Cats and Dogs: The Holistic Approach'; 'Using Brain-Balancing Techniques to Strengthen Your Writing'; 'The Art of the Celebrity Interview'.

With no ambition to be a rock or movie star manager, I signed up for the 'Stardom Strategy' course because I had been reliably informed that the class always included at least half a dozen or so actresses looking for 'career guidance'. The course, which cost $195 for six meetings in a large lecture hall was instructed by Ken Kragen, a Hollywood manager who built the careers of Lionel Ritchie, Burt Reynolds, Kenny Rogers and country singer Travis Tritt. Shortly before the first class, he had helped co-produce the Clinton Inauguration showbiz concert. As with the Peter Guber class, a condition of enrolment is that you are forbidden to contact Kragen outside course hours.

As it is one of the most popular UCLA Extension courses, everyone had to fill in a 'contact' form detailing their 'career history' along with their home address and telephone number to faciliate smooth networking. The 'class-bonding' process was also aided by a twenty-minute snack break half way through the lectures, when people urgently tried to match faces to potted biographies. The list was a strange document. Shannon Lee Aunsoe, for example, described herself as 'Actress/writer – interested in chatting about any or all. Always interested in networking, new friends are hard to find.' Over the next few weeks I received about half a dozen let's-get-together phone-calls from people on my course.

On a cold night in February, I fulfilled my second teenage ambition. I had been watching a repeat of *Grease* on late-night television, when it occurred to me that I had been living in LA for more than a year, had probably made over a hundred trips to the cinema, or screenings, but had never been to a drive-in movie theater. I had, in fact, never seen a drive-in. I didn't even know whether they still existed.

In fact few outdoor movie houses now exist around LA, but after some detective work, I tracked down the Pacific drive-in theater in Van Nuys – a faceless low-rent valley suburb of oversized neon signs, autodealers, fried chicken eateries and unmodernised motels. I fixed myself up with a date from my course – an unsuccessful thirty-something actress – to see the new Tom Cruise film, *A Few Good Men.* I didn't tell her exactly *where* we were going to see it.

I had been told that people only go to drive-ins today as a frugal economy measure – the unemployed, or families on a tight budget. Not exactly the right impression for a date, you might think. But after months of watching films in fussy little air-conditioned studio screening rooms, I didn't care. I was looking forward to a sense of spectacle for a change.

The show began at 7p.m. Being a chilly night, there was no

queue. It was not a place of beauty. The rough London equivalent would be a disused car-park the size of a football stadium in north Wembley. I pulled up at a cage-like sentry box and paid $8 for our tickets. We were handed our Cine-Fi sound instructions. This informed us that we were forbidden to drink alcohol – and to sit or lie on the ground, although sitting *on* the car was permitted, so long as it did not interfere with the line of sight of cars to the rear. There was no danger of this. The vast car-park had just a dozen cars in it.

The screen was fifty-foot high. To get sound you were meant to attach what resembled a thick plastic telephone cord to your car aerial, and tune into your AM dial. But since somebody had stolen my aerial – routine in LA – we were reduced to using an old portable radio whose wavy antenna I stuck out through the sunroof. Reception was good. The movie was enjoyable enough trash. Every fifteen minutes or so, the flashing red tail-lights of an aircraft descending towards the local Burbank airport came into view, flapping across the top of the giant screen like a slow-motion firefly. The evening was more enjoyable than almost any other trip to a film in LA. Movie people get ridiculously self-important and it is considered a serious *faux pas* to mumble any words of disparagement when you leave the studio screenings room. It is all taken so personally. Everyone hurries out, their faces screwed up with tension, as if they had just failed their driving test, or performed badly in an important written exam. So many people in LA seem to have forgotten that entertainment is meant to be fun.

The success of UCLA Extension has been to shed the jokey stigma that lingers around the idea of higher education in Britain. That you are in the habit of listening to an Open University professor talk on quantum physics at 5.30a.m. on a Saturday morning, or spend your Wednesday evenings down at the local poly discussing Ted Hughes, is probably the sort of thing you keep to yourself in England. In LA, if you ask somebody to dinner when they have a UCLA nightclass, you sense a certain smugness in their voice when they reply:

'I'm very sorry – but I have my Frank Lloyd Wright architecture class that night – it's with Virginia Kazor – you know, the curator of the Hollyhock House, in fact she's a friend so it would be kinda difficult to get out of . . . and, anyhow, I find Wright just so *interesting* . . .'

'How about next Wednesday?'

'That's my last class in The Operas of Richard Strauss and Hugo von Hoffmannstahl – with David Fox – you know, the music critic . . .'

'Monday?'

'William, I'm real sorry – I have my Soufflé Workshop class.'

* * *

Today, the teaching of screenwriting has become a lucrative cottage industry. In addition to film-schools, weekend movie-writing seminars are booming – with bookshops and computer stores piled with various how-to-write-a-million-dollar-script DIY books and soft-ware. The classified pages of *Variety* are now crammed with ads for such quack-doctor courses as 'Sex, Lies and Screenwriting', or 'Michael Hauge's Screenwriting For the Nineties' so far presented to over 8,000 people in forty-five cities around America and Britain.

But with *alumni* like Kirk Douglas, John Cleese and Mel Smith to boast about, the best-known guru remains the leather-jacketed Robert McKee, a burly former New York actor/waiter who has made a fortune from preaching the wisdom that comes from years of failing to get your own movies made (the only formal qualification seemingly required to actually teach scriptwriting). After four years jet-setting between LA, New York, Rome and London with his weekend 'Story Structure' course, the former failed Hollywood hack – he has the odd *Columbo* TV credit – is now a Tinseltown micro-celebrity himself.

Some years ago, after paying £260 to attend McKee's seminar, I walked inside the Royal Chemistry Society's lecture rooms – off Savile Row in London – to find myself queuing for registration behind an off-duty Barry Norman. Beside him, a familiar face from the *Late Show* looked uneasy as he was asked to clip a plastic name tag to his David Bailey suede jacket. Half the editorial staff of *Private Eye* stood stiffly in the biscuit queue.

Yet such seminars are, frankly, amateurish. Over the weekend, I sat eating my salad lunch next to a City solicitor, a former *Daily Mirror* news editor, an Open University sexual therapist and a retired Welsh accountant turned translator of Spanish verse for Faber & Faber. I doubt very much that any of them have even got so far as receiving an agent's rejection slip. The idea of being able to sell an unsolicited script for $1 million, thousands of miles away in LA, is as improbable as successfully performing open-heart surgery after attending a Women's Institute first-aid course.

Rather than carrying on slipping into UCLA lectures, or wasting my money on a weekend scriptwriting course, I thought it was about time I met some real Hollywood screenwriters. What rather disturbed me about such self-appointed screenwriting gurus as Richard Walter or Robert McKee was the awkward fact that despite professing to be such experts, they had both failed – from no lack of trying – to get any of their own *original* scripts actually made into movies.

Joe Eszterhas is the highest paid screenwriter in Hollywood history. His most recent film, *Sliver*, starring Sharon Stone as a kinky New York publisher, was his eleventh script to be made into a film. These days, nobody wants to pay $1 million for an Eszterhas script. That would be too cheap to be good. He sold *Basic Instinct* to Carolco for $3 million. He did no research. The 110-page script was pounded out on a manual Olivetti in three weeks. In April 1993, former Columbia head Jon Peters was reported to have paid him $3.4 million to write and produce the screenplay for *Gangland*, a *Godfather*-style story of the rise and fall of the John Gotti's Gambino crime family.

Eszterhas, a grizzly looking six-foot Hungarian immigrant

with a Hell's Angel beard, leather-thonged sandals and Elvis black sunglasses is perhaps the best example of the change in status now being enjoyed by the Hollywood screenwriter. Having come to America when he was six, unable to speak any English, the former reporter for a Midwestern daily (he used to get so bored he would sneak out of the newsroom in the afternoon to watch a film), who went on to become a senior editor at *Rolling Stone*, is now a chain-smoking multi-millionaire who gets sacks of fan-mail, and doesn't even need to visit LA for meetings – studio executives fly up to San Francisco to his stately red-brick colonial mansion looking out over the San Francisco Bay.

I asked him why he didn't live in LA.

'Physically, I have a problem with LA' he said. 'It's too zippy for me. It's too fast lane. I get the sense of a hundred suburbs in search of a city. I feel a certain emptiness just being around it. Up here, the people are more human.'

His office looks like an Ivy League professor's study. His desk is surrounded by twenty-foot high shelves of books, and framed posters of his most successful films – *Flashdance, Jagged Edge, Basic Instinct.* Bootlegged copies of his scripts now sell on the blackmarket for up to $100.

'Who buys them?'

'I guess they're bought by guys who want to figure out how the hell you can be paid millions of dollars for a few weeks' work.'

On a table under a bookshelf is a framed *Los Angeles Times* cartoon of Mike Ovitz, who once famously threatened to ruin his career if he left CAA to join ICM. Eszterhas quoted Ovitz as saying 'My foot soldiers who go up and down Wilshire Boulevard each day will blow your brains out.'

That Eszterhas is expected to earn over $10 million in 1993 – he was paid $2 million in cash in November 1992 by producer Charles Evans for a one-page idea for a rock n' roll musical about Las Vegas showgirls – is clearly sweet justice for Eszterhas. His career has, in fact, been even *more* successful since leaving CAA.

'What I really enjoyed was a man [Ovitz] who said he was going to bury me, and six months later I set a new record in Hollywood for a screenplay. I was able to buy my house, and I felt overjoyed about that. To have a man with that sort of power, and then to essentially make him eat it.'

Eszterhas is regularly invited to lecture at film-schools like UCLA – but always refuses. 'My lawyers have advised me to decline such offers,' he sighed. 'Just as I have to send back any scripts that I get sent. They said that if I wrote about something that had vaguely come up in conversation with a student, we could wind up in court, sued for a fortune, and looking like a bunch of idiots.'

Screenwriters have, of course, always been paid absurd amounts of money. In 1926, Ben Hecht, a Chicago newspaper reporter and one-time Dadaist poet, was lured to LA by a cable from Herman Mankiewicz, who co-authored *Citizen Kane* with Orson Welles: WILL YOU ACCEPT THREE HUNDRED PER WEEK TO WORK FOR PARAMOUNT PICTURES? ALL EXPENSES PAID. THE THREE HUNDRED IS PEANUTS. MILLIONS ARE TO BE GRABBED OUT HERE AND YOUR ONLY COMPETITION IS IDIOTS. DON'T LET THIS GET AROUND.

But despite becoming the richest screenwriter in pre-war Hollywood (for fixing *Gone With the Wind* in a week, he received $15,000 from David Selznick), Hecht never allowed himself any illusions about the lowly rank and exploitive nature of his factory-line hackery. 'The movies pay as much for obedience as for creative work,' he wrote in his memoirs. 'An able writer is paid a larger sum than a man of small talent. But he is paid this added money not to use his superior talents.'

When P.G. Wodehouse was hired to write dialogue for $2,000 a week by MGM in 1930, he invariably found that he was working with eight collaborators and that fifteen or sixteen people had already meddled with the story. Under the studio system, writers were placed under iron-clad contracts

– at Warners, for example, it was a sackable offence for a writer to be on a set without written permission. If he wanted to see his own films, he was obliged to queue up and pay his money like anyone else.

This cliché of the luckless screenwriter has long been fuelled by their depiction in films themselves. Just as the long-suffering writer in *Sunset Boulevard*, ends up dead, floating among the leaves in a Hollywood swimming pool, so, in Robert Altman's *The Player*, the repudiated screenwriter is killed by a ruthless studio executive and left in the gutter of a Pasadena cinema car-park.

Whilst misfortune may remain the lot of many would-be screenwriters who descend on Tinseltown, the future has never looked brighter for the nineties generation of writers, such as Eszterhas, Shane Black (*Lethal Weapon*), Nora Ephron (*Sleepless in Seattle*; *When Harry Met Sally*) or Michael Tolkin (*The Player*).

Not only are they also being paid ever-spiralling sums, but, significantly, they are also gaining increased creative control, critical respect, and fast becoming as famous as the actors and directors they write for.

Perhaps the best-known screenwriter is William Goldman, who wrote *Butch Cassidy and the Sundance Kid* and *All the President's Men*. But whilst the success of his waspish Hollywood memoirs, offering an unromantic view of two decades of screenwriting, has helped to push his basic fee to $1 million for just rewriting a script – the studio must send a limousine to pick him up from his house in Connecticut, fly him first class to LA, and pay for his usual Beverly Hills Hotel luxury suite – Goldman views himself as simply an overpaid hack. The studio's word is his command. As he advises: 'There is one crucial rule that must be followed in all creative meetings: Never speak first. At least at the start, your job is to shut up.'

The Eszterhas school would beg to differ. Dancing on the grave of the *auteur* theory of film-making which decreed that the director was the sole author of a film, today's most commercially successful writers (and writer-directors like Oliver Stone and David Mamet) are finding themselves fêted, in turn, by a new generation of movie-critics eager to make their presence felt.

'Each generation of critics needs to notch its gun-belt in terms of a specific,' said Eszterhas. 'Partly for their own reasons of self-aggrandisement, we are seeing younger critics saying, wait a minute, surely the writer of a movie is important. The change is as revolutionary as when the *auteur* theory began.'

'The most misunderstood aspect of film-making for many years,' he continues, 'has been that if the director is dealing with an original screenplay, the genesis of the film – in terms of idea, character and plot – belongs to the writer. When critics used to review my films, they related exclusively to the director. Now they pay more attention to the writing.'

Goldman's whore-like attitude is, he contends, partly the reason that so many films coming out of Hollywood today are so mediocre. They are made by committee – with scripts minced to pieces by the politics of compromise. What angers Eszterhas is that the Goldman school appear so proud of selling-out – and that generations of young screenwriters have been affected by this attitude.

He refuses to play the studio hustler, saying that he now aims to simply write original scripts for auction. 'That way you don't have to talk some schmuck into it.' The studio knows what it is buying. It doesn't get to influence them so much because the development process is by-passed.

Despite the level of his success, he has not always been able to sell his work. From 1980–92 he wrote seven screenplays on spec – three of which (Magic Man, Platinum and Checking Out) nobody wanted.

'It's a heart-breaking process when you wait for the phone to ring and nothing happens. People don't realise this, but three of my screenplays just didn't sell. Nobody came to the party. I loathe pitching. I don't do it. I did it at the beginning and I'm bad at it.'

'Why?' I asked.

'Because it's like selling shoes. You're trying to sell your work and, personally, I find it a demeaning experience. There are people in town who pitch three different ideas a day – I mean how the fuck can you really want to do something, if you are selling five different things.'

But the real problem is that screenwriters don't fight for their work. 'You always get to a point where you disagree with the director or producer – and most writers say, "How do you want me to change it?" They don't say "I'm not changing it." But everybody has that choice. I've been very public about the fact that if I feel I'm right, I'm really going to fight. People are very careful about changing my work.'

'What about *Basic Instinct*?' I said. 'You wanted to change the script to placate the gay community,'

'I was a schmuck,' he said. 'I should never have done that. Paul [Verhoeven] said he wouldn't make the changes. In retrospect, I think he was absolutely right.'

The other difficulty is that whilst everybody today has a great idea for a movie, the vast majority of would-be Oscar winners hasn't the least idea how to write a script. This is one reason why so many gifted writers – Scott Fitzgerald, William Faulkner, Brecht – flunked in Hollywood.

Eszterhas is quietly dismissive of the vogue for film-writing schools. 'The danger with film-schools is that it all becomes very in-bred with film references,' he said. 'In most cases students would be better off dealing with real life than going to film school. The scripts that I've read from film-school students lack a certain sort of primal reality. They're too intellectualised. Very academic and formulaic.'

With around 45,000 scripts circulating in Hollywood each year, to be taken at all seriously as a screenwriter you usually need, in fact, to have a proven film-related professional training or background. In 1974, after a book he had written had just been shortlisted for the National Book Award, Joe Eszterhas received a call from an executive at United Artists.

'You write well,' she said. 'Do you have any interest in doing a screenplay?'

After six months, Eszterhas came up with a 380-page script about the rise and fall of an American union boss. 'I didn't know a tinker's damn about screenplays. It was totally crude.' Taken under the wing of director Norman Jewison (*In the Heat of the Night, Moonstruck*), Eszterhas was tutored for eighteen months in the craft of screenwriting – finally reducing the script to 110 pages, which ended up as *F.I.S.T.*, starring Sylvester Stallone. 'It was the best kind of graduate course you could ever get. I didn't know how lucky I was.'

As a respected former journalist and author who, along with Tom Wolfe and Hunter Thompson, wrote for *Rolling Stone* in the seventies, Eszterhas admitted to being depressed by the poor standard of most journalism coming out of Hollywood – loaded up on the back of the studio PR juggernaut.

'As someone who comes from journalism,' he said. 'It's whoring and sucky. Its largely because of the PR people. They have an insane amount of power today.'

'Such as.'

He gave me an intriguing example. After he had written *Betrayed*, his lawyer at the time, Barry Hirsch turned to him and said: 'You're writing all these scripts, and having all these movies made – but nobody knows who you are. I'd like you to come down and meet someone.' So he went to lunch and met with publicist Pat Kingsley – head of Hollywood's most notoriously strong-arm PR firm, PMK.

'What did she say?' I asked.

I knew all about Pat Kingsley. My own dealings with her had been far from amicable.

'She gives me this rap,' Eszterhas said. 'You know, a lot of people should *know* who you are. You're clearly very successful, very talented, why don't you let us handle you? We can set people up to interview you. And I said, how do you know anybody will want to? And she said, well, if we suggest they interview you, and if they also want to interview some of our other clients, then they *will* interview you. And if you're worried about what they're going to write, that's not a problem either, because in many cases they turn their manuscript in to us before they send it to the publication.'

'What did you say to that?'

'I said no way. That really blew my mind. I was a journalist, and I certainly didn't know that sort of thing was going on. I refuse to have a publicist. I deal with everything myself.'

I asked if he thought the celebrity journalism coming out of Hollywood today was patronising towards the public.

'I do. One of the things that is very wrong with Hollywood today is that it always underestimates the intelligence of the public. With *Basic Instinct*, for example, people were always saying you couldn't do an ambiguous ending. You can't do a movie filled with ambiguity, the old cliché goes, because who are you going to root for? I hate that cliché. I mean it's not a goddamn football game. It's a movie. Its supposed to be drama.'

'So what's the secret of writing a $1 million-dollar script today?'

'You are supposed to know who the good and bad guys are. That's all bullshit. My movies show you don't have to do any of that. My theory is that the public has been manipulated and force-fed for so long – the buttons have been pressed for so long – that if you can stand a genre on its head, and give them something unique, they are starved for it – really ready for it.'

* * *

Martin Amis is sipping a dry vodka and Negroni cocktail in the Century Plaza Hotel lobby bar on the Avenue of the Stars in Century City. As a grand piano tinkles away over the discreet evening chatter in the ritzy *salon*, with its black-and-white marble floor, gilt Louis XIV armchairs and neo-Egyptian art, he slowly rolls himself a cigarette from a plastic pouch of Old Holborn. He is the only person smoking.

They were arriving, I began to discover, every week. Literary luvvies in search of a piece of the cultural action.

Their latest scripts, neatly bound with three brass tacks, buried at the bottom of their suitcases – along with the Dunhill sunglasses and sun oil. Just as in the twenties and thirties, when Americans like Pound, Hemingway and T.S. Eliot flocked to the bohemian bars and cafés of Europe, so flying out to LA seems to have become *le dernier cri* of literary London. And not just get-rich-quick hacks flying on Virgin but internationally acclaimed *authors* – droves of them – such as Martin Amis, William Boyd, Ian McEwan, Tom Stoppard, Christopher Hampton.

In front of Amis, on the bar, is a copy-proof of a book review which he is trying to read and correct. But he's not concentrating. He's jumping the lines. He's sipping his drink again, nibbling those cheese savouries, wheezing on his cigarette – enjoying this crazy cartoon of LA around him.

At forty-two, Amis is dressed not unlike a professional gigolo. Armani-style designer jacket, open-neck cream shirt and tight, faded Levis. Peanut-butter tan. Expensive gold watch. The thick hair is suavely scooped back Travolta-style to make his toadish eyes pop out at you like a pair of marbles. The gnomish head is freakishly large, the voice gravelly and patrician. He's a small guy – but relaxed, affluent, in shape.

Amis was, indeed, for hire in Los Angeles. Taking a break from literary fiction, he was writing a Tri-Star sci-fi/action adventure film, called *Mars Attacks*, produced by Jon Davison (*Airplane, Robocop*) that he was now the latest screenwriter on.

'It's an updated version of *War of the Worlds*,' he drawled, 'except that they don't come to mess us up. They come in search of new markets. They talk and dress like Californian businessmen and bring all kinds of benefits – like cancer-cures.'

The future has always troubled Amis – an avid sci-fi fan. After discovering the joys of Space Invaders on holiday in the South of France in the seventies, he wrote a book about the craze with an introduction by Steven Spielberg (it is now a valuable collector's item). His only previous screen-credit is for *Saturn Three* (1980), starring Kirk Douglas and Farrah Fawcett, involving a maniac who builds a robot on an obscure space station which goes berserk. 'I was superseded by another writer and then re-hired on a weekly basis. You get a kick seeing your ideas given this hard-ware reality.'

Mollycoddled, revered and spoilt rotten as the precious darling of literary London, Amis seemed to relish his mercenary status in LA. Whilst his number of fans in America has grown into a loyal army since *London Fields*, his following remains essentially high-brow rather than mass-market. Put another way, most people in Hollywood haven't heard of him.

He joined the *Mars Attacks* project after *Premiere* magazine asked him to write a piece about *Robocop 2*. Amis and Davison hit it off in the interview. 'It was the idlest of coincidences, really. We chatted, I was impressed how much he loved it and wanted his film to be good. He then said he had an idea, which he had been wanting to do for some time – and would I like to try and write the script?'

He quashes any idea that he is 'bored' with writing novels, or that he has turned to scriptwriting as fiction has become marginalised by the imaginative scope of cinema. 'There may be writers who feel like that. I don't feel like that one bit. In fact, I feel this is getting to be a distraction from what I really want to do – and I won't want to do it again for three or four years.'

'To write for the movies is not a literary ambition, it's a social or financial ambition,' is how Amis sums up the allure of Hollywood for the literary novelist – quoting Ian McEwan, whose *The Innocent* was being filmed in Berlin and whose original screenplay, *The Good Son*, was being turned into a psycho-thriller by Twentieth Century Fox.

'I feel perfectly happy with the number of readers I reach,' Amis continues. 'I think one is attracted by mass culture, and not because of anything that Julie Burchill has been saying, but just because it's fun. The trouble is that writing scripts gets very much less "fun". By the final draft, you certainly feel you've earnt every cent.'

But Amis isn't in Hollywood for the money. His next two-book deal with Random House in America is worth in excess of $500,000. You get the feeling he doesn't even much *like* money. Doesn't care about it. Isn't interested in it. Pays someone to pay his bills. 'Money isn't really it,' he admits. 'I mean if Steven Spielberg rang – which he hasn't – and said "I want you to write a screenplay" – I could say I wasn't going to waste my time with screenplays because I was already going where the real money was, which is the Literary Novel.'

William Boyd arrived in LA to deliver his new version of the 1954 French classic, *Les Diaboliques* to Warner Bros during the worst floods and mud-slides in California this century. He was flown first class from London and stayed in a vastly expensive hotel for a week. He had one meeting with the studio. It lasted forty minutes. Boyd, who, unlike Amis, has had seven of his scripts made into films (his most recent being *A Good Man in Africa* and *Chaplin*), taught himself film-writing by wading through scripts of old movies he liked. It's very much easier for a bad writer to produce a screenplay, he contends, than for a bad novelist to have a bad novel published. If a script is properly bound, people believe that they actually *are* screenwriters – with fragile egos consoled by the fact that only a miserably small proportion of even studio-commissioned screenplays are ever made into films. 'My uncharitable theory is that the screenplay is not an art form,' sniffed Boyd. 'It's a highly developed craft.'

When in LA, Boyd says he keeps the fact he is a novelist a bit quiet. 'What people are impressed by in Hollywood' he added, 'are, first, how much money did your last film make and second, have you had any scripts made into film? The brutal perception is that if you've got scripts made into movies then you are probably worth hiring. What they don't want to hear is you saying that you are a novelist who has been translated into twenty-five languages. It is utterly irrelevant.'

Despite his lack of screen credits, the place of the movie writer in the transatlantic literary world clearly intrigues

Martin Amis. The week before the *The New Yorker* had published a mischievous short story of his, *Career Move*, set in LA and London, in which he transposes the role of poets and screenwriters.

'It's a ridiculous story,' said Amis smirking, 'but I think it works by portraying screenplay writers struggling away in garrets writing stories with absurd titles like "Offensive from Quasar 13" for little magazines that pay tiny cheques that bounce.' His jet-setting poet Luke drives a Celebrity Chevrolet and is 'developing' a multi-million dollar poem called 'Sonnet' with his agent from Talent International.

It's not just a clever joke. For all the cultivation of his laid-back image as Mid-Atlantic literary hipster Amis takes his work *very* seriously indeed. He would love to write a really successful movie – preferably, you get the feeling, something a bit nasty. 'Sick is back since *Silence of the Lambs*,' he said gleefully. 'I used to take a lot of girls to *The Exorcist*. It was simply a dating mechanism. Afterwards, they were too scared to sleep alone. I can't have been the first to discover that.'

Like many novelists, Amis's first attempt at a screenplay – adapting his first novel *The Rachel Papers* years ago – was an ego-crushing experience. 'I wrote the script. And I was very pleased with it. And then the would-be director and producer came around to talk about it and they started off with what they didn't like and I was close to tears. Of incredulity and disgust. I had written it. There it was. What *were* these people talking about?'

As Amis frankly admits, the collaborative nature of making a movie wholly contradicts what being a writer is all about. 'Screenwriting is really anti-writing,' he sighs. 'I would distrust any writer who can look me in the eye and say that he isn't most alive when alone. That is what being a writer is.'

Amis is a control-freak. When he says writer, he means novelist. He reserves the same brand of condescending scepticism for journalism – 'every stage in the experience seems to involve a lot of people' – as he does for screenwriting. 'In Hollywood, you're dependent upon what other people think,' he says 'You have no control. You're dependent on market forces that haven't come up for me for twenty years as a writer of fiction. But it does get you out of the house. It's fun and it is exciting – you know, the idea of it happening on the screen. And I like hotels – who doesn't?'

Which is just as well as he has been spending rather a lot of time in swanky American hotel suites recently. Book-signings. Late-night TV appearances. Limousines. In-room video messages. Amis loves this stuff. He has difficulty viewing Los Angeles as part of America – it's more like another country.

'I hated LA the first few times – but I do rather like it now. I used to feel ill when I was here, that's probably why I didn't like it. My best friend here died recently, so I was rather expecting to enjoy it less this time but, in fact, I do like the rhythm of it. I don't really know it well. Not like I know New York. It's exotic.'

He does, however, find he is received with more good-will in America than in London. 'In England, I'm in a special situation because of my father. I've exhausted the good-will there in a general sense. And the forces of resentment lock in earlier.'

What seems to irk Amis is that celebrities in America are usurping the role of writers, as advice-givers, interpreters of the American condition. As Saul Bellow has argued, most Americans today regard novels as 'how-to books' about life. The writer is no longer a 'curer of souls'.

'Writers are here to interpret America – to tell us what America is – is it just a collection of people from all over Europe and Africa and Mexico, is it the melting pot? Or is it really a country? Does it have an identity? What is America?'

The fear of the American writer, he says, quoting Don de Lillo, is the moment when the person steps out in front of the crowd with that smile that he has been rehearsing for years, the fan to whom your books have spoken in strange and interesting ways, the fan who has taken it all a bit seriously. 'The difference being that in America he will have a gun rather than the fist. I've had the fist. I got attacked by a fan.'

The mallet-like blow that Amis received from his 'fan', who used to follow him into restaurants, was, he says, directly described in *Money*, when John Self is punched 'like no blow I had ever felt'. 'It was a very strange experience. It was someone I vaguely knew at Oxford, who flipped. He came into my father's house and started smashing things up. I don't know what he had in mind for my father but he had plenty in mind for me. He was paranoid. It was very unpleasant.'

Although Amis himself has profiled such Hollywood swells as Hugh Hefner, Steven Spielberg and Brian de Palma he says that nowadays he wouldn't want to bother. 'Occasionally a magazine like *GQ* rings me up and says "Do you want to do Clint Eastwood, or Boris Becker?" Well, the way I would *do* them now is I wouldn't interview them. I mean what are you hoping you're going to get? All you are doing is examining their publicity machine.'

'I would rather just hang around them for a bit. I'd rather watch them being interviewed than interview them. It's post-modern now. You have to take a step back. You write about their PR act, because that's as close as you're going to get. To be quite honest, I have long thought that the interview is a completely dead form.'

Ah.

14

Walking on Sunset

'WELL. I DROVE DOWN SUNSET Boulevard one afternoon. That was my mistake,' begins Joe Gillis shortly after he is fished out of Norma Desmond's Beverly Hills swimming pool.

Nobody, of course, has ever walked anywhere in LA – although so many people do now seem to be *running*. Running up debts. Running away from the past. Running into trouble. Running out of time. It occurred to me that to walk the length of Sunset Boulevard – from Downtown to Malibu – would be the LA equivalent of canoeing up the Amazon.

Like most people living in LA, I had clocked up so many hours driving down Sunset that its garish blur of nondescript buildings and giant movie hoardings had gelled together in my mind into a few cheap neon landmarks. Stretching westwards from the Union Station to the ocean, Sunset Boulevard's twenty-six zigzagging miles seemed to sum up much of both the hope and despair, triumph and tragedy, of modern America – the neon-lit arcade supposedly leading into the heartland of the American Dream.

Simon agreed to walk with me. As a pair we were not wholly unqualified for this trip. Before Billy Wilder had come to Hollywood in 1934, aged twenty-eight and dangerously low on cash, he had been a newspaper reporter in Berlin, after studying law at Vienna University. Like the unemployed hack in *Sunset Boulevard*, Simon was a heavily debt-ridden screenwriter without any credit – either screen or financial – to his name. (Six months later he won the 1993 BAFTA Screenwriting Fellowship.) With four unsold scripts circulating around town, it was no secret that he was coming along with me primarily for the free meals.

We set off as the sherbert-pink dawn broke over the skyline of Downtown LA on the Friday morning of the XXVII Superbowl weekend – with the Dallas Cowboys taking on New York's Buffalo Bills in front of 100,000 people at the local Rosebowl in Pasadena. Los Angeles was overflowing. Our breakfast at Union Station had consisted of sugary custard doughnuts, each like an over-sized rotten pear, and a plastic cup of weak filter coffee.

To reach the first block on Sunset we passed under a graffiti-sprayed freeway bridge overhung with shaggy vine-gourds, next to the thick and windowless walls of the Los Angeles Central Jail. Rising above the Los Angeles River, the old city gaol – crammed with around 6,300 prisoners – bulged under the early morning sky. The spaghetti of steel railway tracks spilling from the station glinted in the hazy sun as they hugged the jail walls. I had read somewhere that the over-crowded male prison, many of whose inmates slept on patches of squalid cell floor, housed several of the most violent and deranged criminals in America.

Weaving through the colourful Mexican street market at the start of Sunset, I paid $15 at a leather stall for a souvenir of the urban trek ahead – a thickly studded Clint Eastwood-style belt with a chunky metal buckle. Other travel items, stuffed into my jacket pocket, included a fold-up map of the city, an instamatic camera and our equivalent of Baedeker – *The Ultimate Hollywood Tour Book: The Incomparable Guide to Movie Stars' Homes, Movie and TV Locations, Scandals, Murders, Suicides, and All the Famous Tourist Sites* by William A. Gordon.

Just down the street was the federal courthouse where the historic civil rights trial of the four officers in the Rodney King beating case was to start the following week. As we crossed over the 101 Hollywood Freeway, which swerved away from Downtown like a figure-of-eight track, and headed west out of the fringes of Chinatown towards Dodger Stadium, we entered a two-mile no man's land – a grim landscape of auto-dealers, overgrown car-parks piled with rubbish, under-stocked liquor stores, crumbling fifties houses and door after door of illegal sweatshops, each smelling like an overheated second-hand carpet-shop and bustling with families of shawled Oriental women, aged from eleven to eighty.

We headed up through the tatty vicinity of Echo Park towards Silverlake; Sunset began to take on a run-down but homely feel. In Monopoly terms, we were trudging along a litter-strewn Whitechapel Road early on a windy Sunday morning. People no longer just scurried past us with eyes like dead fish. As we passed a bearded black man sitting in a smashed-up old Toyota whose bonnet was somewhat desperately fixed to the bumper with a large chain he grinned and wished us good morning ('Hey guys,' as he put it, 'have a good-one'). Local garage mechanics, or residents washing down their old cars parked on the street – well-kept old Lincolns and Oldsmobiles – waved at us keenly. Some stopped to study us more closely as if we were a scruffy pair of an exotic zoological species (*homo pedens*).

About a mile or so further on, the surreal LA headquarters of the Church of Scientology – whose Tinseltown acolytes include the likes of Tom Cruise – loomed above Sunset like a pyramid-palace hewn from cliffs of royal-blue quartz. After being instructed to watch a fuzzy video about Life Orientation, a thirty-something woman with designer glasses, dressed like an Iraqi traffic warden, led us into a bare third-floor ante-room and attempted to read the images flowing through my mind whilst I gripped two clammy and warm metal tubes shaped like lavatory rolls. She sat behind a desk peering at a series of digital red LED meters that were supposedly tuned into the combusting ganglia and synapses of my brain. In her soft and reassuring tone she told me to relax; her blinking machine could locate the source of mental barriers that prevented people having confidence in themselves. Through the Science of Mental Health I would become a Clear – a person with increased self-respect, able to achieve my worldly goals and discover the key to lasting, perfect relationships. The bad experiences of one's past, she stressed, limited our happiness potential. As we left, she handed me a leaflet on the book *Dianetics* – a mental force so powerful, I read, that it could protect the body against damage from atomic bomb-flash.

At around 1.30p.m., we entered the tawdry fringes of Hollywood, with its tacky $29-a-night motels, twenty-four hour supermarkets, Denny's restaurants – the graveyard of the old studios and movie-theatres. I passed the dilapidated white neo-classical building, headquarters of KTLA TV – where I uneasily remembered having made my own Tinseltown screen debut on *Love Connection*. Deciding where to have lunch was not difficult. Next to the former Columbia studios was the Columbia Bar and Grill, used by director Robert Altman to film scenes of a crowded LA power-lunch in *The Player*. Having made our reservation from a battered pay-phone directly across the street (making it clear the noisy background traffic was being picked up on my car-phone as we drove down Sunset), we were led to a table in the corner surrounded by tropical plants.

We crossed Vine Street, only a block away from the Alto-Nido Apartments on Ivar Avenue in which Joe Gillis had his poky bedsit. Already an undesirable address by the early 1950s, the apartment building today has the dingy feel of a soon-to-be knocked-down hotel on London's Vauxhall Bridge Road.

It was still too early in the day for the street girls – most of whom now carry pagers (and some cellular phones) which bleep when their regular clients call them up. At around 11p.m., around the intersection of Mansfield and Sunset – where there can be around thirty girls in knee-high white boots touting for business – the street can sound like a

Nintendo game shop. You can always tell the difference between LA's up-scale escort agency girls, based in Beverly Hills, and the cheap hookers working the Strip – or so I was once told by the owner of an expensive LA hair salon – because the escort girls always get paid by the thousand: ten hundred dollar bills stapled together.

Strewn along the empty pavement were a scrofulous medley of unshaven and sunburnt tramps and street beggars, asleep on benches or dozing in the sun whilst zealously guarding their supermarket trolleys loaded high with either glass bottles or an assortment of squashed aluminium drink cans, for which they are paid cash, or a mountain of black plastic bags containing their ragged possessions. Known locally as 'sidewalk cadillacs', some are ingeniously fitted out with such features as battery-operated headlights for wheeling around backalleys in the dark, as well as collapsible giant umbrellas (borrowed from the garden tables of local pubs) for use in the rain, or as a shade in extreme heat. In addition, such vehicles often came complete with a bicycle chain and combination lock – for security at night.

Many of the best examples of LA's talent for self-destruction exist along the twisting length of Sunset Boulevard – a good instance being the original site of Schwab's Pharmacy, formerly the most famous drugstore in America. In 1939, the song *Over the Rainbow* came to composer Harold Arlen as he walked past the store after a bibulous dinner. He used the light from its window to scrawl down the famous melody before he forgot it.

Today, Schwab's Pharmacy is pretty well forgotten. As the late afternoon traffic shuddered past us at the corner of Sunset and Crescent Heights, we looked for some sort of plaque to mark where the framed establishment had stood until it was bulldozed by property developers in 1988. But there was nothing. In its place stands a banana-yellow Virgin Records mega-store.

In November of 1940, F. Scott Fitzgerald blacked out with a heart attack at the counter of Schwab's whilst buying a pack of cigarettes. The next month, on 21 December, forty-four-year-old Fitzgerald – by now an unemployed screenwriter – suffered a second heart attack, which killed him. Back in June 1937, when Fitzgerald, desperately short of cash, had finally been lured back to Hollywood by a promise of $1,000 a week from MGM for six months, he had cheered himself for the task ahead by booking into the $400 a month Garden of Allah – just across the street from Schwab's. After opening in 1926 with a party attended by such luminaries as Charlie Chaplin, Rudolph Valentino and Mae West, the Garden of Allah's hotel, villas and bungalows had quickly become one of the most desired and fashionable residences for the Hollywood *haut monde*. The Garden's curious blend of costly luxury and its Butlins-style bungalows, had made it the chosen home of the likes of Frank Sinatra, David Niven, Ava Gardner, Clark Gable, Errol Flynn and Ernest Hemingway in the thirties and forties. Regrettably, the sybaritic carousing took its toll.

By the 1950s the hotel had begun to fall apart, with the pool water resembling a frothy soup, showers not working properly, messages found screwed up behind the piano, cigarette-burns in the carpets, and endless complaints about obdurate waiters. Much in need of a refurbishment, the hotel lost its long-term residents as it gradually went to seed. Its once discreet terrace bar became the favoured hangout of local prostitutes. Harold Ross, a former editor of *New Yorker*, came to describe The Garden as 'a pesthole of pettifogging vaudeville actors and fallen women'. In 1959 the hotel was bulldozed and the valuable site sold to a Savings & Loan for development. Today it is dominated by a drive-in McDonalds.

As the pompadour grandeur of the Garden had begun to fizzle out many of its regular clientele had switched to the cottages and suites of the surreal Château Marmont nestled in the Hollywood Hills above the Strip. Originally designed as a luxury apartment building, the Marmont opened as a hotel in 1929. Marilyn Monroe, Marlon Brando, James Dean, Mick

Jagger, Barbra Streisand, Howard Hughes, Vivien Leigh, Roman Polanski, Warren Beatty and Dustin Hoffman, have all been guests. Resident John Belushi died there on 5 March 1982 from a fatal drug overdose in his two-bedroomed Bungalow 3, set back from the garden with its own little courtyard.

Since Billy Wilder himself had always been one of the hotel's most loyal clients, it was obvious we should spend our first night at the Marmont. Wilder had owned just one frayed suitcase and a dented 1928 DeSoto coupé when he checked into the cheapest room available in the Marmont in August 1934 – a room described in the official history of the hotel as a 'furnished cubicle: small, cramped and dark'. It was hidden behind the back of the building and opened out onto a stony bed of dried weeds, with a rusty hotplate for a kitchen and a pull-out bed that took up nearly three-quarters of the poky room.

For a short period of time – over Christmas 1935 – he had been reduced to moving into a tiny cloakroom next to the women's lavatory on the ground-floor. It wasn't until 1936, after his marriage to Judith Iribe, and a new contract with Paramount that he was able to move into a small suite.

By the time we reached the Château Marmont it was almost dark and the hotel's giant neon sign glowed – the initial letter 'M' had failed to light up for some reason – above Sunset's slow-moving evening traffic like a red-hot branding iron. The popular mythology that has built up around the Marmont – from its celebrity intrigue to erratic service – has long, of course, been part of its jaded charm. A year before, I remember setting off to meet someone who was staying there for a drink before dinner, when my phone rang. I was matter-of-factly asked to bring along a bottle of wine and a corkscrew as the hotel – after sixty years in business – still did not have a liquor license. We drank the wine in bathroom tooth-glasses – in full view of the Front Desk. Nobody cared.

Most of the original antiques and furniture from the twenties and thirties had been either destroyed by residents (guests regularly used Persian rugs and curtains as blankets when the heating broke down), or – more often – simply stolen by people who came in off the street and loaded up with whatever paintings, lamps or tables took their fancy. Until fairly recently, the Marmont was so understaffed and so lacking in any basic security, the only strategy the management could devise to prevent its furniture from disappearing was to ensure that its decor was so truly ghastly that nobody would wish to waste their time removing it.

As we walked through the hotel's Gothic colonnade we were greeted by a team of drilling workmen in the lobby – part of a multi-million dollar facelift. It wasn't long before we were reassured that the hotel had lost none of its special talent for individual flavour – the personal touch – that had helped to earn it such a colourful niche in Hollywood history. The general manager, Mr Philip Truelove, a tall and cheery Englishman with a warm handshake and a twinkly smile, took us up to our suite (I had expressly asked for a twin room). Opening the door – Number 69 – he led us into the spacious sitting room, decorated with fresh flowers.

We followed Mr Truelove down a thickly carpeted corridor.

'And this,' he said with a knowing smile, flashing his clear blue eyes at both of us as he raised his voice just a little for maximum theatrical effect, 'is the master bedroom. . .'

In front of us was one very large double bed.

'As you can see it has a wonderful view of the city . . . ' he continued. 'I do hope everything is to your satisfaction Mr Cash. If there is anything you need simply call the Front Desk. I do hope you have a most enjoyable stay at the Château Marmont.'

There was a brief pause. After sharing a house for a time with Simon we had long become used to people thinking we were gay. Living in a town in which around 30 per cent of the film community are estimated to be homosexual such an assumption was hardly surprising. Since there was clearly nothing we could do about changing our room, we both smiled back.

'Er . . . yes. I mean, everything seems splendid. Thank you so much Mr Truelove. You really have been most kind to arrange . . . er . . . this lovely room. I'm sure we'll both sleep wonderfully – just wonderfully.'

We needed a drink and so dropped in on Nicky Blair's restaurant – packed out with LA's jet-sleaze weekend crowd – where a grey-haired Clint Eastwood was having dinner tucked away discreetly in a corner. Sylvester Stallone, dressed in what resembled a Spanish waiter's outfit and surrounded by an entourage of bodyguards, stood self-consciously at the meet-a-mate bar.

After waiting nearly an hour for our reserved table at Spago, just across the street, we finally, at about 11.15p.m. got round to eating our Wolfgang Puck designer pizzas ($70 for two cheesey pizzas the size of 45rpm singles and a couple of beers). Most of the Mediterranean restaurant – probably Sunset's most famous gastonomic shrine – seemed crammed with shiny-suited tourists, would-be romantic mute young couples and rowdy Superbowl fans. I was relieved, at least, as two men dining together, not to be seated down the end of the room, near the lavatories, where I had found myself on my last visit with a friend from university. We had been squashed up next to a pair of Prince look-a-likes with thick mascara and matching 'His and His' ruby earrings. It is a useful rule, I have discovered, that when eating out with a male friend in LA restaurants you should make it clear you are on business otherwise you are likely to end up seated in what seems clearly designated as the 'Gays Only' area.

Our final stop was Sunset's Roxbury Club, which is the closest that LA has to an established nightclub. According to my *Ultimate Hollywood Tour Guide*, the Roxbury was the city's 'hottest nightclub of the moment and a favorite of Young Hollywood. On any given night, the crowd will probably contain familiar faces from MTV or Arsenio, but they'll be upstairs in the rarified air of the VIP room with Sly and Prince and other one-name stars. Dress to kill and you'll get in, but forget about the VIP room unless you're on The List.'

People who visit LA are usually baffled when I tell them LA has little European-style night life. Most evening entertainment in LA is specifically geared towards ruling out any conversation. I remember once reading a glossy magazine that offered ten tips for successful dating in LA. Top of the list was 'to plan the evening so as to keep the need for talking to a minimum'. This is made easy at the Roxbury, where the main upstairs bar and disco resemble sweaty dungeons. I practically needed a wet-suit and flippers to get a drink, as the bar area – lit up every ten seconds or so by strobe flashes – was practically afloat with spilt drinks and broken glasses. As I stood inside the ropes of the VIP room sipping my vodka tonic, without lemon, listening to the wild jungle-beat around me, I stopped to remind myself that I was standing in the heartland of every Valley Girl's Friday night fantasy.

* * *

As we lolled in the bright morning sunshine outside the hotel ('I do hope you both slept well, Mr Cash' volunteered the beaming Mr Truelove in the morning), film director Spike Lee jogged out of the hotel in his white sneakers to buy a doughnut from the local grocery store. We were approaching the Sunset Strip – where the 'Sunset Slayer' had picked up his victims and shot them as they gave him oral sex in empty car-parks. We were happy to avoid investigating the scenes of his crimes.

Turning right on the King's Road, and walking a steep fifty yards above Sunset, we dropped in for breakfast at the house of twenty-eight-year-old English actress Elizabeth Hurley (star of Dennis Potter's BBC series *Christabel*; her most recent big budget movie was Warner Bros's *Passenger 57* with Wesley Snipes). A large sign saying 'Warning – Dangerous Dog' was fastened to the gate. Like myself, Elizabeth had an Alsatian – called Nico – the only difference being that hers was prone to acts of extreme violence. It had recently ripped a sizeable chunk out of the face of a visiting friend of her housemate, the British film producer and LA socialite Julia Verdin. The man needed over fifty stitches.

'I know this sounds terribly LA,' she said as she whisked up some fluffy scrambled eggs in the kitchen. 'But one reason that I won't be going back to England for quite a while is that I don't think I could leave Nico behind.'

Like most of Hollywood, I had a bit of a crush on Elizabeth. I suppose I was half in love with her. It was rather difficult not to be. Frankly, after nearly two years of living in LA, Californian girls had turned out to be a serious disappointment. Maybe I knew the wrong people. Probably. Elizabeth was the only actress I knew in LA who got turned down for roles because she was 'Too Beautiful'. Besides, unusual for a Hollywood actress, her bedroom resembled a mini-library. Lying on top of her piano – next to an old *Daily Mail* and a coffee-table book of English gardens – was a copy of Nabokov's *Pnin*. On top of the piano was an Edwardian-looking framed photograph of her long-standing boyfriend. Damn.

Towering above the beginning of Sunset Plaza, in the heart of the Sunset Strip, is the old *Playboy* Building, marked by a dinky little *Playboy* bunny motif. In 1992, however, *Playboy* moved its Studio West office headquarters – where many of its most famous centrefolds were shot – from Sunset to West LA. The offices are now up for lease. As a true sign of the times, a fifty-foot-high condom advertisement has been splashed up on one side of the concrete wall – depicting a sexy Roy Lichtenstein-style cartoon character dressed up in a rubber bondage outfit and brandishing a smoking gun. Her cartoon bubble says: 'No Glove – No Love'.

We walked all morning without a stop. We passed through LA's real-life Norma Desmondland – past pair upon pair of imposing wrought-iron gates behind which stood a bizarre series of mock-Tudor English manors, Gothic mansions, French châteaux, Moorish castles and fifties bungalows. By about 3p.m., after a slice of cake and a Coke at a wedding reception held on a patch of Sunset Boulevard public lawn, we reached the boarded-up entrance of the Beverly Hills hotel – recently closed for a $50 million face-lift.

Owned by the Sultan of Brunei, who paid $185 million for it in 1987, the Beverly Hills hotel seemed to have lost its glamorous edge, its once fashionable Polo Lounge little more than a tea-room for Old Hollywood. I peered through a crack in the wooden boards at a lone security guard sitting on an oil drum by the empty pool. The balmy days of Marilyn Monroe's reported affairs in the hotel with both John and Robert Kennedy, or of billionaire Howard Hughes asking the staff to hide his roast-beef sandwiches in trees for him to find, were clearly well over.

Walking on towards the Holmby Hills, with the sun fading behind the darkening afternoon clouds, the pavement disappeared altogether as Sunset began to resemble a dual carriage-way. With no side-walk, we were forced to scramble along the motorway embankment, at times so steep that we were reduced to crouching down and crawling through the muddy shrubbery, littered with old beer cans, smashed wheel-hubs and the odd piece of discarded underwear, as the traffic thundered past below us.

By late afternoon we reached the 10100 Sunset Boulevard – Jayne Mansfield's eighteen-room 'Pink Palace'. Now owned by Engelbert Humperdinck, the place looked beleaguered and lifeless. As we stood on tiptoe peeping over the wall (this is locally termed being a 'lookie-loo') a car drew up behind us. Both passengers were buried behind a large 'Map of the Movie Stars' Homes'. They did not get out of their car – appearing to have read the bold warning at the beginning of the *Ultimate Hollywood Tour Guide*: 'If you approach a celebrity at his or her home, he or she may construe the approach as a hostile act and act accordingly. Remember: not all celebrities are as volatile as Sean Penn or Sean Young. But why take a chance?'

Simon and I certainly didn't see any 'stars' – either out jogging or clipping their hedges – in the few hours we spent trudging along Sunset in the Holmby Hills. Despite the giant houses we passed – most with their shutters down and encircled by twenty-foot-high walls, and more security cameras than on the Iraqi Embassy in London – there was no sign of human life. Apart from the odd lost tourist, we saw nobody for nearly three miles. After passing by the 1950s modern apartment building on Wilshire Boulevard in which eighty-two-year-old Billy Wilder lives today in a modest-sized twelfth-floor flat surrounded by his valuable collection of modern art, we finally arrived, exhausted, at the Bel-Air hotel. By the time that evening's heavy tropical storm really started, we were sitting drinking vodka tonics by an open fire in the bar.

By a quirky coincidence, Sir Andrew Lloyd Webber happened to be staying that week – visiting Los Angeles to decide on a theatre for the American première of his musical *Sunset Boulevard* in the autumn. When I faxed him a note saying that we were walking the length of Sunset, as a sort of mock-pilgrimage to *Sunset Boulevard*, he invited us to have cocktails with him before dinner.

He arrived dressed rather like a Tunbridge Wells solicitor – thick cords, jacket and loose tie, and his wavy, pudding-like black hair flattened as if having ridden to work on a motorcycle. He was chatty, switching subjects – the Pre-Raphaelites (in particular his own collection), Churchill, Prince Charles's sex life – like an excited teenager swopping discs on his brand-new CD player. Although not an especially good listener – he has an odd habit of breaking into your conversation, suddenly changing the topic completely – he was engaging company, if in a slightly dotty sort of way. He told us, for example, how he had made the English *faux pas* of asking Billy Wilder to have lunch during the Superbowl.

Lloyd Webber seemed to think our journey was a bit nutty. But he was sufficiently surprised that we had made it so far to lead us back to his flash suite with its walnut piano for a screening of a number of the songs for *Sunset Boulevard*. As we sat in the front stalls – i.e. the king-size double-bed – Lloyd-Webber paced nervously around the room eating peanuts as we watched the fuzzy home-video tape. It had been recorded in a stage rigged up in what looked like the old stables of his country house in England. The impromptu preview ended with the number *With One Look*.

'That really was splendid,' gushed Simon afterwards.

Lloyd Webber looked more relaxed now – and was squatting down on the white carpet, trying to locate the VCR stop button as the tape squiggled on fast-forward.

'I wrote that song in LA,' he replied. 'Here, in fact – right here, on my piano in the Bel-Air.'

As we continued along Sunset Boulevard, a simple lesson emerged. To survive in LA, you either have to reinvent or resurrect yourself (Gloria Swanson, the Château Marmont) or you die (Schwab's, the Garden of Allah). And that, of course, was the point of Billy Wilder's black satire: a bitter-sweet elegy to The Vanity of Hollywood Wishes.

The following evening, shortly before the sun set over the Pacific, we reached the beach in Malibu. With our feet aching, we took off our shoes and socks. Rolling up our trousers, we waded into the cold blue water. For a while, as darkness fell from the air, we walked along the beach. After three days together we had exhausted most avenues of conversation.

'Time to go home?' said Simon finally.

It was nearly dark.

'Soon,' I said.

After one last look at the ocean, I dialled a taxi.

Epilogue

The Death of Celebrity

IN TINA BROWN'S FINAL EDITORIAL for *Vanity Fair*, she wrote of leaving to edit *The New Yorker* at 'this defining moment in the American culture'. By this she was referring, I think, to what is likely to become *the* cultural debate of the *fin de siècle*: the place of American mass culture in the critical statusphere.

For years, popular culture was consigned to the cultural back-yard, condescendingly sniffed at by Manhattan Upper East Side, Paris XVI or London W8 bourgeois high-brows as at an unsightly heap of junk that was spoiling their lofty view of civilisation. As George Steiner stated just two sentences into his T.S. Eliot Memorial Lecture at Kent University, his response to *Notes Towards the Definition of Culture* – Eliot's post-war plea for cultural order – 'Not an attractive book,' Steiner woefully proclaimed. 'One that is grey with the shock of recent barbarism. . .'

That was in March 1971. Tina Brown was skinny and seventeen. She had already been expelled from three boarding schools and – as an enrobed Steiner stood at the wooden lectern delivering his cultural post mortem to Britain's assembled intelligentsia – was probably bleaching her hair as the wail of Keith Richards' guitar crackled from a mono record player on the floor of her suburban London bedroom. Just over twenty years later, the former Queen of *décolletage* – who gave us Joan Collins in a blonde wig, Demi Moore's pregnant belly and a 3,000-word critique on Ivana Trump as literary débutante – was sitting enthroned behind her West 43rd Street mahogany desk as the high priestess of metropolitan culture. What's more she was George Steiner's editor.

Presiding as circus ringmaster, the Zuleika Dobson of Metroland, her magazine had transported the reader in a glass hydraulic lift from the lowest basement to the highest penthouse of the post-modern American experience. The panoramic ride, which a million Americans took in their armchairs every month, either made your stomach turn – or left you blinking and starry-eyed, looking up to the Swish Alps of Hollywood as the new cultural capital of the world. By the nineties, it seemed, all the world was a sound stage. The mark of a true high-brow was to be culturally bi-lingual: to find as much cultural significance in Bart Simpson as Bartok, in *Wayne's World* as *The Way of the World*. Hollywood suzerain Mike Ovitz, for example, now sat on the board of the Metropolitan Museum of Art. Mass culture, once the concern of the anorak and long-bearded 'cultural studies' brigade at midwestern colleges and northern polytechnics, had been awarded a cultural upgrade. Popular entertainment was not simply America's second biggest export: it was becoming the hip baby of the cultural and social elite.

What, as someone living and reporting in LA, did seem to be adding up to a fairly radical re-alignment of the cross-cultural axis was confirmed by a trip I made to New York in spring 1992. I was staying – thanks to a friend – at a small club. A remarkable bastion of New World civilisation, its walls hung with more field sport prints, stuffed beasts and polished silver trophies than an Indian viceroy's hunting lodge during the palmier days of the Raj. The oak panelling in the bar resembled a row of public school lockers – only each had the name of a dog printed on it in large letters. The library bulged with such well-thumbed volumes as *How I Shot My First Crocodile*.

At around 6.30p.m. I was sunk downstairs in a deep leather armchair sipping a whisky and soda, when various members strolled in – rich, patrician, Ivy League. I was introduced to Wall Street gentlemen bankers in Sulka ties and polished black Oxfords. And what do we talk about? The British general election? Fox-hunting in Shropshire? Partridge shooting in Spain? Bill Clinton and Gennifer Flowers? *Wrong*. An hour of earnest discussion on the new season of Tinseltown films – along with a complex technical theory, worthy of footnotes in *Cahiers du Cinéma*, about why *Casablanca* was better seen on television than at a cinema.

The next morning over breakfast I read a lavishly illustrated article that devoured over half of the op-ed page of the *New York Times*. It was by the cultural critic Camille Paglia and was about 'Rock As Art'. The piece argued that rock stars and music are one of the most neglected parts of America's national heritage. She advocated special scholarships for rock groups to be set up at colleges and universities. 'Popular music and film are the two great art forms of the twentieth century,' wrote Paglia. 'In the past twenty-five years, cinema has gained academic prestige . . . But rock music has yet to win the respect it deserves as the authentic voice of our time.'

Authentic voice of our time?

Later that afternoon I walked through a misty Central Park and visited the *American Rococo, 1750–75: Elegance in Ornament* exhibition at the Metropolitan Museum of Art. It was in its final weeks and the dimly lit second-floor rooms were almost deserted. The few, mainly elderly, or academic looking, visitors shuffling around the hushed corridors looked pretty bored. They may as well have been dead.

Whilst looking at one exhibit my attention was diverted by two museum attendants, each standing by a carved pillar, one on either side of a wide doorway, who seemed to be having some sort of argument. Both were in their mid-thirties and educated looking; judging by their badly fitting blue uniforms they probably worked part-time. Each time one wanted to force a point, he paced over to the other's pillar and whispered loudly into his ear. I stood still, pretending to peer at my exhibit, whilst listening to their discussion. After a few minutes, I learnt what the fuss was about: impassioned disagreement over the respective merits of David Bowie's recently released, and re-mixed, *Ziggy Stardust* and *Young Americans* albums onto compact disc as compared to the original vinyl. Greatest art forms of the twentieth century? The authentic voice of our time? Perhaps Paglia was *right*. Her *Sexual Personae* advocated that mass culture mirrored the classical pagan themes, and looked to Hollywood as the modern Babylon, a charismatic shrine to the enigma and power of Western personality. The sweeping hold of cinema, and celebrity and fashion, over the Western imagination represented the triumph of image over word, spectacle over narrative – a return to the pagan cult of the eye.

Not that there was, of course, anything very new or original about many of her claims. The high–low debate had been quietly simmering for nearly half a century. Dwight Macdonald had called pop culture a spreading ooze back in the fifties. What did seem new, however, was the scale of intellectual attention and respectability extended to such ideas – the boosted level of artistic prestige now being accorded to mass culture. Just a fortnight before Paglia's *New York Times* piece on Rock as Art, for instance, Gore Vidal had been invited by various grandees of Harvard University to deliver the 1992 *William E. Massey Sr Lectures in the History of American Civilization*. The subject of his three lectures, two of which were delivered from the Forum chamber of the John F. Kennedy School of Government, and attended by dozens of the most respected scholars in the land, was Hollywood movies – and the filming of history.

Again, what Vidal said was far from revolutionary. To any semi-informed post-modern critic, it was yesterday's news. Films were, he argued, the lingua franca of the twentieth century. It was a universal phenomenon, he said, that whether one visited Harvard, Oxford or the University of Bologna, after the polite and dreary exchange of academic small-talk, the conversational ice never really breaks until somebody brings up the movies. Movies – what he called the 'Tenth Muse' – were the cultural adhesive that bound civilisation together. It was impossible now, he contended, for a novelist to be properly famous, however well he was known in media circles, when the novel itself meant so little to the civilised, and almost nothing to the general public. Literary fame was dead. Books could no longer be really famous as they were not widely talked about in the way that a popular film is *talked about*. Movie fame was, in fact, the only true fame existing today. Or, put another way, Hollywood's stars were the only celebrated people that the public swooned over today. 'Today, where literature was movies are,' Vidal proclaimed. 'Whether or not the Tenth Muse does her act on a theatre screen or within the cathode tube, there can be no other reality for us since reality does not begin to mean until it has been made art of.'

* * *

Meanwhile, in London, in a seedy top-floor flat across the street from a discount jewellery shop in Shepherds Bush the *Modern Review* was born – the new quarterly 'high-brow review of mass culture' launched in September 1991 by Fleet Street journo-queen Julie Burchill and her smart mob of cultural snook-cockers, led by *chef de bande* and editor Toby Young.

Cyril Connolly boasted that the first issues of *Horizon* in 1939 were edited from Stephen Spender's two-room flat in Bloomsbury, with furniture and books moved aside to make room for galley proofs. Twenty-seven-year-old Young was equally proud of the editorial offices of the *Modern Review*: the bedroom of his student flat in which each issue was put together on a prehistoric Macintosh. To save money on curtains, a pair of sheets was tacked up across the windows with drawing pins. The smelly room, with bare and sickly lime-green walls, was swathed in darkness much of the day. There were no chairs. For editorial meetings, the staff –

including Burchill – had to sit on his unmade bed.

Possibly not since Hugh Hefner scrounged $600 off friends to start *Playboy* in 1953, editing it on his kitchen table in Chicago, has a new magazine grabbed so much attention in direct disproportion to its low-budget origins. Founded on just £500, with Burchill staying up all night licking subscription envelopes, the *Modern Review* was soon rubbing spines with the *New Republic* on the racks of Sunset Boulevard's trendy Book-Soup bookshop, and exhibited on intelligentsia coffee-tables beside the latest unread issue of *The Economist*. Just as the sixties had *Esquire* and *Rolling Stone*, the seventies had *New Musical Express*, the eighties *Vanity Fair* and *The Face* – so the *Modern Review* saw itself as being the zoom lens of the nineties *Zeitgeist*. 'If Shakespeare were alive today,' declared its opening editorial, 'it's not inconceivable he'd be working in Hollywood.'

In the same way that Wyndham Lewis' *Blast* earned notoriety in 1914 as the *belles-lettres* of its day with its celebration of the machine and its misanthropic flaying of such establishment nobs as Augustus John, so the *Modern Review* crashed into the cultural spotlight by declaring American mass culture the new avant-garde. It claimed to be the first non-academic magazine to treat the latest movie blockbusters, bestsellers and pop records with the same intellectual and critical attention that is applied to painting, opera and theatre.

What was truly unusual about the first issues of the magazine was that the contributors were paid absolutely nothing (contributors are now paid £50). They sent in their sweated-over 3,000–5,000 word essays, with by-lines that looked as if they belonged in the *New York Review of Books* (*New Yorker* film critic Pauline Kael – not paid; *New Republic* editor Andrew Sullivan – not paid; Julie Burchill – not paid; Cambridge English don Eric Griffiths – not paid; *Guardian* fiction critic James Wood – not paid; and so on) until you noticed the subject matter was Arnold Schwarzenegger, Axl Rose or *Alien*^{3}. The pieces were written with the sort of excited and eager enthusiasm you might associate with youthful efforts to get published in a university magazine. But the *Modern Review* seemed to be on to *something*. Odd donations began arriving. John Le Carré, for example sent a cheque. The Rt Hon. Alan Clark MP wanted to subscribe. Every newspaper wrote about it. *The Late Show* carried a twelve-minute item whose studio discussion was cut short after a fight broke out between Toby Young and author Jon Savage. Mary Sackville West, a *Late Show* producer, later wrote to Young: 'I've never had so many calls about an item – they all wanted to know where to buy the *Modern Review*.'

That was a sensitive question. There was *no* proper distribution. No advertising – no marketing department. No PR. The difficulty of obtaining early issues helped invest the magazine with *samizdat* status in certain media salons. It was, indeed, a form of guerilla publishing. Unable to afford even to design the first issue of the magazine, Young's staff had broken into the high-tech offices of Robert Maxwell's *European* newspaper on New Fetter Lane. For forty-eight hours, whilst the paper was closed for the weekend, Young had squatted in the arts editor's suite using Maxwell's state-of-the-art equipment for free.

It wasn't long before New York tuned in. Despite the *Modern Review* having dismissed *Vanity Fair* as 'in essence, a philistine journal', and sniffing at Tina Brown ('her brilliant career has blinded her to the banality of her product'), Brown was interested. She flew *Vanity Fair* media columnist James Wolcott to London to interview Julie Burchill and her co-founding editors. Young adamantly refused to let Wolcott see their grotty premises. They lunched at the Groucho Club – and the piece ran across three glossy pages. By this time, Jay McInerney, who held his own generation of critics in contempt for being hostile to the serious intellectual claims of popular culture, was already having issues dispatched to him in New York by his London editor, Liz Calder. 'Nothing has happened in America for a long time that is comparable to the *Modern Review*,' he told me. 'I used to lie awake at night waiting for these things.'

* * *

In Tom Wolfe's bruising *Harper's* essay of 1989, *Stalking the Billion-Footed Beast*, about the wimpish failure of American writers to wrestle with the 'rude beast' of social realism, he wrote: 'Of one thing I am certain. If fiction writers do not start facing the obvious, the literary history of the second half of the twentieth century will record that journalists not only took over the richness of American life as their domain but also seized the high ground of literature itself.' He was, of course, expanding on the theme of *The New Journalism*, which declared that non-fiction had displaced the novel as American literature's 'main event'.

But when I dutifully waded through my monthly mountain of general interest and entertainment magazines and newspapers (*Time, Esquire, Vanity Fair, Rolling Stone, Newsweek, GQ, Premiere, Entertainment Weekly, People, Interview, New York Times, Los Angeles Times* – and so on) which were supposedly chronicling the 'richness of American life', I became pretty sure of something myself. From living in LA, I knew that Hollywood is about as wild, ripe and exuberantly comic a subject as existed on earth. There was no chance, as Wolfe put it, of running into the damnable problem of *material*. But if the bottomless swamp of spineless, crass and vapid celebrity interviews and entertainment features I was reading – and many magazines often seem stuffed with little else – was the 'high ground of literature itself' then I began to conclude that civilisation was perhaps worse off than I imagined. It had, in fact, to be getting dangerously close to running on empty. It wasn't real journalism – in contrast, for example, to some of the zinging and zestful reporting that I was reading of, say, Michael Kinsley, Michael Lewis, Christopher Hitchens or Dominick Dunne, in political, financial or social spheres. It was as pathetic as watching a mini-bus load of tourists taking on a tribe of jungle cannibals with a golf-bag of pop-guns. It was, of course, journalism reduced to the level of the *commercial*.

After six months of living in LA, meeting dozens of studio executives, actors, actresses, directors, producers, screen-writers, critics, journalists and publicists – in fact, spending my whole life snooping around the entertainment community, observing the engine-room of the celebrity machine, the bulk of most Hollywood punditry began to seem absurd. After a while, a single fact became glaringly evident about the weekly avalanche of 'Posh Pop' editorial commentary and magazine celebrity profiles I was reading. With the exception of a few fairly small circulation magazines like the *Modern Review*, and the occasional *Spy*, *Movieline* or *Harper's* article, most seemed myopic about the reality of nineties Hollywood – particularly the machinery of its marketing and publicity militia. Not unlike the clueless generals of World War I, naïvely pontificating from their creaky club chairs in London, most celebrity and movie-based journalism – and there was an awful lot of it – seemed wildly at odds with the racket that was really *going on*.

Of two things, in fact, I became certain. The media, who often seemed to gawp at Hollywood as if it were the Delphic oracle, were being duped. The legion of trendy commentators and celebrity profile writers are as star-struck – *gobsmacked* – as the masses who camped out all night to get a seat in the stands on Oscar night. They had lost their critical senses. (What are good films? Who are interesting people? Films that movie-goers go to see. Actors that people see on a screen.)

At a time when so much space and attention is being lavished on the cinema and the intellectual claims of popular culture, the quality of films coming out of Hollywood has never been so bad. As one senior studio mogul confessed to the *New York Times* shortly before the start of the 1993 summer movie season, the industry's mood was of 'self-loathing'; the movies being made were 'a lot of formulaic, by the numbers, cliché-ridden, high concept garbage'. Despite the first six months of 1993 bringing in a cumulative gross of $2.25 billion, too many Tinseltown productions remained almost unwatchable. The juggernaut of marketing and publicity was rendering critical judgements largely redundant. Worse, the self-important and delinquent tendencies of so many actors and pop-singers crossing the tinsel-rope bridge from non-entity to 'celebrity' has never been more crudely apparent.

Secondly, film-making was being increasingly reduced to instant visual gratification backed by a heavy-muscle publicity machine that had the world's media fooled into believing that Hollywood executives and celebrities have some mystic hotline into the souls and value of society. The normally scabrous British media, for example, seemed to grant American stars a form of immunity – with chat-show hosts treating them with obsequious and risible reverence. People seemed to have forgotten they are just movies – aimed mainly at an audience of sixteen to twenty-four year olds.

It struck me as odd. Whilst wizard technology and market competition had helped raise the standards of the best TV and print journalism to such a high level, the media's febrile and disingenuous coverage of the high comedy of modern Hollywood, in particular its celebrity circus – which probably takes up more combined space in the world's newspapers and magazines than any other subject – seems an anachronistic hangover from the days when H.L. Mencken charged American journalism of the 1920s with being 'feeble and vulgar'. Celebrity journalism is lagging back in the dark ages – with editors and journalists finding access to movie actors or pop-stars more difficult than access to presidents or dictators, enduring SS-style attempts at censorship, and invariably writing with a caution and timidity once reserved for birthday odes to Nero.

* * *

For some years it has been difficult to open a newspaper or magazine – and not just *USA Today* or the *Daily Express* – without the pearly white teeth of a Hollywood celebrity glaring smugly out, accompanied by 1,500 words of unctuous prose. Wherever you go, magazine racks are piled high with an endless row of celebrity covers. Flick through the channels on the TV, and you are likely to see some movie actor or supermodel plugging his or her new film, ghost-written novel, autobiography, perfume, restaurant, clothing chain, fitness video, salad dressing, condom label, self-help guide, Aids charity . . . or *whatever*. Not so long ago, such news as came out of Hollywood was invariably confined to the gossip columns, film reviews, or, occasionally, to a fluff piece at the bottom of the home or foreign pages. Nobody took actors and celebrities – or what they had to say – very seriously.

That has changed. Films and celebrities are now taken so seriously by the media that the line between 'entertainment' and 'news' has become otiose. This has long been demonstrated by programmes like *Entertainment Tonight* which are formatted exactly like a local news bulletin – as if the only news today happens in Hollywood. During most of the 1992 Republican convention, CNN's Headline News made Woody Allen's love-life its lead story. When somebody accidentally stepped on the toe of a drinking companion of *Beverly Hills 90210* teen-actress Shannon Doherty in an LA nightclub the incident became international news. If Madonna spoke out about Bosnia, Arnold Schwarzenegger opened a hamburger restaurant or Barbra Streisand decided not to ski in Aspen, it was now world headlines rather than showbiz gossip.

Perhaps the most disturbing recent example of all came in March 1993. Rodney King's testimony in the federal trial of the four LAPD officers charged with beating him and depriving him of his civil rights coincided with the week of actress Kim Basinger's breach of contract suit in Los Angeles Superior Court, a few blocks away in Downtown LA.

Basinger was being sued for $5.6 million by Main Line Pictures after she dropped out of a film called *Boxing Helena* – about a girl whose arms and legs are amputated and kept in a box – just four weeks before shooting. On the *opening* day of Rodney King's historic testimony, in which he testified that he thought the police officers were going to kill him, almost all British newspapers gave considerably more news coverage (the *Daily Mail*, for example, gave it almost a whole page) to Miss Basinger's first day in the witness stand.

Coverage of Hollywood is shifting away from the entertainment pages to the news and editorial pages. The *New York Times*, for example, ran at least twenty separate articles on the Oliver Stone film *JFK*, including six on its op-ed page. *Newsweek*, *Esquire* and *Life* (and a thousand other American and European magazines) ran marathon-length cover articles. The feeding frenzy repeated itself with Spike Lee's *Malcolm X* and *Jurassic Park*. *Four* months before the opening of Steven Spielberg's dinosaur epic, the *Wall Street Journal* ran a long front-page story devoted to the minutiae of the film's marketing campaign (ranging from Jurassic Park Foam Soap with Moulded Dinosaur Topper to JuJu Dinosaur Eggs).

The yards of serious newspaper columns and TV space given to such films serve, of course, as a stamp of cultural validation, seeming to legitimise the dubious notion that political, sociological and historical truths can be learnt from visiting the cinema. More importantly, perhaps, the studios have been quick to realise that engineering media controversies is a cheap and hugely effective new way of marketing films. As *Harper's* noted a few weeks before *Jurassic* opened, in 1993, Hollywood's New Auteurs are its marketeers – the executives with the job of enticing an increasingly disillusioned and bored movie-going public into the cinemas. As the public and critics grow less patient with Hollywood's product, the studios have learned to assume that their big-budget movies will be savaged by word-of-mouth, the magazine declared. As a result, 'studios need to bring in huge crowds on the first weekend, when the only 'word' on a film is created by Hollywood publicists, ad-writers and merchandisers'.

Most newspaper and magazine editors are gullible and happy accomplices to the 'Event Movie'. The problem is that practically no raw reporting is really being done from the front-line. Instead there is a vast array of armchair pundits, from Chicago to Hampstead, many of whom have never been to LA. As Kenneth Tynan noted back in 1959, when guest theatre critic of *The New Yorker*, pundits wrote as supposed experts not only in their own specialised subject, but also in what is referred to as the 'American experience' or the 'American situation' – setting themselves up as cultural and sociological referees, interpreters and trend-spotters. 'They speak *ex cathedra*,' he wrote, 'and are listened to with a respect that borders on awe, even though – and this is the odd thing – they frequently have little or no official status.' Apart from a few lone and belligerent madmen on the entertainment trade journals (*Variety* and the *Hollywood Reporter*), which the public never reads, few reporters in LA – with a few exceptions, like Bernie Weinraub of the *New York Times*, seem very interested in hammering on the studio gates, hounding agents or flame-grilling publicists, in asking the 'Talent' the *right questions*.

Nobody dares hold up a mirror to Caliban. Apart from finding LA both morally and aesthetically bankrupt, what irked Waugh most about his safari trip into the great Hollywood reserve, where the moguls stumbled and basked under the palm trees, was the way that Tinseltown's 'insurmountable barrier of financial prosperity' clouded over all critical distinctions between films. 'No film of ours is ever a failure,' a studio executive had told Waugh. 'Some are greater successes than others, but we reckon to get our money back on everything we produce.'

By the nineties, little has changed. Of the hundreds of American newspapers published each day, only three (according to the *Blu-Book*, at least) have staff correspondents in LA – *New York Times, Wall Street Journal* and *Washington*

Post. The Hollywood Foreign Press Association, as I've shown, is a joke. The vast majority of 'journalism' coming out of Hollywood is, in reality, being written by freelance 'entertainment' writers, usually far too busy making a tidy fortune from syndication rights – or worrying about having their celebrity access cut off – to be troubled too much about the fact that their copy is empty-headed tripe. A great deal of Hollywood journalism is, in fact, not coming out of Tinseltown at all. It is the result of a star-dazzled throng of suede-jacketed super-hacks being summoned for a hasty interview (six to eight minutes with an actor is normal at most 'junkets'; Clint Eastwood, say, will be interviewed over fifty times in a day) in a ritzy New York or London hotel suite, fluffily carpeted VIP trailer, or – if the publicist thinks you sufficiently important – sitting on the foldaway seat in the back of an airport-bound stretch limousine. It makes little difference. The celebrity robotically spouts whatever spiel he or she has been told to say. The fact is that wherever this gunk is pounded out, most celebrity journalism reads like an unofficial organ of the studio public relations industry. The result of all the global attention that has recently been lavished on Hollywood is that Tinseltown has become too big for its boots. The cult of celebrity amounts to a spurious con-trick on the public.

The con works like this: a small number of suitably vetted 'journalists' are given exclusive access to film sets, stars, directors, producers and the executive suites of studio chiefs, because there is a tacit understanding between the publicists and the publications that no unfriendly copy will be published. Not only are photographers and journalists asked to submit examples of past work for inspection but publicists are known to independently screen journalists by employing a research agency to track down unsubmitted examples of past work on a Nexus computer data-base.

These studio-sponsored articles are then syndicated *en masse* to hundreds of magazines in America and around the world. The price of publishing 'negative' copy, and not playing along with this journalistic bootlegging, is instant blacklisting and excommunication. Phone calls not returned. Access cut off. Legal proceedings initiated. Anyone attempting to wrestle with the 'rude beast' swiftly finds – however prestigious or important their publication – themselves swotted down like a fly. The most ludicrous recent example was when Columbia threatened to cut off the entire staff of the *Los Angeles Times* from *all* access to its executives and film sets unless the newspaper barred a particular journalist from even so much as uttering the word Columbia again – after he wrote a piece claiming that a screening of *Last Action Hero* had been poorly received by a preview audience.

In recent years, the editors of the *New York Times* have had a policy of appointing a well-seasoned and experienced reporter to the beat. Far from being a fluff-assignment, they want a hardened journalist who wouldn't be messed around with, or have the tinsel pulled over his eyes. Someone, in fact, like Larry Rohter, a highly cultured former Afghanistan war correspondent with *Newsweek*, who, after years in the field, has witnessed all forms of official corruption from the Far East to darkest Peru.

After considerably less than a year of being in Hollywood, however, Rohter made the highly unusual request of asking to be relieved of his assignment. Despite the heavy clout of the *New York Times* behind him, he became fed up with the constant barriers, pernicious threats and attempts at blacklisting he encountered in dealing with the Hollywood publicity machine. In his first week in Hollywood, for example, a well-known producer rang him up and asked him if he had thought of writing a screenplay. The money was good – he knew a major studio that might be interested. Before Rohter blew the whistle on such unusual journalistic perks he was hastily appointed the *New York Times*'s Miami bureau chief. The transfer was quietly hushed up. 'If I can interview Ferdinand Marcos about fraudulent elections in the Philippines, with him answering any question I fire at him,

I fire at him, then I really don't see why I can't ask some two-bit actor about his marriage or finances,' Rohter told me. 'Marcos may have been a scoundrel, but at least he didn't try interfering with questions. Hollywood likes to compare itself with Washington, but it's so much, much, worse.'

Recently, the growing power of many Hollywood publicists has become a subject of bitter acrimony. Fed up with being dictated to, many editors, journalists and photographers are now spoiling for a fight. A bitter and bloody war has, in fact, been in the making for years. Editors, journalists and photographers have become increasingly impatient with the presumptuous and high-handed handling methods of a new breed of publicists. As Nixon discovered with Watergate, you can't beat the press.

Celebrity journalism, as I have said, is languishing back in the twenties and thirties. As Graham Greene discovered, rather to his surprise, when appointed film critic of *The Spectator* in 1939, studios seemed to regard journalists as little more than greedy children, disciplined into line with a few fancy invitations, some free cigarettes and fizzy drinks. Greene regularly received two telegrams each week, delivered to his home, from an American film company summoning his presence the following day at the Savoy, when a 'film personality, sometimes of remarkable obscurity', would 'hold court' – followed by refreshments (champagne, sherry, cigarettes or, occasionally, a four-course lunch). Greene expressed bewilderment over the invariable assumption that film journalists – as opposed to book reviewers or drama critics – craved alcohol by 10.30a.m.

Whilst you get Evian water instead of champagne at most studio screenings today, and certainly won't get a free pack of cigarettes, little has changed. The Tinseltown publicity machine now increasingly steam-rolls critics, lavishing its sweetest attentions on 'entertainment writers', who are regarded as much easier to control. Studios are worried less and less about reviews, knowing that if they create enough honeyed prose outside the review columns the masses will queue up around the block on a Friday night. Like Greene, many critics I talked to blame much of this erosion of critical standards on the rising power of publicity and marketing executives. As Peter Rainer of the *Los Angeles Times*, chairman of the National Society of Film Critics, told me: 'They dictate the shots because no one is willing to stand up and say "No, we'll choose our own writers, thank you." Newspapers or magazines know that if you don't take the story, a rival will get it and you won't get the next story. You are not just going to get a big cover story. You have to pay for it. There is extensive collusion going on between studio marketing departments and the media.'

* * *

During my time in Hollywood I have met dozens of major 'stars' – at premières, *aprés*-award show parties, interviews, junkets, tennis courts, cricket matches, dinner parties, barbeques, brunches, cocktail parties, screenings, gala benefits, nightclubs, dry-cleaners and so on. Many are about as interesting as a glass of soda water left out for two days by the swimming pool. Some are dull and crass, some are crude monsters, most are quite ordinary. William Boyd, who is no stranger to LA and has met many of its most celebrated inhabitants, admitted: 'I've met quite a lot of stars, and a lot of the time when actors become celebrities they become quite terrible human beings. Most are completely neurotic, or their egos are out of control. When you put a star on the cover of a magazine and it doesn't sell any more copies you begin to realise that people are probably interested in other things.'

In a survey of British schoolchildren, asked what they want to be when they grow up, 95 per cent replied: 'to be famous'. 'Fame – I wanna live for ever' went the theme song to the TV show. For the media to so often idolise today's celebrity circus like a bouncing troop of teenage cheerleaders, invariably suffering from acute critical paralysis, is puerile. Significantly, in its first two years the *Modern Review* has not run a single celebrity interview. Yet, for most magazines, the quest for celebrity has become the Holy Grail of the twentieth century. If you are born Tom Mapother, dyslexic, poor and with an absentee father, then Hollywood is meant to represent the New Wonderland in which everyone can escape their unhappy past. Dim the lights, roll the cameras – and action! Suddenly, there you are, up on the screen: Tom Cruise.

A popular myth about today's celebrity circus is that 'stars' enjoy being drooled over on TV chat-shows, interviewed and photographed for newspapers and magazines. The vast majority of Tinseltown celebrities don't. Far from leading glitzy lives, the majority of successful actors tend to work very hard, have a few close friends, go to bed early and – significantly – are either painfully shy of, or simply loathe the accoutrements and trappings of the celebrity circus. As Jodie Foster once told *Time*, 'I became an actress because I like to act, not to get my picture in the paper and have people wonder what colour socks I wear – and not to get the best table at the Polo Lounge.'

Most – particularly the more talented – dislike being incessantly interviewed, snapped, posing with fans, repeating themselves on chat-shows, being *looked* at, *smiled* at, *loved* by millions. Such publicity demands are, incidentally, written into their contracts: many would simply refuse to do it otherwise. Clive James, author of the BBC series *Fame in the 20th Century*, frankly admitted to me, 'Human beings are simply not designed to deal with the effects of being recognised by everybody.'

Just as the celebrities themselves are now increasingly weary of the demands of the publicity treadmill cranked up for each new film or album so the public have also tired of the tedious and unchanging menu of junk journalism and unctuous TV chat served up each week. Every month it is the same thirty or forty celebrity faces smiling fakely from the covers of the same magazines – or re-hashing the same spiel on TV, whether it is for Jay Leno, Arsenio Hall, David

Letterman or Jonathan Ross. Nothing is ever really said, there is no conversation. All the viewer sees is a comic robot. Instead of dwelling on what might be of interest about a famous person – namely, their work, achievements or thoughts – interviewers tend to drool over trivial details about the actors *themselves*, on the assumption that they must have some wonderfully intriguing and multi-layered personality. Unfortunately, the fact that they haven't, or don't much like the one they've got, is very often the reason that they become actors or stand-up comics in the first place.

Marlon Brando, interviewed in April, 1978 by *Playboy* on his private island of Tetiaroa, forty miles north of Tahiti, was lucid and candid on this subject. The island had no phone and the interviewer stayed ten days.

Playboy: What about acting as an art form?
Brando: In your heart of hearts, you know perfectly well that movie stars aren't artists.
Playboy: Do you consider any people in your profession artists?
Brando: No.
Playboy: So you have never considered yourself an artist?
Brando: No, never, Kenneth Clark narrated a television series called *Civilisation*. It was a remarkable series. It was erudite, communicative, polished, interesting to listen to. There was a man who knew who the artists of the world were. He didn't talk about any paltry people that you and I might mention. He talked about great *art*. He certainly didn't refer to the art of film . . . If Kenneth Clark said I was an artist, I would immediately get him to a neurosurgeon.

Brando's contempt for film acting went so far as having his script-lines Sellotaped to the forehead of his co-star during shoots as he couldn't be bothered to learn them. A significant part of the 8,000-word *Q & A* interview with Brando, who rarely spoke to journalists, concerned his revulsion at the inanity of the bulk of celebrity journalism, in particular the profile industry. Most actors, he said, simply had no wish whatsoever to open up the private details of their lives for public consumption. 'It's not absorbing or meaningful or significant, it doesn't have much to do with our lives. It's dog-food conversation,' said Brando. 'I guess I have a burning resentment of the fact that when people meet you, they're meeting some asshole celebrity movie actor, instead of a person. This *idiot* part of life has to go in the forefront of things as if it's of major importance.'

Back in 1967, in her essay 'Movies on Television', written before the invasion of satellite and cable-television channels into our sitting-rooms, Pauline Kael lamented the demeaning of the exotic magic of the cinema by the gamut of re-repeated second and third-rate old films at all times of the day and night on television. She drew attention to their visual incoherence – being all jumbled together out of their historical sequence. What may once have been assured a worthy rank in film history was now dishonoured by being so available, so meaninglessly present. In the other arts, she argued, something like natural selection took place, with only the most influential or excellent works surviving. 'There's a kind of hopelessness about it,' she wrote, 'what does not deserve to lasts, and so it all begins to seem one big pile of junk . . . Watching old movies is like spending an evening with those people next door. They bore us, and we wouldn't go out of our way to see them; we drop in on them because they're so close. If it took some effort to see old movies, we might try to find out which were the good ones, and if people saw only the good ones maybe they would still respect old movies.'

A similar sense of *ennui* has, I would argue, set in with the bland and packaged ubiquity of the modern cult of celebrity. The nasty surprise received by Kim Basinger in March 1993 when the Los Angeles Superior Court ordered her to pay $8.9 million for dropping out of *Boxing Helena* is indicative of the extent to which the public have become jaded with Hollywood. Likewise, Arnold Schwarzenegger was thought to be invincible at the box office. The 'main event' of the 1993 summer movie season, confidently declared the *Los Angeles Times* in May, would be 'Arnold "Last Action Hero" VS. T–Rex "Jurassic Park".' Arnie was, in fact, given top billing. The embarrassing flop of *Last Action Hero* proved to be yet another symptom of the public's lassitude with Tinseltown's publicity militia. After Columbia's marketing team, headed by Mark Gill, failed to *manage* the media's response to the $90 million action-fantasy bomb, Peter Guber – who, as head of Sony, oversees Columbia – predictably remarked: 'Failure is not the End Game – it is an almost inevitable cul-de-sac on the road to success.'

It is no longer enough to say that distinctions between fame, talent and notoriety are blurred to the point of irrelevance. If, as Vidal suggests, conventional types of fame (military, scientific, literary) have been marginalised by the green-eyed monster of modern movie fame, then what happens when today's celebrity-style movie fame ceases to fascinate, ceases to convey any sense of mystery or magic and is consumed simply because there is nothing else better to do? When every form of deliberately offensive and gratuitous publicity stunt has been exhausted? When distinctions between fame and fandom are mocked by the 'instant celebrity' possibilities of the camcorder and karaoke machine? When distinctions between news and entertainment are warped to the extent that John Lennon's assassin is interviewed as a personality – naturally, plugging a book – on the TV talk-show circuit? When viewers and readers have lost their capacity to be morally, visually or verbally shocked, or even surprised? When the cult of celebrity has become pretty well meaningless?

There was a time when the stars were distant types who were photographed in sharply contrasted black-and-white studio portraits that suggested a hard, erotic glamour. It meant something because it seemed so unobtainable. Before TV helped to demean the sense of mystery that went with the cinema, distinctions between the public and the stars were clean-cut. Now, just as distinctions between fame and notoriety have become blurred, so have distinctions between fame and fandom. Both have lost a sense of their allure despite the fact that, as Kenneth Tynan once observed, film is the most difficult art to be bored by.

Now the big-budget movies so often seem visually incoherent, devoid of all narrative drive, with sequel after sequel coalescing. To enter the old darkened theatres, with their luridly extravagant oriental or Egyptian designs, was to enter into a fantastic world. Today's new cinemas are built like faceless corporate office blocks. As Salman Rushdie observed in his 1986 review of *Debrett Goes to Hollywood*, few stars today can generate enough power to dazzle us, partly because the television screen has made them smaller than we are. 'We channel-hop while they kiss,' he wrote, 'we push the fast-forward button on our videos when they bore us.'

With the 'Death of Celebrity' – if that doesn't sound too bold a phrase – I envisage a return to a rather more exacting idea of fame that invests some meaning and mystique to being well known. A post-celebrity culture revolving less around the marketing of fame as a publicity-fuelled commodity, a trite form of advertising which is making the stars, the media and the public all yawn with its bland and meaningless ubiquity – to one with a more demanding critical standard.

The world mania for celebrity is a testament to modern society's own erosion of identity and self-confidence, the loss of any shared consensus of cultural values – the cultural adhesive that binds society together. As movies are an American product, you might argue that is fair enough for a celebrity culture to thrive so extensively in the United States. But for this movie-fame to be dictating serious news and cultural values to such an extent around the rest of the world seems less desirable. By the year 2,000, the major studios expect foreign audiences to provide up to 70 per cent of their business – against just 30 per cent in 1980. Jack Valenti, president of the Motion Picture Association of America, has called the foreign market the 'locomotive' that will haul the movie industry into the next century.

Films and celebrities have risen to fill the cultural void as the lowest common denominator. Ask about Oliver Stone or Sharon Stone around the dinner table and you will doubtless get a lively – and informed – discussion. Movie and celebrity culture are increasingly the only culture – if that is the right word – that many 'educated' people have to talk about. An Arts Council Survey of British adults in 1991, for example, revealed that seeing a film was easily the most frequent 'culture' enjoyed by 80 per cent of the public, with only 48 per cent regularly reading books. In the United Kingdom, cinema admissions doubled to over 100 million in 1992, partly because 400 state-of-the-art screens were built, chiefly in shopping centres, from 1985–91. Significantly, the survey revealed that only 54 per cent of those who went to the movies said they were interested in them.

If mass culture is really going to start filling the cultural void – it is too early to say whether popular film and music *will* be known as the great twentieth-century art forms – it is certain that a more exacting critical standard will be both demanded and required. Both Tinseltown and the media have underestimated the basic intelligence of the public. One of the reasons for the booming cult of celebrity in recent years is that Hollywood often seemed practically the only good news coming out of America. In bleak, slumped and insecure economic climates – i.e. the 1930s or 1990s – popular interest in celebrities is always high. This is partly because they are viewed by magazine editors and TV producers as comforting symbols that give people something to smile about and provide a form of communal focus that reassures them that – despite the swamp of unsettling images and soundbites from around the world – the world is not spinning out of control.

But there are more pernicious reasons for the yards of column inch space devoted to Tinseltown – notably to do with the cross-fertilisation of media empires. Take Warner Bros's *Batman Returns*: in 1992, it was the fastest grossing film ever ($46 million in the first three days), mainly thanks to a swamp of media hyperbole. It was also one of the worst films in years, which dropped like a stone – a month after release it had been practically forgotten – when word-of-mouth got around amongst the regular public that it was utterly devoid of plot or point.

Warner Bros (owned by Time-Warner) sank an estimated $80 million into making *Batman Returns*. *Time* (owned by Time-Warner) devoted several glossy pages to a shameful review by its normally adroit critic Richard Corliss that likened the film to the 'soar of pure poetry'. *People* magazine (also owned by Time-Warner) published exclusive photographs of the *Batman Returns* première party (other media were not invited). *Entertainment Weekly* (owned by Time-Warner) gave the film a glossy cover, accompanied by eleven pages of junk prose.

Michael Keaton (Batman) *comes to the door of his home dressed in a bathrobe and nothing else. The doorbell has startled him out of his shower. After excusing himself, he pulls on gray gym shorts and a white polo shirt, then reappears, padding barefoot across the airy living room. Leading me into the kitchen, he confronts a new coffeemaker, a model to which you add water and whole beans . . .*

Drivel. But carried along by a $250 million juggernaut of licensed merchandising (from Batman cereal to McDonald's Bat-frisbees), the media hype built up with such a fireball effect that a week after its première in LA a serious news item appeared from New York in the foreign pages of the *Daily Telegraph*, regarding some very minor protests at alleged anti-Semitism in the film. Even more bewildering, perhaps, was that Warner Bros sponsored a classroom guide for *Batman Returns* – written by a London based organisation called Film Education – which was ordered for use at thousands of British schools, although the studio decided not to produce an equivalent for use in America.

* * *

On a summer night in London in 1806, twenty-eight-year-old William Hazlitt sat up until dawn drinking and arguing with a group of young literary friends in Charles Lamb's barrister's chambers in Mitre Court, a cobbled alley close to Fleet Street. The discussion, which Hazlitt wrote up in a quirky essay called 'Of Persons One Would Wish to Have Seen', revolved around a whimsical parlour game. The idea was to nominate famous figures – painters, musicians, writers, politicians, philosophers, terrorists, murderers – and decide whether they would be worth meeting in real life.

The critical standard was uncompromising. The only English statesman that anyone expressed the least desire to see was Oliver Cromwell. Locke and Newton were dismissed as prissy bores. Milton, too starchy and puritanical. Spenser, a romantic pansy. Dryden, a vulgar show-man. Fielding, Hobbes and Hume, tedious and dull. After Boswell's *Life*, there was nothing more to know about Dr Johnson. Chaucer, Ben Jonson, Bunyan, Guy Fawkes, Handel, Shakespeare, Pope, Hogarth: approved.

When I came across the essay in LA, I was struck by the fact that of nearly one hundred candidates proposed throughout the night only one was an actor – David Garrick. And even though he was also a prolific writer, producer, director and stage manager, a friend of Hazlitt's swiftly attempted to blackball his nomination, grumbling that 'it was a shame to make all this rout about a mere player and farce-writer'. Twenty years later, when Hazlitt published his best selling *The Spirit of the Age, or Contemporary Portraits* – the first collection of modern day celebrity profiles – the volume contained no mention of any actors, despite nineteenth-century popular interest in the London theatre being comparable to that of Hollywood film releases now.

With the ready availability of books and newspapers, followed by the rise of the mass media, came a crucially important new power: being able to appeal over the heads of coercive patrons – to the public itself. Coupled with the high new level of financial reward, this signalled the death of patronage. As Hazlitt wrote, 'An author nowadays no longer hangs dangling on the frown of a lord, or the smile of a lady of quality . . . but throws himself boldly, making a lover's leap of it, into the broad lap of public opinion on which he falls like a featherbed.'

In *The Frenzy of Renown*, Leo Braudy argued that modern fame is the 'democratic descendant' of 'honour' – with the vastly increased number of ways of being known today making our celebrity mania the antithesis of the classical notion of fame. Fame used to be reserved for the few – as reward for noble public deeds: military, political, dramatic. This concept of fame, he argued, has become grotesquely distorted. He drew attention, for example, to the disturbing letter that a serial killer in the Midwest wrote to his local police complaining that he wasn't getting enough publicity. 'How many times do I have to kill before I get a name in the paper or some national attention?'

Yet this idea that Tinseltown somehow represents the democratisation of idolatory remains probably the most disingenuous popular myth about Hollywood today. Tinseltown is no meritocracy. It is a town whose day-to-day business methods would frequently gall even the most unscrupulous Wall Street dealer or Washington lobbyist. For all LA's trendy and liberal cosmopolitan image, the studios remain medieval-style fiefdoms where executive power is absolute – and money is enthroned as the divining rod of success and merit. Hollywood is more feudal than democratic, with personal patronage as entrenched in the power-play as in the city state of fifteenth-century Rome. Because of Hollywood's high media-profile today, the small mafia of publicists who hold the levers of power controlling access to the Tinseltown celebrity machine have become especially despotic. The media are seen as existing for the primary purpose of being manipulated, exploited and controlled.

One evil, it is increasingly argued, of the American profile industry is the cult of personality. But in a sense the problem is not that there is too much 'personality' about – rather there is too little. Too little sense of the real *person* being interviewed. Too much deference to celebrity protocol. Too much reliance on the impersonal, artificial and unreliable modes of discourse that have become the sources of the modern interview.

The novelist A.S. Byatt, among others, has expressed concern about this – now that the telephone has replaced the letter, and the celebrity profile and TV chat-show are going to be the main sources of the future biographer. Each time a celebrity is interviewed, it seems, their faded cuttings are photo-copied and then dutifully re-hashed. Vladamir Nabokov always refused to be interviewed unless he was allowed to write out his answers by hand. Far from wishing to curtail this slide into a false and disingenuous media reality, most publicists, in fact, encourage this style of interviewing – a glossy 'media-pack' of selected profiles will be biked around to you before your interview; they see it as a form of control. Ultimately, however, it is reductive – and only adds to the reader's sense of boredom.

The first popular myth that needs smashing about this sort of journalism is that the writer is a detective under oath to pursue the whole truth and nothing but. The best journalism, or character profiles, have often belonged as much to the author to his subject. No one has ever suggested for a moment that Crito scribbled down Socrates's last words in 60wpm shorthand, or that Boswell's encounters with Dr Johnson are genuine transcripts of their conversation. Aubrey's waspish and irreverent *Brief Lives* offers more character insights than any mountain of *Life* covers. All used the imagination of memory to create a coherent artistic picture – not a shapeless jumble of junk prose. It is the quality of imaginative extension that distinguishes real journalism from junk journalism. As Tom Wolfe noted back in the 1960s, the term non-fiction, under which umbrella lurks the modern profile industry, concedes abjectly to the claims of fiction as superior art.

Held up as an archetype of the American experience,

celebrity has now become a pejorative, with actors and pop stars risibly becoming the United States' agony aunts, displacing writers and journalists as interpreters of the American condition. Desperately seeking to legitimise themselves as serious people, they set themselves up as experts on subjects ranging from Aids to Zagreb. Arnold Schwarzenegger, televised talking sport with President Bush after the president had widely been denounced as being a wimp, was used to woo the New Hampshire voters in the primary season. They didn't buy it.

As the 1992 presidential campaign entered its final weeks, the media spotlight glowed with an avalanche of 'Tinseltown and Politics' articles and television 'specials' which dwelt endlessly with the stars' political endorsements and the menu details of their $1,000-a-plate fund-raising dinners. Yet the public doesn't care what Hollywood thinks – and they certainly didn't vote on the absurd basis of which celebrities support which candidates.

The primary reason, in my view, that the coagulating and globular bubble of American celebrity is likely to be harpooned by the media is chiefly because mass culture has become a victim of its own success. Despite the cross-fertilisation of media empires, the media and Hollywood are natural rivals. Not collaborators. Both seek to define how society – Britain or America – perceives the world and its place in it.

Up until quite recently – before Hollywood became a *news* story – that was all very well. Nobody took Hollywood very seriously. But there has been a gear change. As Peter Guber's 'Hollywood and the Media' lectures at UCLA contended: 'It is neither the selling nor the manipulation of world views that either party objects to; it is the success of the competition's point of view that disturbs them'.

Exactly. With Hollywood on the brink of an information technology revolution, and agencies like Mike Ovitz's CAA and ICM poised to provide an endless supply of packaged celebrity talent to supply a hugely exploded film and TV market, the more serious media have every reason to be disturbed by the extent to which Hollywood, rather than itself, is shaping society.

The media backlash against the cult of celebrity will, I believe, happen sooner rather than later, and partly as a direct consequence of the heightened intellectual claims now being made for mass culture. At the root of the problem is the risible notion afflicting too many American journalists – namely that they have a responsibility to protect and defend the idea of 'culture'. With LA having been awarded a cultural upgrade, there is now every reason for bringing the same incisive and rigorous standards of reporting and writing to Hollywood that are applied to the financial and political worlds.

In his inaugural lecture as Professor of Politics and Contemporary History at Birkbeck College, London, Ben Pimlott, the distinguished British biographer, spoke of the dangers of contemporary history remaining so conservative. Pick up any recent political biography, he said, and you will find it built like a Wimpey house, with almost identical segments and proportions. Biographers, he argued, were becoming complacent about their audience. They had forgotten that great portraits – such as Strachey's *Eminent Victorians* – aimed not so much at the abstraction of truth but *understanding*. He has advocated a drastic change in the genre. 'When the moment does come,' he said, 'the revolution will be rapid.'

At 'this defining moment in the American culture', this is precisely what its distant cousin, the booming celebrity journalism industry, also urgently requires.

What is required is for journalists, in this wildest and most comic of twentieth-century cities – this Babylonian cultural colossus – to trade in their pop-guns for sabres. Their edges should be sharpened like linen knives. What is also needed, to paraphrase Pimlott, is for a legion of radical innovators with the arrogance of a Picasso and the genius of a Joyce to smash our encrusted expectations. Celebrities need reminding they are the fleeting parvenus rather than the princes of fame.

Index

Academy Award ceremony 132–4
Academy of Motion Picture Arts and Sciences 118–20, 129, 135
Aids 42, 74, 83–4, 90, 210, 223, 278
Airplane 236
Aladdin 110
Alamo, The 118
Alcoholics Anonymous 223
Alien³ 261
All the President's Men 231
Allen, Woody 196, 265
Allison, Shawn E. 95
Alon, Moshe 'The Brute' 39, 44, 47
Altman, Robert 231, 245
American Civil Liberties Union 166
American Foundation for Aids Research 84
American Photo 40
American Rococo 1750–75 . . . (exhibition) 258
American Rose Society 114
American Star (Collins) 72, 81
Amis, Kingsley 196
Amis, Martin 35, 235–40, 241
Anatomy of Britain, The (Sampson) 31
Anderson, Matthew 199
Anderson, Terry 83, 84
Andre Emmerich Gallery, New York 214
Apocalypse Now 39, 208
Arizona Republic 166
Arlen, Harold 245
Arnstein, Bonnie 195
Arsenio 250
Art of Walt Disney, The 113
Arts Council 274
Asher Dann & Associates 54, 55
Aspen Wallposter 152
Auden, W.H. 208, 210
Aunsoe, Shannon Lee 224

Bacall, Lauren 98
Backdraft (Widen) 221
Bacon, Francis 214
BAFTA 200
Baker, Michael 167
Baker, Detective Stephen 167, 176, 178
Balzac, Honoré de 141
Bambi 109
Bamigboye, Baz 21, 23, 39–40
Bardot, Brigitte 16
Barnes, Julian 142–3
Basic Instinct 71, 78, 126, 228, 229, 232–3, 235
Basinger, Kim 266, 275
Bates, Simon 22
Batman 217
Batman Returns 264, 278, 279
Bayer, Ms Mary 96–7, 99
BBC 4, 31, 124, 188, 189, 192
Beatles, The 87
Beatty, Warren 74, 133, 248
Bel-Air Cap Ferrat 15
Bellow, Saul 196, 239
Belushi, John 199, 248
Berlin, Isaiah 211
Betrayed 234
'Beverly' 23–6, 30, 33–6, 49, 53–4, 59
Beverly Hills 90210 58, 266
Beverly Hills hotel 253
Beverly Hilton 203, 204
Bigger Splash, A 213
Bill and Ted's Bogus Journey 179
Birkbeck College, London 279
Bisset, Jacqueline 136
Black, Shane 221, 231
Blair, Nicky 249
Blaricom, Mirjana Van 123, 124, 130, 132
Blast 261
Blind Date (television show) 68, 71
Bogart, Humphrey 90, 98
Bogdanovich, Peter 197
Bolton, Michael 86, 153
Bowie, David 259
Boxing Helena 266, 275

INDEX

Boyd, William 236, 237–8, 272
Boyz 'N' the Hood 180, 218
Bradbury, Ray 87
Bradley, Tom 1, 5
Brady, Ian 28
Brando, Marlon 247, 274–5
Braudy, Leo 281
Breakfast News (television programme) 188
Brecht, Bertholt 233
Bremner, Charles 31
Bright Lights, Big City (McInerney) 138, 140, 144
Brightness Falls (McInerney) 138, 142, 143
Briseno, Theodore J. 180
British Columbia and Yukon Council of Film Unions 16–17
Bronson, Charles 106
Brown, Geoff 16
Brown, Tina 10, 256–7, 259
Brunei, Sultan of 251
Buffalo Bills 242
Bundy, Ted 28
Burchill, Julie 237, 260, 261
Burgess, Andre 222
Burton, Richard 37
Bush, George 5, 283
Butch Cassidy and the Sundance Kid 231
Byatt, A.S. 282

CAA 120, 221, 229, 283
Cahiers du Cinéma (Truffaut) 256
Cahill, Arthur 92
Caine, Michael 81, 126
Calder, Liz 262
Canby, Vincent 119
Cannes Film Festival 13, 16, 20, 119, 130, 1332, 180
Capital Correspondents Association 173
Capra, Frank 90
Caravaggio 83
Career Move (Amis) 239
Carlton Hotel, Cannes 20
Carolco 228
Carroll, E.J. 157
Casablanca 256
Cassidy, Hopalong 98
CBS 73, 188, 189, 190
Center for Motion Picture Study 135
Chandler, Raymond 85, 135
Channel 4 television 82
Channel 5 television (France) 19
Channel 7 (KABC-TV) 133
Chaplin 238
Chaplin, Charlie 98, 247
Chariots of Fire 119
Charlie's Angels 58
Château Marmont 248–50, 255
Cheers 221, 222
Cher 100
Christabel 251
Christopher-Michael 104–5
Church of Scientology 243–4
Citizen Kane 213, 230
City of Night (Rechy) 49
Civilisation (television series) 274
Clancy, Ray 29
Clancy, Tom 133, 201
Clark, Douglas Daniel ('Sunset Slayer') 27–31, 35, 165, 250
Clark, Sir Kenneth 274
Clark, Alan Rt Hon 262
Cleese, John 227
Cleopatra 36–7
Clinton, Bill 110, 160, 224
CNN 64, 200, 266
Cohen, Martin 206
Collins, Jackie 72–82
Collins, Joan 76, 81, 137, 256
'Colonial Club' 202
Columbia studios 217, 228, 244, 270, 276
Columbo (television series) 227
Connaught, Duke of 15
Connolly, Andrew 133
Connolly, Cyril 260
Contact 119
Coppola, Francis Ford 208
Corliss, Richard 279
Costner, Kevin 126, 221
Crawford, Cindy 74, 106
Crisp, Quentin 68
Crittendon, Vernon 173, 175, 177
Crosby, Bing 58, 98
Cruise, Tom 74, 126, 127, 129, 225, 244, 273
Crying Game, The 119, 120
Crystal, Chris 179
Curtis, Jamie Lee 126

Dahl, Roald 196
Dahmer, Jeffrey 27, 28
Daily Express 122, 124, 265
Daily Mail 21, 40, 124, 205, 266
Daily Mirror 28, 228
Daily Telegraph 31, 124, 201, 279
Daily Variety 218
Dallas (television series) 106
Dallas Cowboys 242
Damme, Jean Claude Van 204
Darby, Jonathan 119

Index

David Hockney: A Portrait (Webb) 213
Davis, Barbara 42
Davis, Geena 126
Davis, Marvin 42, 136
Davis, Nancy 153
Davison, Jon 236–7
de Lillo, Don 240
De Niro, Robert 17
de Palma, Brian 241
Dean, James 199, 247
Death Becomes Her 205
Death of a Centrefold 197
Debrett Goes to Hollywood 277
Deighton, Len 196
Demetriou, Pete 182, 183, 184
Deneuve, Catherine 134
Dennis Davidson and Associates 19
Denny, Reginald 184
Diaboliques, Les 238
Diana, Princess of Wales 69, 201
Dianetics 244
Dickens, Charles 82, 163–4
Diller, Barry 42, 44
Directors Guild 90, 135
Disney, Walt 90, 100, 102, 115
Disney 57, 86, 100, 101, 103, 104, 108–16, 120
Disney World 109
Disneyland 101–6, 109, 113
Doherty, Shannon 266
Dôme, Le 72
Donner, Dick 72, 73
Douglas, Kirk 227, 237
Douglas, Michael 78, 136, 204
Down and Out in Beverly Hills 110
Dunne, Dominick 58, 81, 263
Dynasty (television series) 57, 58, 106

Eastwood, Clint 122, 127, 135, 249, 269
Eaton, Dr Hubert 87, 90–91, 92, 94, 95
Eber, José 42, 106
Ebert, Roger 119
Economist, The 32, 107, 261
Eisner, Michael 57, 100, 110, 134
Electric Kool-Aid Acid Test, The 48
Eliot, T.S. 236, 256
Eminent Victorians (Strachey) 284
Emmanuel, Elizabeth 201
Encyclopaedia of Modern Murder, The 27
Entertainment Tonight (television programme) 21, 218, 266
Entertainment Weekly 263, 279
Entrekin, Morgan 142
Environmental Protection Agency 110
Ephron, Nora 231
Esquire 261, 263, 267
Eszterhas, Joe 111–12, 228–9, 231–5
Euro-Disney 100, 111
European 262
Evans, Charles 229
Evans, Donald Leroy 27
'Everage, Dame Edna' (Barry Humphries) 106
Everett, Rupert 21, 22
Executioner's Song, The (Mailer) 164
Exorcist, The 239

Face, The 261
Fairbanks, Douglas 213
Fame in the 20th Century 273
Farrell, Nicholas 16
Faulkner, William 141, 233
Fawcett, Farah 237
Fear and Loathing: On the Campaign Trail '72 (Thompson) 160
Fear and Loathing: On the Campaign Trail '92 (Thompson) 160
Fear and Loathing in Las Vegas (Thompson) 150, 154
Ferris, Hugh 138
Few Good Men, A 225
Fields, W.C. 90
Fink, Mitchell 137
Fisketjon, Gary 141, 142
F.I.S.T. 234
Fitzgerald, Scott 195, 233, 246–7
Flashdance 229
Fleming, Ian 196
Fleming, Peter 32
Fling, Reverend Bill 169
Flynn, Errol 90, 247
Fonda, Bridget 130–31
Ford, Anna 192
Ford, John 118
Forest Lawn Memorial Park, Glendale 89, 90–5
Forest Lawn Memorial Park, Hollywood Hills 85–9, 93
Forsythe, John 106
Fortensky, Larry 33, 37, 42, 45, 103
Foster, Jodie 126, 133, 273
Fox Television 64–6, 68, 180, 181
Franckenstein, Clement Von 204–5
Franckenstein, Sir George Von 204
Freak Power 152
Frenzy of Renown, The (Braudy) 281
Friedman, Robert G. 217, 218
Fry, Benjy 222
Furstenberg, Diane von 42, 44
Futterman, Steve 174–5, 178

Index

Gable, Clark 90, 247
Gabor, Eva 42
Gangland 228
Garden of Allah 247–8, 255
Gardner, Ava 247
Garrick, David 280
Gates, Daryl 182
Geeson, Judy 206–7
Geffen, David 42
Gere, Richard 106
Getty, John Paul 196
Gilbert, John 57
Giler, David 72, 82
Gill, Mark 276
Gilmore, Gary 164–5
Givens, Robin 21
Globe 38, 40, 44
Goday, Happy 111
Goldberg, Whoopi 87
Golden Globe awards 118, 121–5, 127, 128, 132
Goldman, William 117–18, 222, 231, 232
Gone With the Wind 230
Good Man in Africa, A 238
Good Son, The 237
Gordon, William A. 243
GQ (magazine) 240, 263
Graves, Robert 196
Gray, Linda 106
Gray, Thomas 93
Greene, Graham 267, 271
Griffin, Merv 42
Griffith, Melanie 205
Griffiths, Eric 261
Groucho Club 262
Guardian, the 31, 124, 261
Guber, Peter 216–191, 224, 276, 283
Gustaitis, Algirdas 128–30

Hackman, Gene 127
Hampton, Christopher 236
Hanson, Marla 142
Hard Rock Café, London 150
Harding, Don Eugene 166
Harlow, Jean 90
Harney, Corinna 2, 3
Harper's 263, 264, 267
Harris, Daniel 167, 175
Harris, Robert Alton 163–7, 169, 172, 173–9
Harris, Scott 43
Hawn, Goldie 205
Hazan, Jack 213
Hazlitt, William 280–1
Hearst, Randolph 98
Hecht, Ben 230
Hefner, Hugh M. 1–6, 74, 193–8, 241, 261
Hefner, Kimberley 6, 193, 194
Hefner, Marston 195
Hell's Angels (Thompson) 150
Hello! (magazine) 73, 75
Hemingway, Ernest 236, 247
Henry, Chuck 133–4
Henson, Jim 110
Hepburn, Audrey 136
Highlander (Widen) 221
Hill, Benny 174
Hirsch, Barry 234
Hiscock, John 31
Hitchcock, Alfred 98, 200
Hitchens, Christopher 263
Hockney, David 34, 35, 42, 44–5, 49–50, 203, 207–15
Hoeflin, Dr Steve 42
Hoffman, Dustin 221, 248
Hogarth, William 34
Hollywood and Beverly Hills Cricket Club 205
Hollywood Foreign Press Association (HFPA) 121–5, 127–32, 269
Hollywood Husbands (Collins) 80
Hollywood Reporter 119, 136, 268
Hollywood Reporter *Blu-Book* directory 117, 124, 131, 268
Hopkins, Anthony 126
Hopper, Dennis 22
Horizon 260
Hotel du Cap d'Antibes, Cannes, 1, 16–19, 26
Houston, Whitney 74
Howards End 118, 120, 135
Hudson, Rock 83
Hugh Hefner: Once Upon a Time (video) 192–3
Hughes, Howard 248, 253
Humperdinck, Engelbert 253
Hurley, Elizabeth 251–2
Huss, Judge William 113
Huston, Anjelica 74

Iacocca, Lee 153, 154
ICM 229, 283
Imaginary Homelands (Rushdie) 11
In Living Color (television show) 64
Indecent Proposal 222
Independent, The 32, 124
Independent Spirit Awards 120
Indochine 134
Innocent, The 237

INDEX

International Variety 123
Interview 263
Ipcress File, The (Deighton) 196
Iribe, Judith 247
Irons, Jeremy 126
Isherwood, Christopher 82
ITN 31, 64, 190, 191
Ivens, Martin 30–31, 32

Jack the Ripper 28
Jackson, Glenda 117
Jackson, Michael 36, 37, 39, 41, 42, 44, 45, 105, 106, 203
Jagged Edge 229
Jagger, Mick 205, 248
James, Clive 273
Jenkins, Simon 14, 33
Jewison, Norman 234
JFK 267
John, Augustus 261
John, Elton 57
Jones, David 41
Jones, Quincy 42
Jurassic Park 267, 276

KABC-TV 133
Kanally, Dave 101
Katzenberg, Jeffrey 110, 111
KCBS Channel 2 174
Keaton, Michael 279
Kael, Pauline 261, 275
Kelly, Charles 166
Kelly, Gene 136
Kelton, Simon 216, 217, 221, 222, 242, 249, 252, 253
Kendle, Kip 177
Kennedy, John F. 253
Kennedy, Robert 253
KFWB 182, 184
Kiley, Sam 31, 152
Killing of the Unicorn, The 197
King, Jack 17
King, Rodney 1, 10, 32, 172, 180–81, 185, 186, 243, 266
Kinsley, Michael 263
Kinglsey, Pat 234
Kitaj, R.B. 210
KNBR radio station 171
Koon, Stacey 180
KQED-TV 168
Kragen, Ken 224
KTLA TV 70, 189, 245
KTTV 184

LA Law 221
La Survival Guide 49, 50, 63
LA Weekly 53
Lady and the Tramp, 112
Lamb, Charles 280
Last Action Hero 270, 276
Late Show 227, 262
Laurie, Annie 93
Lawrence of Arabia 194
Lazar, Irving 'Swifty' 136
Lazich, Bob 171–2, 176
Le Carré, John 262
Lee, Peggy 112–16
Lee, Spike 251, 267
Leigh, Vivien 248
Lennon, John 276
Leoncavello, Edoardo 100
Lerman, Oscar 73
Lescoe, Susan 94–5
Lethal Weapon 72, 221, 231
Levin, Bernard 51
Levine, Barry 38–9, 41
Lewis, Michael 263
Lewis, (Percy) Wyndham 261
Life magazine 211, 267, 283
Lindsey, Don 27
Lloyd Webber, Andrew 254–5
London Fields 237
Long, Rob 221–2
Los Angeles Central Jail 242
Los Angeles Pet Memorial Park 96–9
Los Angeles Police Department (LAPD) 1, 10, 32, 172, 180, 182, 183, 188, 263
Los Angeles riots (1992) 1–7, 109, 181–92, 200
Los Angeles Times 10, 45, 55, 59–60, 63–4, 95, 167, 176, 205, 229, 263, 270, 272, 276
Love Connection (television show) 67–71, 189, 245
Loved One, The (Waugh) 85, 89–90, 96, 199
Lucas, George 102, 220
Lucraft, Howard 131
Lungren, Dan 175
LWT 68, 71
Lyne, Adrian 222
Lyne, Susan 218

McCartney, Paul 87
MacDonald, Bill 126
Macdonald, Dwight 257
McDonnell Douglas 202
McEwan, Ian 236, 237
McInerney, Helen (née Bransford) 138, 139, 141, 144, 146, 148–50

Index

McInerney, Jay 138–46, 148–50, 262
McKee, Robert 227, 228
McKellan, Ian 216
Maclaine, Shirley 106
Madonna 7, 13–16, 18–25, 47–8, 56, 84, 122, 136, 221, 266
Mailer, Norman 140, 196
Main Line Pictures 263
Majestic Hotel, Cannes 19, 24
Malcolm X 267
Mamet, David 232
Manilow, Barry 84, 106
Mankiewicz, Herman 230
Mansfield, Jayne 253
Marcos, Ferdinand 270–1
Mars Attacks 236, 237
Matisse, Henri 209–10
Maupin, Armistead 82–4
Max (ABC news producer) 168–9
Maxwell, Robert 262
Mayeski, John 167, 176
Meaning in Star Trek 88
Mencken, H.L. 265
Merchant-Ivory 110
Metropolitan Museum of Art 257, 258
MGM 230–2, 246
Miami Vice 221
Michelangelo 93
Micklethwait, John 32, 107, 124
Midler, Bette 84, 126
Millo, Aprile 45
Minogue, Kylie 100
Miramax 110, 121
Mission, The 119
Mitchell, Aaron 170–71
Modern Review 260, 261, 262, 264, 272
Mogambo, Prince 22
Money (Amis) 35, 241
Monroe, Marilyn 200, 247, 253
Moore, Demi 256
Moore, Roger 137
Morain, Dan 176
Morgan, Piers 21
Morris, Todd 169
Morris, William 221
Motion Picture Association of America 218, 274
'Movies on Television' (Kael) 275
Movieline 264
MTV 250
Muggeridge, Malcolm 196
Muppets 111
Murdoch, Rupert 64, 65, 68, 136
Murphy, Eddie 22, 100
Murphy, Tony 133
My Beautiful Laundrette 83
My Left Foot 134

Nabokov, Vladimir 252, 282
NASA 88
National Book Award 233
National Enquirer 38, 43, 44, 105, 106–7
National Society of Film Critics 272
National Theatre 216
NBC 174, 192
Nelson, Bruce 55–9
New Musical Express 261
New Republic 102, 261
New York Review of Books 261
New York Times 31, 119, 123, 132, 218, 258, 259, 263, 264, 267, 268, 270
New Yorker 143, 239, 247, 256, 268
New Zealand television 190–91
News International 32, 64
Newsday 81
Newsweek 195–6, 263, 267, 270
Nice-Matin 18
Nicholson, Jack 161
Nicolson, Rebecca 15
Nimoy, Leonard 85, 87
Niven, David 247
Nixon, Richard 160, 271
Nolte, Nick 126
Norman, Barry 228
Northampton, Earls of 91
Notes Towards the Definition of Culture (Eliot) 256

Oakland, San Francisco (firestorm) 54
Of Persons One Would Wish To Have Seen (Hazlitt) 175–6
Olinka, Juliana 127
Onassis, Christina 38
One Hundred and One Dalmations 109
One's Company (Fleming) 32
Open University 218, 226, 227
Orion 117
Orwell, George 175
Osborne, Robert 136
Oscars 117–21, 128, 129, 133–6
Over the Rainbow (Arlen) 246
Ovitz, Michael 120, 221, 229, 257, 230, 283

Pacino, Al 128
Paglia, Camille 258, 259
Pakistan television 191
Palm Beach Club Casino 13, 14, 20, 21
Palm D'Or (at Cannes) 119
Palmer-Slater, Gail 152

Paramount Pictures 85, 140, 222, 247
Paris-Match 18
Parker, Alan 22
Passenger 57 251
Patel, Marilyn Hall 166
Paterson, Graham 28
Peck, Gregory 42, 55, 106
Peck, Veronique 42
Penn, Sean 253
Pennies From Heaven 196
Penthouse 196
People magazine 74, 126, 137, 263, 279
Peters, Christopher 126
Peters, Jon 228
Pets magazine 97
Pfieffer, Michelle 122
Phillips, Julia 79–80
Physique Pictorial 210
Pimlott, Ben 284
Planet Hollywood restaurant chain 18
Playboy magazine 2, 3, 4, 193, 195–6, 197, 252, 261, 274
Playboy Enterprises 1, 192
Player, The 231, 245
PMK 234
Pnin 252
Point of No Return 130–31
Polanski, Roman 23, 248
Porter, Cole 196
Potter, Dennis 196, 251
Pound, Ezra 236
Powell, Laurence M. 180, 181
Premiere magazine 218, 237, 263
Pretty Woman 110
Prevention of Cruelty to Animals (Los Angeles chapter) 99
Prince 79, 250
Private Eye 228
Project Angel Food 84

Race to Erase Multiple Sclerosis, The 153
Rachel Papers, The (Amis) 239
Rain Man 217
Rainer, Peter 272
Ramey, Phil 40
Random House 144 237
Rano, Kip 40
Reagan, Nancy 42
Reagan, Ronald 39, 171
Rechy, John 49
Reed, Christopher 31
Reeves, Phil 32
Reitman, Ivan 153
Repo Man 221
Reynolds, Burt 224
Rhinoceros Films 24
Rhys-Jones, Griff 16
Rich, Gerry 121
Richard III (Shakespeare) 216
Richards, Keith 256
Richardson, Tony 90
Rickman, Alan 133
Ritchie, Lionel 224
Ritts, Herb 42
Ritz-Carlton Hotel, Aspen 154
Roberts, Peter 32
Robinson, David 16
RoboCop 221, 237
RoboCop 2 236
Roddenberry, Gene 85–9
Rogers, Kenny 224
Rohter, Larry 270–71
Rolling Stone 42, 229, 234, 261, 263
Rooney, Mickey 98
Rose, Axl 261
Rosenberg, Liz 18, 19
Rosencrantz and Guildenstern Are Dead (Stoppard) 135
Ross, Jonathan 274
Ross, Harold 247
Roth, Joe 110
Roxbury Club 250, 251
Royal Academy 212
Royal Opera House 212
Royal Pet Mortuary Inc 98
Rufus-Isaacs, Alexander 205
Rushdie, Salman 11, 277
Ruuth, Marianne 123–4

Sackville West, Mary 262
St Pierre, Monique 197
Sampson, Anthony 31
San Diego Trust and Savings Bank 167
San Francisco Chronicle 83
San Quentin State Prison 27–30, 163, 166, 168–79
Sands, Julian 205
Santa Barbara County Police 39
Sassoon, Vidal 56
Saturn Three 237
Savage, Jon 262
Scent of a Woman 128, 129–30
Schatz, Stephanie 98
Schiller, Larry 164
Schlesinger, Peter 2101, 213
Schwab's Pharmacy 245–7, 255
Schwarzenegger, Arnold 18, 261, 266, 275, 283
Scoop (Waugh) 9
Selznick, David 57, 230

Seymour, Jane 136
Shakespeare, William 259
Sharif, Omar 194
Sharpe, Tom 43, 99
Shatner, William 87
Sheldon, Sidney 81
Sheraton Universal 203, 204
Shields, Brooke 42
Shining Through 204
Silence of the Lambs, The 27, 28, 117, 239
Sinatra, Frank 112, 247
Singleton, John 180, 218
Six O'Clock News (television programme) 192
Ski Association of America 157
SKY 68
Sleepless in Seattle 231
Sliver 126, 228
Sly 250
Smith, Dennis 200
Smith, George Washington 55
Smith, Liz 44, 45
Smith, Mel 227
Snipes, Wesley 251
Solomon, Judy 123
Son of Sam 28
Songs of the Doomed (Thompson) 159
Sony Picture Classics 120
Sony Pictures Entertainment 216–17
SOPHIE (Save Our Pets' History in Eternity) 99
Spago restaurant 250
Spectator, The 271
Spelling, Aaron 58
Spender, Stephen 260
Spielberg, Steven 236, 238, 241, 267
Spirit of the Age . . ., The (Hazlitt) 280
Spiro, Ian 201
Spy 264
Stallone, Sylvester 234, 249
Star, 38, 42, 105
Star 80 197
Star Trek 85–9
Star Trek: The Next Generation 87, 221
Star Wars 220
Steiner, George 256, 257
Stern 18
Stewart, Patrick 89
Stewart, Rod 34, 54–5, 56–7
Stone, Oliver 120, 136, 221, 232, 267, 278
Stone, Sharon 78, 126, 137, 228, 278
Stoppard, Tom 135, 236
Story of My Life (McInerney) 142
Strachey, Lytton 284
Stratten, Dorothy 197
Streep, Meryl 205
Streisand, Barbra 55, 127, 133, 248, 266
Studs (television show) 64, 68
Sullivan, Andrew 261
Sun, The 21
Sundance Film Festival 119
Sunday Telegraph 16
Sunday Times, The 31, 124, 152
Sunset Boulevard 62, 96, 231, 242, 254
Superman 72
Susann, Jacqueline 81
Swanson, Gloria 96, 98, 255

Tales of the City (Maupin) 83, 84
Tartikoff, Brandon 85
Tate Gallery 214
Taylor, Dennis 187–8
Taylor, Elizabeth 33, 36–48, 84, 102, 103, 104, 106
Telluride (Colorado) Film Festival 119
Terminator 2 18, 64
Thief of Baghdad 213
Thompson, Douglas 122–3, 124
Thompson, Dr Hunter S. 150–62, 234
Thunder 126
Tigret, Isaac 150
Time 196, 263, 273, 279
Time-Warner 279
Times, The 2, 5, 14, 16, 27, 28, 31–3, 64, 65, 106, 124, 125, 149, 165, 172–3, 187, 203
Times Saturday Review, The 15
Tolkin, Michael 231
Top Gun 112
Travolta, John 23, 75, 140
Tri-Star studios 217, 236
Tritt, Travis 224
Truelove, Philip 249, 251
Trump, Ivana 42, 256
Trumpler, Lisa 'Lisalotte' 131–2
Truth or Dare 13, 21, 24, 25
Turner, Tina 21
Twentieth-Century Fox 42, 110, 237
Twilight Zone 221
Tynan, Kenneth 196, 268, 277
Tyson, Mike 21, 38

UCLA 216–24, 226, 228, 283
Ultimate Hollywood Tour Book . . ., The (Gordon) 242–3, 250, 253
Unforgiven 127, 135
United Artists 233
Universal Studios 34, 35

University of Southern California (USC) 220
Updike, John 196
USA Today 266

Valenti, Jack 218, 277
Valentino, Rudolph 98, 247
Vanity Fair 10, 28, 58, 74, 110, 138, 139, 256, 261, 262, 263
Variety 119, 120, 123, 128, 132, 268
Vasquez, Daniel 179
Verdin, Julia 251
Verhoeven, Paul 233
Vidal, Gore 140, 196, 259–60, 276
Vonnegut, Kurt, Jr 196

Wall Street Journal 218, 220, 264, 267, 268
Walter, Professor Richard 219–22, 228
War of the Worlds 236
Warner Brothers 82, 86, 127, 217, 221, 230, 238, 251, 278, 279
Warwick, Dione 106
Washington Post 268
Watts riots 181
Waugh, Evelyn 9, 85, 89, 90, 96, 199, 268
Wayne, John 118
Wayne's World 257
Webb, Peter 213
Wefald, Vernon 29
Weinraub, Bernie 123, 132, 218, 268
Weisberg, Judge Stanley 181
Welles, Orson 213–14, 230
Wenner, Jann 42
West, Mae 247
When Harry Met Sally 231
White, Lord Gordon 136, 137
Who's Afraid of Virginia Woolf? 48
Widen, Gregory 221
Wilcox, Jerry 178
Wilder, Billy 62, 81, 242, 248, 254
William E. Massey Sr Lectures in the History of American Civilization 257
Williams, Robin 126
Williams, Willie 10
Williamson, Marianne 44, 84
Willis, Douglas 172
Wilson, Colin 27, 28
Wilson, Gregory & Aeberhard 15
Wind, Timothy E. 180
Witchell, Nicholas 189–90
Wizard of Oz, The 64
Wodehouse, P.G. 196, 230
Wolcott, James 144, 262
Wolfe, Tom 4, 48, 141, 234, 260, 263, 283
Wonder, Stevie 45
Wood, Graham 149
Wood, James 261
Woolery, Chuck 71
Woolley, Steve 119
Working Title 83
World is Full of Married Men, The (Collins) 73, 74

You Only Live Twice (Fleming) 196
You'll Never Eat Lunch in this Town Again (Phillips) 79
Young, Robin 15
Young, Sean 253
Young, Toby 260, 262

Zadora, Pia 123
Zeffirelli, Franco 42
Zenger, Alan 104, 105, 107, 109